T0231676

GAME OF X V.1

GAME OF X V.1
XBOX

RUSEL DEMARIA

CRC Press
Taylor & Francis Group
Boca Raton London New York

CRC Press is an imprint of the
Taylor & Francis Group, an **informa** business

CRC Press
Taylor & Francis Group
6000 Broken Sound Parkway NW, Suite 300
Boca Raton, FL 33487-2742

© 2019 by Rusel DeMaria
CRC Press is an imprint of Taylor & Francis Group, an Informa business

No claim to original U.S. Government works

Printed on acid-free paper

International Standard Book Number-13: 978-1-138-35017-5 (Hardback) 978-1-138-35016-8 (Paperback)

This book contains information obtained from authentic and highly regarded sources. Reasonable efforts have been made to publish reliable data and information, but the author and publisher cannot assume responsibility for the validity of all materials or the consequences of their use. The authors and publishers have attempted to trace the copyright holders of all material reproduced in this publication and apologize to copyright holders if permission to publish in this form has not been obtained. If any copyright material has not been acknowledged please write and let us know so we may rectify in any future reprint.

Except as permitted under U.S. Copyright Law, no part of this book may be reprinted, reproduced, transmitted, or utilized in any form by any electronic, mechanical, or other means, now known or hereafter invented, including photocopying, microfilming, and recording, or in any information storage or retrieval system, without written permission from the publishers.

For permission to photocopy or use material electronically from this work, please access www.copyright.com (http://www.copyright.com/) or contact the Copyright Clearance Center, Inc. (CCC), 222 Rosewood Drive, Danvers, MA 01923, 978-750-8400. CCC is a not-for-profit organization that provides licenses and registration for a variety of users. For organizations that have been granted a photocopy license by the CCC, a separate system of payment has been arranged.

Trademark Notice: Product or corporate names may be trademarks or registered trademarks, and are used only for identification and explanation without intent to infringe.

Visit the Taylor & Francis Web site at
http://www.taylorandfrancis.com

and the CRC Press Web site at
http://www.crcpress.com

Contents

Part I: Betting Billions

Part II: Xbox Gets Connected

Epilogues

Foreword

Championships aren't won on SportsCenter.

They're not won by a single player, a single game or even in a single season. Championships are won through years of experience, hard-work, planning, scouting, recruiting, practice, analysis, financial investment, persistence and determination.

Like successful sports teams, successful businesses and products don't happen overnight. Nor are they the result of one, or even a small number of peoples' ideas, work, leadership or creativity. We all know this in our hearts, so why are we so quick to eulogize (or vilify) the heroes manufactured by the media?

Here's why.

Most of what goes into winning a championship, or birthing a new business or creating an innovative product is boring. It lacks the drama, the conflict and the heroics that sells papers, magazines and clicks. The media craves dramatic characters, soundbites and a good ol' fashioned bar fight.

Stories that don't fit a marketable narrative structure, find the trashcan quickly. This leaves fans, followers and fanatics little insight to how these businesses or products came to be, how they navigate the critical challenges or the breadth of the team behind them.

Just 19 months and 1 day elapsed between the day the Xbox project was approved and it was on store shelves across the U.S. By any standard, it was a massive accomplishment – birthing 3 new billion dollar businesses for Microsoft and challenging entrenched rivals.

Xbox wasn't simply one of the fastest-to-shelf "version 1" products in Microsoft's history, it remains the fastest business to reach a billion dollars in sales. The iPod, considered the most successful consumer electronics product of all time, launched just one month before of the original Xbox, but would take 4 years before it overtook our installed base.

Halo, a game that the media universally criticized at its first E3 appearance would defy critics to become a $5 billion dollar franchise. Bungie's first 3 installments would rack up nearly 250,000 years of gameplay and over 20 billion battles on Xbox Live.

Xbox Live connected millions of gamers together across the globe, birthing a third billion dollar business – and it even won an Emmy. It would take

Nintendo and Sony over a decade to catch up with the work that the Xbox team did to lead the industry towards a connected future and to make online gaming a seamless experience.

These successes weren't accidental. The team, while enormously talented, incredibly committed and ruthlessly focused started with a detailed plan and a stacked deck.

As a kid growing up on videogames, I read everything that I could get my hands on. Unlike my friends, my childhood hero was not Neil Armstrong, but Nolan Bushnell. There were a few books written, but in truth, the category had yet to be taken very seriously by anyone. On top of this, Japan was the "Hollywood" of the industry. The history of videogames, for a 12 year old fanboy without Internet was sparse.

Most of what eventually did get written about the early days were written well after the fact and starred only a few very public players.

These first generation consoles were designed by dozens of engineers and games were created by 2-5 people. By the time Xbox would be delivered in 2001, over 10,000 people from more than 50 companies were involved in getting the console and launch titles to shelf.

Be assured that this origin story does not fit neatly into 140 characters.

When we started the Xbox project in 1999, I proposed the idea of having a writer on staff to memorialize our journey. Having been involved in several early Internet efforts at Microsoft, I knew that it would be near-impossible to reconstruct the quest after the fact.

My peers rejected the idea, arguing that it may compromise our strategy, could distract the team or was rooted in egotistical motive. Knowing there would be more important battles to win with this new team, I moved past the decision. As a result, we allowed much of the history to evaporate.

15 years later, Rusel approached me with the idea of his new book. As a longtime historian of gaming, I knew that his interest and intentions were sincere, so I took the call. He expressed that the few attempts to capture the story behind Xbox came up short.

He told me that he wanted to tell the story from the beginning, where the taproot of the narrative was DirectX. The fan in him experienced the evolution from Flight Simulator to Halo and the historian knew that there was much more to the story.

After leaving Microsoft, I had declined all requests from journalists. To me, the media as a necessary evil and something I never enjoyed. It was especially difficult working with media and seeing our success, or failure be credited repeatedly to a very small number of people.

As the proverb goes, "After the game, the king and the pawn go back into the same box." To me, nothing rings more true.

The team is the heart and soul of any product, brand or business. And somehow, our team always managed to get marginalized by the press. Add memory bias and PR spin into the mix and the story that shoots out the other end is about as honest as a Hostess Twinkie.

So, I made a deal with Rusel. I told him I would participate exclusively under the condition that he invite a couple dozen (unknown to media) team members to participate in the book. I urged him to gather diverse perspectives, and give others the chance to share their stories too.

And, after 3 years, here it is. Two massive volumes with stories, insights and details from nearly 100 contributors that helped create the Xbox.

An avid reader, I can't recall ever reading a book quite like this before.

I was definitely too close to the topic fully enjoy it as a new reader. As I fact checked the first draft, something frustrated me about the book. After the first 200 pages or so, I found that frustration transforming into something that I really came to enjoy and appreciate.

You see, the story of Xbox doesn't all fit together in a neat, tidy package. It's not a typical 3 act narrative or 12 stage hero's journey. It's rough. Messy. It's littered with unresolved conflicts and contradictory statements. And, it provides stage to some strong opinions and selective memories without judgement or rebuttal.

That grit is a real part of any team or quest. There is internal strife, frustrations and heartache that contributes to the creative process. There are perspectives that don't align (and may never). There are opinions and players which veer off of the gravitas of the effort and misfits that try to sabotage others' efforts. Most writers and editors will painstakingly filter these elements out of the story, transforming "reality" into a "good read".

Thank you Rusel, not just for hunting patiently for these details and grit, but for having the courage, decency and respect for leaving these messy details in.

For each of the many personalities and players exposed in this book, there were dozens of others not named. When I said we started with a stacked deck, I was also referring to a lot of players and roles barely even mentioned here - there would be no Xbox without these key contributors as well.

First, we must thank Bill, Steve and Paul for creating a company and a culture that celebrated risk-taking, was unafraid to reinvent itself, dove fearlessly into new categories and hired world-class talent. The chance that they took on this newly formed team might have happened on February 14th, but the spirit that enabled that decision was decades in the making.

While DirectX and Microsoft Games Studios may have paved many of the direct roads leading to the launch of Xbox, we must also acknowledge the creative minds across Systems, Research, Services, Hardware and Applications that contributed code, patents, ideas and key talent to bring Xbox to life.

We also must celebrate the oft overlooked supporting cast of Legal, Finance, Operations, Manufacturing, HR, Administration and Sales. Unlike a true "startup," this fledgling product team was able to rely on decades of experience, knowledge and insight from these rock-solid organizations who were nimble enough to match our cadence.

Finally, our partners. While we designed Xbox, the software and the services, Flextronics and Foxconn manufactured it. The core processing was powered by chips by Intel and Nvidia. Microsoft promoted it, but Best Buy, GameStop, EB, Target and WalMart actually sold it. Of course there were dozens more companies that lended their expertise to our plan as well.

Most importantly to our success was the game creators. People don't buy a console because of what it can do, they buy it for the games it plays. Thousands of amazing game creators brought their visions, stories, puzzles, characters and challenges to life on Xbox. We just gave them the canvas. Backing these creative teams were dozens of publishers that took huge financial risks not just on these creators but also our first-generation platform.

It was an honor to be part of the amazing Xbox family and to be invited to share some of my memories about the journey we all shared for this book. It was fun to be reminded of some of these great times, tough mistakes and unforgettable personalities.

Never once did I feel that what we were doing was perfect, but I always believed it was magic. It was the passion of the many incredible people in these pages that made Xbox magic. Thank you all.

J Allard
(HiroProtagonist)

About This Book

This book began when I was updating my game history book *High Score Expanded*. I called Ed Fries, former head of Microsoft's game division and asked him about the real story of Xbox. That's where it began. Ed steered me to Otto Berkes and Ted Hase. I followed the trail, which led to a years-long effort and a two-volume story based in large part on interviews with 93 people, all of whom had played a role in the long road to Xbox and the promotion, approval, and ultimate launch of Xbox and Xbox Live. This is the Xbox part of the story. Volume 2 contains the prehistory, or as I like to call it, "The Prequel."

Just So

When I was young, I remember reading Rudyard Kipling's *Just So Stories*. Like *How the Camel Got His Hump*, *How the Leopard Got His Spots*, *How the Elephant Got His Trunk*. You might think of this book as **How Microsoft Got Its Console**.

In a very real sense, I'm beginning this book at a crucial moment of an ongoing story. I chronicle the long road taken to this point in *Game of X v.2: Prequel*, which is full of stories about people and events, technology and company culture, accidental successes and colossal failures. It's a look at the DOS and early Windows era as seen by the 40-plus people I interviewed for that book alone. And in the end, that road leads to this moment, a moment of relative calm and quiet at Microsoft. It comes after the initial furor over the Department of Justice anti-trust actions and after years of controversy over graphics standards has blown into a war of words and recriminations. It comes after the departure of one of the most outrageous, polarizing, controversial, and effective figures in Microsoft's history. When Alex St. John was finally fired, his talent for disruption left with him. But a little of it remained, and as we'll see, not everyone was willing to go back to "normal" at Microsoft. There was more disruption to come, and it started with a couple of guys talking in the hallway.

Online Appendix

For the fullest enjoyment of this book, we recommend exploring the extensive Appendix compiled for this book, with many original documents and further technical details online at https://www.crcpress.com/ 9781138350168.

Acknowledgments

Game of X v.1 could not have happened if it hadn't been for the many people whose stories and insights and sharing of materials made this book possible. For this volume, I want thank the following people:

Otto Berkes

Ted Hase

Seamus Blackley

Kevin Bachus

Nat Brown

Mike Calligaro

Lit Wong*

Alex St. John

Jason Robar

Jay Torborg

Jon Grande

Robbie Bach

Rick Thompson

Ed Fries

Brad Silverberg

Bob McBreen

J Allard

Cam Ferroni

Colin McCartney

Drew Angeloff

Rob Wyatt

Don Coyner

Jon Thomason

Bernie Stolar

Chris Phillips

Stuart Moulder

Mike Abrash

Boyd Multerer

Dave McCoy

George T. Haber

John O'Rourke

Todd Holmdahl

Pete Isensee

Chanel Summers

Mikey Wetzel

Lorne Lanning

Sherry McKenna

Jonathan Sposato

Alex Seropian

Marty O'Donnell*

Peter Tampte

Brett Schnepf

Jordan Weisman

Beth Featherstone

Andrew Walker

Jennifer Booth

Sandy Duncan

Jeff Henshaw

Dinarte Morais

Quoted or supplied support, but not interviewed.

Prologue - The Boardroom

They gathered in Bill's boardroom. The meeting was, in some ways, nothing remarkable—just another high-level decision-making discussion aimed at resolving issues in the Company. However, two things made this a particularly memorable meeting. First, it occurred on Valentine's Day. Second, and far more significantly, the single issue on the agenda was a highly risky, multi-billion dollar decision. If that decision went one way, then a year of time, resources, and dreams would have been wasted. If it went the other way, it would usher in a radical course change for the Company.

The Boardroom was not opulent, nor was it especially large. In fact, it was a singularly unprepossessing room for one of the richest and most powerful men in the world. The room was largely dominated by a rectangular table that could seat perhaps ten to twelve people. There was a large display screen at one end of the room, which could be enclosed in a cabinet when not in use. There were two doors along one wall, one at each end of the room, and two windows between them that looked into the bare walls of the main hallway. The windows sported drapes that could be closed as needed. The two other walls were bare. There was room for a few overflow chairs along the back wall.

Bill was late. The others were all there—a combination of brilliant visionaries and pragmatists, leaders all. Among the executive team members were Paul Maritz, Rick Belluzzo, Craig Mundie, Rick Rashid, Robbie Bach, Ed Fries, Rick Thompson, J Allard, and Steve Ballmer.

Bill Gates walked into the room at ten minutes past 4.

"This is a fucking insult to everything I've done at this company," he said loudly and angrily, slamming the printed slide deck onto the table.

And so began the so-called Valentine's Day Massacre at Microsoft. It was do or die, the moment of truth, the "go/no go" moment for Xbox. It didn't start particularly well.

PART I:

BETTING BILLIONS

~1~
Back to "Normal"

In terms of games and graphic standards, Microsoft had recently gone through some heated and often acrimonious battles. The Developer Relations Group, particularly the trio of Alex St. John, Eric Engstrom, and Craig Eisler, had used every tactic available to them to push through the game enabling technology, DirectX. They had also fought battles over browser technology and competing graphics standards, which once again would be critical to games. They did this, in large part, to counter Apple's dominance in multimedia, and to prevent Microsoft's competitors from ultimately dominating living rooms all around the country. It was in some sense coincidental that games became their focus, but the work they did to support game development on Windows, especially after the launch of Windows 95, would have profound impact on the future of the PC game industry. and it would have a profound impact on the subject of this volume—Xbox.

In the aftermath of the Talisman/OpenGL vs. DirectX battles, and with Alex St. John's departure (all of which, and more, are chronicled in the companion volume to this book, *Game of X v.2*) life and work at Microsoft largely returned to normal. "Normal" meant that the biggest perceived threat to Windows was Sun Microsystems and Java, and, although DirectX had prevailed and the games division was growing, video games and the rising success of PlayStation were mere blips appearing far in the periphery of Microsoft's strategic radar.

"Normal," however, was not for everyone. There were people who sought something that would kindle their passion, and some of those people found their passion and purpose in the area of games. And, as it had been with DirectX, the path forward involved competing visions and a good bit of trench warfare. How it all came about depends on who you talk to. "Success has many fathers..." and over the years some books and a multitude of articles have been written, often claiming to identify one person or a very small group as the "creators of the Xbox," but in reality, there were many creators who often get overlooked, and others who had ideas for consoles, but never acted upon them.

My purpose in writing this book was always to tell the story from as many perspectives as I can, and the following narrative will sometimes present alternative points of view, based on how the people directly involved remember certain events that culminated in Microsoft's multi-billion dollar bet.

Moving Forward with Games

Ed Fries

Ed Fries made his first forays into the game development in 1982 as a senior in high school. "I started working in BASIC but moved to assembly language when BASIC was too slow. I wrote a clone of the arcade game Space Wars and then a copy of Frogger that I called 'Froggie'". Froggie made its way through the bulletin boards and was noticed by a game company called ROMOX, who somehow tracked him down and made him a development deal. His first commercial game, Princess and Frog, came out just as he started college and was credited to "Eddy Fries." Fries went on to create a Dig-Dug inspired game called Ant-Eater and another called Sea Chase, both of which came out on Atari 800 cartridges. His fourth game, Nitro, was never released because ROMOX (and a lot of other companies) went out of business in 1984.

Fries soon found gainful, non-game-related employment at Microsoft, and started a career that had nothing at all to do with games for the most part (see Bogus Software (*Game of X v.2*, pg 20). Ten years later, a chance encounter with a colleague at the airport changed all that and had a huge effect on Fries' future, and arguably on the future of his employer—Microsoft. That's when he learned about an open managerial position in the games division. The game side of Microsoft had never been a high priority for Microsoft, but when Ed Fries was offered a chance to head a division of his own after 10 years working in the

Office software division, it was that open position in games that he requested, firing off a letter to Patty Stoneseifer, the head of the Consumer division, to express his interest in the open position. "My decision upset some of the executives, who had different plans for me. I got hauled into the offices of a couple of vice-presidents, and they told me I was committing career suicide. They said, 'Why would you want to leave Office, one the most important parts of the company, to go work on something nobody cares about?'"

Fries had his reasons. He still retained his interest in games and the memories of being a game developer himself. That was one reason. But he also knew that in the game division he would be able to work without the intense scrutiny he would have to endure as the head of just about any other division. The thought of independence and creative freedom figured strongly into his decision, counterintuitive as it might have seemed to his superiors.

Ironically, it was increased attention that Tony Garcia (see also *Game of X v.2* Chapter 9) credits with his decision to move on, essentially creating the opening for Fries to take over. "We were able to be nimble, we moved quickly, we grew fast, and I think it's harder to do that kind of thing when you are also part of bigger initiatives that may not have the same agility. You know, it's much more fun to work with the people that you've assembled—that whole team feeling—that part is the best part. Especially when you see people succeed and go on to do their own thing. That's all very rewarding. Beyond that, it's all politics that I'm just not interested."

Garcia had gotten the ball rolling, and he had put together a great team, including Laura Fryer, Shane Kim, Bonnie Ross, Ed Ventura, John Kimmich, Shannon Loftis, and Jon Grande, all of whom continued to have long, successful careers at Microsoft and beyond. He had also tried to get some better titles done, working with proven developers like Larry Holland, who had designed games like Secret Weapons of the Luftwaffe for LucasArts, and with Jez San's Argonaut Games, but their games didn't pan out. Then Ed Ventura discovered Ensemble Studios and their game, Age of Empires, and brought them to the table with Microsoft. Before he left, Garcia worked out a deal, including ownership of the IP for Age of Empires, the game that finally put Microsoft on the map as a PC game company.

In March 1996, Fries took over the Entertainment Business Unit (EBU), which later became Microsoft Game Studios. At the time there were about 75 employees and an equal number of contractors, and Garcia had already left.

Fries never even met his predecessor. He moved into an empty office with no remaining sense of its history. "Tony was like a ghost I never met." Fries completed the contract with Ensemble and eventually negotiated the acquisition of the company, but he says, "I often get too much credit for Age of Empires. That was Tony and Stuart Moulder who put the deal together, even though I did complete the contract."

Fries came into his new position with a genuine interest in games, what some people called a Jedi talent for listening and asking the right questions, and, honestly, he was a fan. When he spoke with game developers, they knew his interest was real. Moreover, Fries was a genuinely likeable guy, so no matter how much you wanted to hate Microsoft, you couldn't feel that way about Ed. One of the first things Fries did was hit the road. "You know, I did what probably any gamer would do, which is, I went all over the world and met with all my heroes… game designers that I had the most respect for. I tried to put deals together with them, get them to work with us."

The ultimate acquisition of Ensemble Studios and the successful launch of Age of Empires gave Microsoft a clear PC gaming success. Fries also helped with the transition of Flight Simulator developers, the Bruce Artwick Organization (BAO), onto the Microsoft campus and acquired FASA, along with Jordan Weisman and FASA's Mech Warrior, Shadowrun, and Crimson Skies franchises. In addition, Fries helped both Chris Roberts and Chris Taylor start up their new companies, Digital Anvil (1996) and Gas Powered Games (1998) respectively.

Absorbing FASA

Microsoft's acquisition of FASA, and Jordan Weisman along with it, was announced on January 7, 1999.

Weisman grew up in Chicago, and was severely dyslexic. He credits a second grade teacher for recognizing the problem at a time when it was not well understood, but even more, he credits Dungeons & Dragons directly, and also tangentially for inspiring him (or almost requiring him) to read the entire *Lord of the Rings* trilogy. "I had been given the tools to read because of the luck of having a good teacher, but it was almost physically painful. Not actually physically painful, but it sort of felt like it was physically painful, so you avoid it. Just naturally, you avoid it. And now all of a sudden there was something that I wanted, and there was no way around it except to read."

Jordan Weisman

At college, Weisman was able to "tour" a $50 million ridge simulator that sparked his imagination. So he dropped out of school and began experimenting. "I was positive that I could reproduce that $50 million mainframe simulator by networking together Apple II computers." There weren't any networks to work with in 1979, so he began trying to connect Apple II computers together serially from their motherboards, "which was a really good way to fry motherboards."

Fortunately, before too many motherboards had been crisped, he realized that he was on the wrong track with the Apple IIs, but that there was still a way to accomplish his goal of networked gaming. He refined his concept and approached investors, whose response he sums up as, "Let me get this straight. You're a college dropout, never done anything, and you're talking about net-work computers to create a virtual environment that people are going to buy tickets to… like they buy tickets to a movie to come play. So we think you're just high." So Weisman switched gears once again. "I thought if I started a pen and paper roleplaying company and I'd be rich overnight, and then use the funds from there to build the electronic thing I wanted to build."

That was the beginning of FASA in 1980, where Weisman designed long-running franchises like Battletech, Shadowrun and a pen and paper Star Trek game. Fast forward to 1987: Now Weisman and his team believed it was time to revisit the original concept of networked games, so they started ESP… Environmental Simulations Project. They sank a lot of money into the project, which ultimately cost four times more than anticipated. They had to create their own network and graphics cards. "Only really naïve people would have tried it," says Weisman. However, by the end of 1988 they had created one of the first networked multiplayer immersive environments based on BattleTech, and in 1989 opened the first public BattleTech center (in Chicago) with two more in Japan in 1990 and 1991. Then, in 1992, the Disney family, led by Tim Disney, bought the majority interest in the company "and then together we built a chain of those around the world."

In 1996, Weisman and L. Ross Babcock founded FASA Interactive and Virtual World Entertainment as subsidiaries under the corporate entity Virtual World Entertainment Group. FASA Interactive published the PC game MechWarrior in 1998, and was subsequently purchased by Microsoft. Weisman and his whole team, at that point a part of Microsoft, moved from Chicago to Bellevue, Washington following the acquisition. Ed Fries is quoted in the press release: "'The acquisition of FASA Interactive reflects our commitment to growing our business with a smaller portfolio of top-quality games,' said Ed Fries, general manager of Microsoft's games group. 'The MechWarrior franchise is one of the best-selling series of PC games in history and is synonymous with groundbreaking technology and compelling gameplay. We're excited to continue the growth of the BattleTech property as part of our portfolio.'"

http://news.microsoft.com/1999/01/07/microsoft-acquires-fasa-interactive/

No Mario for Bill

According to Weisman, his move to Microsoft might have been very brief. "I think I'd been at Microsoft less than three months or so, and we were having our first Bill review up at Division. You sweat bullets about those. And so every team was working to present their product. So he walked down the line and he saw each of the games that were in development, and then we sat down and it was just Bill, Robbie Bach and Ed Fries and myself, and a couple questions. And then he asked, 'Well, why don't we have a Mario? Where's our iconic character? Like a Mario Bros.' And he looked at Robbie, and Robbie looked at Ed, and Ed looked at me. Okay! And I turned to Bill and I said, 'You can't have one.' I thought that would be an engaging way to tell Bill that he couldn't have something but it turned out to be way pretentious. And he said, 'What do you mean I can't have one?' I said, 'Because we're a PC game company, right?' And I explained the difference, at the time, between PC games and console games. Over the years this has totally changed, but at the time PC games were always world centric versus console games that were character centric. And so I just did a couple of minutes explaining that, and he thought about it, and then said, 'Oh okay, that makes sense.' I figured it could have been a very short career at Microsoft to start with the sentence 'You can't have that.'"

FASA's Rough Assimilation

Weisman became the creative director for the games studio, and so was not specifically leading the FASA team during the transition. However, he was involved and acutely aware of the challenges they faced. The main issue was the wide disparity between the game studio culture and the traditional development culture at Microsoft. At the time, he says, "Microsoft Games had kind of been the place that you put old developers out to pasture. It was a reward for good years of service in other divisions that you got to go play with games. And it was primarily people who liked to play games rather than people who knew how or were dedicated to making games." Ed Fries was changing this situation, but Weisman further observes, "like anything in a big company, it doesn't change overnight." One difference he notes was that, in contrast to the game developers at FASA, the Microsoft people "didn't live and breathe to make games."

Another cultural shock was the argumentative nature of life at Microsoft, which Weisman explains. "Microsoft development culture was all about features. Different groups would go off and develop different features, and then the leaders of those groups would get together and argue. And I do mean argue. They'd have these long, drawn out battles, fighting for their features to be included in the product. You know, there's a reason that Microsoft products feels like a grab bag full of features thrown together. Because that's how they're built."

Game culture is different according to Weisman. "They start with a singular vision and often a singular vision holder, who then works in successive layers to build teams around that vision. And of course that vision changes over time as people contribute to it, but it is all about contributing to a singular vision. There isn't a 'Well, let's do a first person shooter. You go do the movement system. You do the story. You do the combat system.' And then you don't get together and argue... otherwise it's like a Frankenstein assembly of

parts. So, it's a fundamentally different way of approaching product development. One very design focus centric and the other very feature centric. And it took years to get the culture to kind of learn that."

Weisman doesn't fault Microsoft or Fries for the problems they faced. For one, these kinds of acquisitions between very different cultures were inherently complex. Nobody had bad intentions, but there was a learning curve, and what Fries and Weisman learned from the FASA experience would come in handy later on when one of Microsoft's biggest game company acquisitions of another Chicago studio was on the line.

Reputation

In addition to misconceptions about the differences between PC games and consoles, there was the problem of perception. Games and business software had vastly different identities. They existed in diametrically opposed worlds, and the clash between them became evident soon after Ed Fries took over the EBU. While business products had acceptable, if unexciting names like Windows, Excel and Word, video games had names like Hellbender and Deadly Tide. At the time, the initial problems occurred with the games' names, and less in the content. Fries says that the issue was about public perception and Microsoft's reputation. "They knew we were never going to make the kind of money that they were making, and so their biggest fear about the games business was that we would somehow bring shame on the rest of Microsoft or somehow piss people off."

In the case of Hellbender, people in the business units were concerned that having the word "hell" in the title would potentially offend people, even to the extent of having their products banned. "Will that make, say, the Catholic church ban all Microsoft products and be really expensive?"

The case of Deadly Tide is even more whacked. Both Steve Ballmer and the company's head of marketing, Bob Herbold, came from Procter & Gamble, whose best-selling product was the laundry detergent Tide. Herbold, who had come more recently to Microsoft, was especially concerned about combining "dead" or "deadly" with the word "Tide". And so they brought these two issues to Bill Gates. It was a small meeting with Gates, Ballmer, Herbold and Fries with his marketing team. It started out with a demo of the two games. "We tried not to put all the focus on the games," says Fries. "When we're done, we look around and Steve and Bob Herbold in particular do not look happy, but the first person to pipe in was Bill, of course. And Bill basically says, 'They look great. I love the names. I think it's fantastic. You guys keep doing what you're doing.' And you can just see Steve and Bob Herbold bite their lip. They have to say basically nothing because Bill jumped in first and said it was all great. And that was the end of the meeting. But it gives you a sense of why, if somebody says we're going to publish Quake in roughly that same time, that was never going to happen. That took years of working our way up through edgier and edgier content until we were in a position to do something like that."

While the game division steadily grew over time to nearly 500 people, the enterprise software divisions were still the primary focus of the company. However, while Fries was having success building up the public face of video games at Microsoft, people in diverse areas of the company were starting to talk about something new, something that everybody knew "could never happen here." And yet it did.

Trouble Comes Easy

Before we continue our story, Fries offers an annectdote to illustrate how easy it is to make trouble, which he said happened all the time. "There's actually something that happened years before. The very first version of Excel for Macintosh had a kind of copy protection built into it where it would write this hidden file onto the Mac that would check to make sure it's there. And the guys who were working on it, were guys named Bill, Bob and Steve. They used their initials to make up the filename because they couldn't think of anything better. And so the filename ended up being Bostbeval. So anyway, you could pronounce it as "boss be evil." And so some preacher in Africa discovers this evil file—and it's not even evil spelled like evil—but anyway, he discovers this evil file on his Mac. It's a hidden file, and it says Bostbeval, and so, in his letter he writes that he's discovered this hidden file, and then he renamed it from Bostbeval to "Bestbgood," and then Excel wouldn't work anymore. And so this was clearly the work of the devil, and he was telling all his parishioners not to support Microsoft products."

~2~

"It Could Never Happen Here"

"How does Xbox get started? There's actually no one good answer to that question."

–Robbie Bach

"I think it's difficult to tell the story of something like Xbox because it involved so many different people, all of them have a small piece of it, all of them have their perspective. So it's kind of a Rashomon-style thing to try to piece this sort of thing together."

–Kevin Bachus

Microsoft's business model is to take our fixed costs and turn them into annuity, not take somebody else's fixed costs and turn them into an annuity for them.

–attributed to Bill Gates from a speech he gave every year.

According to Otto Berkes, who in the late 1990s was in charge of DirectX and OpenGL development at Microsoft, it all started with some hallway conversations he had with DirectX evangelist Ted Hase. Berkes and Hase were musing about the future and potential of DirectX as a platform. "The conversations naturally led to looking at the console market… looking at it through the lens of business, technology and the developer ecosystem. You know, at that time, Sony was in its ascendancy. PlayStation was the hot new thing." To be clear, these original discussions, radical as they were when compared with what was normal at Microsoft, didn't focus on a Microsoft console so much as a hybrid approach that combined some of the strengths of a PC system and some of the attributes of the console market and technology… something similar to what Microsoft had tried with Dreamcast (see *Game of X v2* Chapter 16). What happened next involved a steady evolution in people's thinking, based on a variety of factors and events.

Flashback to 1994, years before the conversation between Berkes and Hase, when Kevin Bachus was invited by Sony to a secret meeting. "A bunch of people brought us into a room and showed us the original PlayStation. I thought it was really cool, and I think a lot of people thought it was really cool that a company like Sony was getting into the game business. And after they were so successful, you find yourself wondering who else might build a console. And invariably Microsoft would come up in conversations, but very quickly everybody would say, 'Yeah, they'd be great, but it'll never happen.'"

Following a special Multimedia Retreat in 1997 (described in *Game of X v.2*, Ch. 24), Microsoft recruited both Seamus Blackley and Kevin Bachus. Blackley was hired as a program manager to work on a next-generation graphics project called Fahrenheit, which was a collaborative project between Microsoft and SGI, the original developers of OpenGL. By the time Blackley joined, the project was losing steam at Microsoft, and, as Otto Berkes puts it, "for a variety of reasons I felt that it wasn't going to succeed internally or externally. And Seamus had plenty of extra bandwidth. He's a smart guy, with lot of ideas." Bachus became a group manager working under Ted Hase in the DRG, where he "spent a couple of frustrating years" working on promoting a logo program for DirectX and marketing programs for third-party games for Windows. Seeking more perspectives and help in developing their ideas, Berkes invited Blackley and Hase invited Bachus to join their ongoing—and unofficial—discussions. And now they were four.

They began to meet in Building 4, one of the original Microsoft buildings that encircled a duck pond affectionately known as "Lake Bill." Berkes also says, "Building 4 was attached to one of the cafeterias that happened to serve one of the better lunches on campus at the time. So I was always happy to go over and have a meeting, have a lunch." As their ideas began to take shape, they started doing research and documentation to back up and refine their growing concept. "It was literally just the four of us—no sponsorship, completely off the books."

And Four Becomes Five

Nat Brown's title was Software Architect in the Windows division. In late 1998, his work consisted of going through crash logs and customer complaints and fixing application installation problems. To say that he was ready for something different would be an understatement. As he describes it, "Having to fix the registry and how applications install themselves… that's a particularly bad level of hell." Seeking something more interesting to do, Brown had entered some executive training courses, which involved "hanging out with other executives," as well as trips to visit senior managers at partner companies like Dell, participation in long-term planning exercises, and having "sit-downs" with Bill Gates. Through these programs, he had gained a good deal of what turned out to be relevant insight into some of the company's challenges and the attitudes of the partner companies.

In November 1998, Brown's search for something more exciting was about to be fulfilled, starting when he ran into Ted Hase in a hallway. Hase talked about the state of games and graphics at Microsoft, calling them "a cluster-fuck". Then he added, "There are some guys I want you to meet."

Brown remembers what occurred shortly after this ostensibly chance encounter: "They pinned me down in my office, all four of them in my very small office, and they wanted to talk about a plan they had." What they told Brown was that the real problem was Windows 95 CD-ROM, a meaningless logo program, and the only one currently aimed at game developers. The CD-ROM certification for Windows simply meant that a computer system had a CD-ROM drive built in. Nothing more. "Game developers hate it," they told him. "Graphic card developers hate it. And in the next couple of years, this hardware is going to go bananas. Soon we're going to cross a threshold where we're going to be at 30-60 frames per second of real 3D graphics of the kind that most people haven't seen outside of academia.'"

They got Brown's attention with this information because his passion in college had been in computer graphics, whereas, since joining Microsoft, "the most exciting graphics we did was like putting bevels on 2D rulers to make them look a little more 3D and doing some vector-based sprites, which are truly horrific, for animating characters like Microsoft Bob."

Still, they hadn't gotten to the point, and Brown asked them why they were so excited, which is when Hase pulled from his back pocket a well dog-eared copy of *Made in Japan*, the autobiography of Sony founder Akio Morita. He said, "Read this."

Reading *Made in Japan* helped Brown understand some of what Sony had done well, and even though some of their divisions were struggling at the time, the work ethic and design skills of the company were clear. One thing that stood out for Brown was their management of the supply chain. What this meant is that, like all consoles, it would lose money in the first year, but PlayStation would become cheaper to produce each year it was being manufactured. Brown noted that this was "a scary characteristic to have in a competitor if you were going to build a console."

Brown was inspired to learn more. He requested the past several years of technical/financial analysis of Sony from the legal and finance people and dug deeper into Sony's finances, passing along what he was discovering to upper management. Gates already knew a lot about Sony, and had visited their offices often, as he did with other companies. What Brown uncovered from his research that Gates did not know was that the PlayStation division consisted of about 1200 employees out of a total of 250,000 worldwide, yet that tiny percentage of the workforce was contributing 60% of their corporate profits!

By the beginning of 1999, Brown had become a regular attendee of this unofficial, unnamed group's meetings, where he got a more complete sense of what was being proposed. Their thinking at that time centered on a logo program that set the bar higher each year, branding what a Windows gaming PC would be. It would specify what was required to display the logo, including: minimum standards for CPU, memory, hard drive capacity, input device control, and backward compatibility. At the time, there was no serious discussion of Microsoft getting into actually building any hardware. Their plan was to convince OEMs (Original Equipment Manufacturers) to create gaming machines with Microsoft's certification—a meaningful certification that game developers and makers of 3rd party peripherals like graphics and sound cards would appreciate and support.

As a company, Microsoft's primary focus was still on their enterprise software—Windows in particular. Despite the fact that games were among the top activities of consumer Windows users, Microsoft's philosophy up until that time was to stay out of hardware for the most part (other than mice and some peripherals) and just sell lucrative retail upgrades to Windows and their other software solutions. The logo program seemed the best approach to enhancing games for Windows at the time, but attitudes were about to evolve.

Give It a Name

In early 1999, soon after Brown joined the group, the idea of their project's name came up. Blackley had been calling it Midway, which carried with it the context of a significant victory over the Japanese in World War II. As a codename it had validity, but the time had come to seek something that was a bit more Microsoft-y and less military.

Brown remembers writing on the white board in his office. Because the original idea was to create a logo/compatibility program, something like "DirectX NN Compatible" or "Best with DirectX NN", the whole idea was clearly derived from DirectX. Various versions were proposed and written on the board, after Brown had erased a diagram of a rocket engine left over from a previous job interview he had conducted. ("I had interviewed some candidate who debated rocket propulsion with me and tried to argue that rockets were not simply propelled by the opposing force of the ejection of the mass of their propellant: no-hire that guy, not for being wrong, but for being a stubborn dick and also wrong.")

Written on the board were several early ideas, such as DirectX-Box, DirectXXX-Box, XXX-Box.

The XXX versions were Hase's joke, as he correctly pointed out that both Sony and Nintendo were very closed to adult content, which he observed was a factor in the demise of Sony's Betamax vs. VHS back in the videotape era. In the original vision, where outside PC vendors would produce the products, Hase reasoned, their XXX-Box would have the advantage of more open content.

For months, alternate spellings of the name appeared in various reports and other writing, the most popular one being X-Box, but the one that the group itself adopted at the time was xBox with a cap on the "B." According to Brown, "The initial secrecy and, later, the period of not wanting to send anything specific in email to prevent the Dolphin/WebTV* folks from getting their hands on it, meant we talked with a lot of folks internally and externally purely by phone and just said 'xbox'. It got interpreted however they thought it was spelled." Correct spelling hardly mattered, though. It was always intended to be a code name, never the actual product name, and everybody knew what they were talking about, regardless of spelling.

*Dolphin/WebTV represented competitive technology and were soon to be rivals to the new xbox idea.

The Original xBox Team

Otto Berkes

Ted Hase

Seamus Blackley

Kevin Bachus

Nat Brown

~3~
Other Microsoft Initiatives

While the small proto-xBox team was exploring their concept of a game-centric logo program, other teams at Microsoft were exploring different technologies. This was business as usual.

Fahrenheit

At some point, SGI decided they needed to develop an Intel based workstation platform to compete with faster and faster PCs from companies like Dell and HP, and according to Jay Torborg, they formed a joint development project with Microsoft. The motivation for the collaboration was essentially two-fold. "The concept was to try to do a really high-level abstraction of 3D, to make it easier to do really powerful 3D applications without really understanding how all the 3D functionality worked. And the other big aspect of it was to try to mend fences with Silicon Graphics, mostly because of Direct3D being competition to OpenGL, and a lack of support for OpenGL in general. So this was a way of trying to mend fences with Silicon Graphics and get them to adopt the Windows platform and move forward with that in their low-end technical workstations."

Fahrenheit was intended to be a new high-level 3D application, "where getting the last bit of performance was less important than fast application development," and was to be based on ongoing efforts already underway at SGI and Microsoft. However, Torborg expressed disappointment with the progress of the initiative. "I'm sure there were some people on the team who were really enthusiastic, but for the most part the engineers at Microsoft weren't super enthusiastic about the idea. Certainly the direct managers were a little bit reluctant to be working on it. So it didn't really ever get significant traction, and ultimately, in part because Silicon Graphics ran into so many problems, and the fact that there wasn't really that much enthusiasm for it, either in the development group or from application developers—third-party developers—it ended up getting canceled."

Ty Graham only remembers Fahrenheit because he and Kevin Bachus had been given the task of running the concept out to the marketing teams and executives at various hardware companies, particularly those creating graphics cards. "We had to tell them why it's ok. I can't even remember what we came up with."

Typically, Alex St. John has a completely contrary view of Fahrenheit. Accurate or not, here's what he has to say about it:

"After the multimedia retreat, D3D had won. That "BLAM" email is the declaration of victory because the multimedia retreat (*Game of X v.2* chapter 24) discredited the Talisman people and bought Craig and Eric time to entangle Internet Explorer with DirectX. That left the OpenGL team, which was a different kind of obstacle because they were really battling over control of the 3D graphic driver layer. Obviously Jay had them lobbying him constantly as well. Fahrenheit was the result of that twisted alliance.

"Jay liked adopting Direct3D as the carrier for Talisman initially because it was not an open standard API, so he was free to mutate it to support Talisman. I don't know how the discussion about Fahrenheit began, but clearly somewhere between the MSFT OGL team and SGI it was realized that Microsoft was going to go D3D if for no other reason than to foist Talisman off on the world if they didn't take action, so they proposed to make a "Talismanified" version of OpenGL called Fahrenheit.

"Jay was probably hedging his bets for Talisman by trying to get it injected into every 3D platform he could. It's hard for me to imagine how SGI agreed to go along with the Fahrenheit idea unless some desperation and/or kibitzing between the SGI OGL team and MSFT OGL team was taking place. Recall that SGI announced that they were dumping IRIX in favor of Windows NT during that period. I don't know exactly what happened there... I just know that Paul Maritz was closely involved with the SGI negotiations over all of that stuff.

"They think it was an effort to merge D3D and OpenGL which it was definitely NOT, the only point of junction from Microsoft's point of view was to inject Talisman into BOTH."

Torborg left Microsoft around that time, before the ultimate cancellation of Fahrenheit, whose main relevance to this story is the fact that initially Seamus Blackley was brought in to work on it.

Pandora

Pandora was an internal project to create a DVR capable dedicated version of Windows with a remote-controlled TV-style interface, no keyboard and no mouse. According to Jay Torborg, who worked on Pandora, "It had a full DVR. It had a cable interface for channel selection. It had the ability to play PC games. You could view your photo items. You could also browse the web, but that wasn't the intended aspect of it. It was really more about things that you would normally do in the living room. It was about having Windows, and it was all about the UI."

Time and effort was dedicated to Pandora, but it never was released. In that distinction, it was not alone.

WebTV

Then there was WebTV, the ex-3DO team that was acquired by Microsoft in April 1997 for $425 million. Their goal was to create a set-top box for browsing the Internet from a TV in the living room. As Developer Relations Group member Jason Robar describes it, "it was supposed to be web for your grandma. A real simple box that's going to let you browse on your TV."

Robar describes an experiment he and Alex St. John performed. "Alex got one of those WebTV boxes and he said, 'Let's try to browse your average website on your television.' But the problem was that you would be sitting 10 feet from a 30 inch television. It was difficult to read, at best. "Televisions weren't high definition, and it was kind of a chicken and the egg problem. Most websites wouldn't author for that type of environment until there was an installed base, and there's not an installed base because most websites can't be read that way," says Robar.

But the WebTV team didn't just go away. They began to view position themselves around games by including a proprietary 3D chip set. And eventually, they came head-to-head with the proto-xBox team. "There were all kinds of rival groups all trying to put a box of some kind with Microsoft operating system APIs in the consumer living room," adds Robar.

The Zone

One of my personal points of career pride was having started the Zone and being a source of a bunch of the talent that went on to do great things and also led the charge in Microsoft's thinking about online gaming.

-Jon Grande

Late in 1994, Jon Grande wrote a proposal in which he suggested a way to create a Microsoft game presence on the Internet. At the time, the Microsoft Network (MSN) was following AOL's "walled garden" approach with its proprietary client model, but Grande and his colleagues thought that was the wrong approach. "We all were strong advocates of building games directly for the internet. Our Trojan horse approach to go after doing that was this wild idea I had where I basically wrote a proposal that went up the food chain. It wasn't supposed to go to Gates originally. I think it was supposed to go to Bruce Jacobson, and it ended up that he forwarded it to Patty <Stoneseifer> and Patty forwarded it to Bill, and it came back down. So we essentially got head count to hire six people and a million dollars to help developers put their games up on MSN."

The Zone was a great incubator for talented people whose careers were on an upward trajectory. Laura Fryer, one of the first people hired, went on to help run the Advanced Technology Group with Seamus Blackley, and at the time of this writing is heading up Epic Games' Seattle studios. Shannon Loftis stayed in the Microsoft Games Group for years and at the time of this writing is a general manager for one of the Xbox One groups. Michael Mott, a senior planner on the Zone, went on to become COO for Microsoft's president Don Mattrick until he left. And the Zone itself had a lasting impact, according to Grande. "The Zone was the first effort at Microsoft that touched online gaming at all, and the Zone kind of split in half, and half of it became part of the nucleus of the early thinking of Xbox Live, and the other half of it went on to become MSN Games."

~4~

The Executive Retreat: March 1999

The 1999 version of Microsoft's yearly executive offsite retreat provided a key moment in the history of Microsoft's move toward a game console, but few people recognized its significance in the moment, and, although several people recall it still, their memories are expressed with slightly different inflections.

According to Bachus, it was at the offsite that Rick Thompson introduced the question that had been nagging Bill Gates for some time: Why had Microsoft been unsuccessful at introducing products under $500, such as interactive television and mobile devices? Gates was concerned about how this problem affected the investments they had made in the game industry, between the hardware and game divisions, as well as DirectX. He wanted to know how Microsoft could become more successful with these investments.

Robbie Bach, who was at the time the president of the Entertainment & Devices division and Ed Fries' boss, also believes that Thompson introduced the concept of a console. "We were doing this process they call 'open space' where people propose topics. Then everybody decides which topics they want to discuss and you go discuss them for a couple of hours. And Rick Thompson proposed that Microsoft do a video game console."

Thompson, who joined Microsoft in 1987 and became the head of the Hardware Division in 1995, recalls the open space process a little differently. "One of the things we used to do was these breakout groups to talk about different things. The way you arranged the breakout groups was, you had a pad of paper—one of those big easel things. You'd write a topic down on it—a few words—and you'd hold it to your chest, and everybody would stand in a big circle and read each other's topics." Thompson wrote something that mentioned Sony, AT&T and AOL and held it up like the others. His topic was meant to explore the potential threat that these three companies posed if they were to collaborate on a multifunction box. Essentially, he posed a question and suggested an answer that was bound to concern people at Microsoft: "What happens with Sony, for the money they put toward subsidizing a game console, AT&T subsidizing cable modems, and AOL offering huge subsidies as well, if they all got together to create a box that was a combination game console, cable modem and AOL subscription box? The amount of subsidies that could be put to that box would make the box free and stacked up at the local Safeway." Thompson didn't expect this collaboration would actually occur, but he thought it a provoking enough idea to spark some good discussion.

At least one person was provoked by the ensuing discussion of Thompson's proposition, and his name was Bill Gates. Following the retreat, Gates fired off an email requesting that people look around the company for potential ways to respond to this possible threat. According to Thompson, people showed little interest in cable boxes, so the discussion began to center on game consoles, which could function as a central unit upon which other functionality could be added.

It was during and shortly after the executive retreat that the first inklings of the conflict to come appeared, as different groups immediately revealed their visions of what Microsoft's response might be—what approach Microsoft should take toward a console or a gaming PC. On the one hand, you had Craig Mundie, an executive vice president who was involved with the ex-WebTV group and the Windows CE people, who at the time were working with Sega on the Dreamcast. On the other hand, you had five guys from DirectX, DRG, and Windows—the very unofficial xBox group.

Around the same time as the executive retreat, Microsoft split the Windows division into separate enterprise and consumer divisions, and consumer Windows was given the task of figuring out what kinds of devices, platforms, or PC appliances they could develop, or influence the industry to produce, that would make the consumer Windows identity successful.

According to Nat Brown, who had already been researching solutions to the problem of sub-$500 devices, one proposal on the consumer side was to create specialty Windows-based PCs. For instance, there might be a kitchen PC that was little more than an electronic recipe box, or a PC that was basically a web browser box. There would be "real" PCs and "non-real" PCs, the difference being whether they could run Office or not. There were also ideas for other types of home devices, such as PCs for students, and, of course, dedicated gaming PCs.

~5~
A Real Danger Emerges

Sony's success with PlayStation was already on the radar at Microsoft, causing emotions like concern and curiosity among the executives, but so far these responses had not quite escalated to great heights of fear and uncertainty. In mid-March 1999, with their preview of PlayStation 2 at the Game Developers Conference, Sony dropped a bombshell that represented a tangible threat to Microsoft's game business. Where there was fear, there was opportunity, and the xBox team harnessed the PS2 boogieman to amp the threat level to Orange, which helped add urgency to the nascent discussions about Microsoft's future game strategy. In doing so, they took advantage of particular Microsoft tendency—a tendency to assume the worst.

Brown and his co-conspirators understood this tendency. "One of the reasons we transitioned from a less aggressive approach to a more aggressive one is that we began to get into a more terrified state of, if Sony executes perfectly, what will happen? It's not a bad way to think about your competitors… to think about what if? The beauty of that thinking is that you think about every possible, wonderful thing they could do. It can cause you to become a little bit over-analytical of what's going on and to do some strange things, but there's a balance point that sometimes Microsoft does really well. The early days of MS Explorer, early days of Windows, Office, early days of Xbox, there were these great points of paranoia and focus."

The original PlayStation's dominance of the gaming landscape meant that the console's next generation was quickly seen as a threat to Microsoft's growing PC game business. In fact, one Sony executive boasted that the PlayStation 2, with its dedicated gaming power and the proprietary Emotion Engine, would make PC gaming obsolete. The PlayStation 2 announcement also caused concern over something that was very important to Bill Gates. "It really was about the perceived threat that Sony was building an operating system for the living room," says Ed Fries, "and Microsoft didn't want to see that happen."

Further fanning the flames, Berkes and Blackley coauthored a white paper entitled *Evolution of Consumer 3D: The new Home of Visual Computing* (See *"Evolution of Consumer 3D"* on page 249). The opening paragraph states:

"Recently, an uncomfortable fact has come to light. It comes not as a surprise—indeed it is rooted in the same commoditization of the PC space that has consumed so much of our bandwidth of late. In fact, the market and technological factors responsible have been obvious for some time. The problem, catalyzed by the announcement of the Sony PlayStation2, is a financial and technological oxymoron: the highest performance graphics machines in the world will soon also be among the least expensive."

The paper included a brief primer on the evolution of 3D graphics, including the groundbreaking work of John Carmack, and the general drivers behind the relentless push for better and higher resolution graphics. But along with the "educational" elements of the paper were statements like:

…Sony has surmised that their next generation console, PlayStation2 (PSX2), must represent more than just a game box. It is, rather, an opportunity for Sony to actually own this new RT3D medium, which can gener-

ate far higher margins for them than any of their legacy media businesses. They also think that they can push the Windows PC out of this space,
and keep it out.

The rest of the white paper details the rapid evolution of 3D hardware solutions, challenges presented by the comparatively slower evolution of CPUs,
and solutions that have been found, such as adding memory and computing
power directly onto graphics boards. At the end, Berkes and Blackley contrast
the approaches that the PC and PlayStation 2 employed in implementing
real-time 3D (RT3D), concluding that the more open PC model has many
advantages over the closed console model adopted by Sony and other console
manufacturers. In essence, they could be seen as making a case for their Windows-based console approach.

The Question of OEMs

In their internal discussions, the xBox team had discussed the living room
strategy, recognizing it as a new competitive arena for Microsoft, which
up until then had primarily focused on business or the home office. They
were looking for a way for Microsoft to harness its investment in computer
graphics and the DirectX APIs, as well as the developer "ecosystem" they had
developed. How could they use their DirectX assets to compete with Sony for
dominance in the living room? And how could the xBox team use Microsoft's
growing concern over Sony to their advantage?

"The perception was that everyone who played a game on a console was
doing so at a risk to Windows," observed Bachus, although, coming from the
game industry, Bachus disagreed with that assessment. He believed that consoles and PCs coexisted because they did very different things, and even the
games played on each platform tended to provide different types of experiences. Despite seeing no direct conflict between the two platforms, Bachus, along
with Blackley, continued to support the idea of a Microsoft game console,
even as unlikely as it seemed. Meanwhile, the unofficial xBox group continued to do research and refine their agreed-upon approach, which was still to
enable gaming PCs built by OEMs, using a proprietary version of Windows
specifically tailored to that purpose.

The more they considered the OEM approach, the more they realized
how rigorous and specific the specifications would need to be, and how

much support Microsoft would have to provide, not only in terms of technology, but also in design and manpower. They realized that they couldn't realistically support very many OEMs and keep the program profitable financially. They started running numbers based on supporting five OEMs, but over time it got honed down to two… just two OEM companies to carry the Microsoft gaming logo and create these gaming machines to compete with Sony.

Another problem was the OEMs themselves. According to Brown, "I had visited these big OEMs and they weren't designing shit. They were basically white boxing, white labeling everything out of China, and I'm thinking, you get 3% and all you're doing is putting a sticker on it. Dell was still doing stuff in-house, but nobody else was. They were just trimming costs and using the cheapest labor in China. Anybody can play that game if they've got enough money for the other side of the game, which is marketing and sales and content."

Despite their growing concerns over how they could implement a successful logo program that was profitable to all involved, they continued along the OEM path. Even as it became more and more logical for Microsoft to build its own console system, they still didn't really believe that was a viable option. On the other hand, Bachus and Blackley, who say that their vision was always to build a Microsoft console system, saw the OEM solution as a sort of Trojan Horse—a smokescreen to keep the conversations going.

With further research they were able to extrapolate Sony's potential dominance in key areas, and they made sure that Gates and the other execs were fully aware of their conclusions. For instance, PlayStation was able to produce an intense and immersive 3D experience, with a fast boot-up time, and even wireless controllers. (They didn't actually have wireless controllers yet, but it was a threat.) On top of that, Sony manufactured a lot of TVs and monitors. It wasn't too big a stretch to imagine what Sony was already implying, that the PlayStation could ultimately become a general computing device and take over the home. Moreover, the more successful consoles like PlayStation became, the more PC game developers might abandon Windows development, an eventuality that became increasingly important as more Microsoft execs came to understand the impact that games had on PC hardware sales. Hase's group verified this fear by conducting surveys in stores, where they revealed that most consumers were purchasing PCs for the home to play games and surf the Web. And as consoles offered multiple uses, such as watching DVDs and streaming entertainment in addition to playing games, they became an even better sub-$500 investment for home consumers.

A Summit

Because the DRG was so deeply involved with Microsoft's game technology, and especially due their role in developer support, they were often consulted on strategies that involved the game industry, and they often attended various planning and strategy meetings outside of those specific to the console debate. According to Bachus, it was at one such meeting in March 1999 that Gates asked them to plan a summit for May, inviting everyone at Microsoft whose interests touched on the game industry. Gates also asked for an analysis of PlayStation 2, especially in how it would compare graphically with where Windows was going. Based on their research, Hase and Blackley created a slide deck, with additional input from Bachus, who remembers, "One of the things that Seamus and Otto put into the slide deck was that we should totally make a console." So, despite the general belief that Microsoft would never make a game console system, they didn't back away from the idea, but sent the document, complete with the console recommendation, to Bill Gates days before the game strategy summit.

Brown explains that the idea of a "summit" was common at Microsoft. "Bill and other folks in upper management were always organizing or asking others to organize summits to get disparate and/or competing groups together to talk things out and/or demonstrate technology to execs or to one another. Summits were often used as a tool to defuse conflict in meetings and punt stuff down the road, sort of like the president appointing a commission to look into gun control or abortion rights and come back with recommendations six months later, by which time the anger or furor over the pressing issue might have passed a bit."

The May summit included a lot of different groups from Microsoft—essentially anyone whose work might touch on games. In addition to the xBox team, Craig Mundie's teams of ex-3DO/WebTV/WinCE people, Ed Fries' Entertainment Business Unit, and Rick Thompson's Hardware division were all represented.

Different approaches were presented at the summit—all of which had been presented in smaller meetings with Gates—including the idea of using Windows CE as a gaming architecture since it was already being incorporated into Sega's Dreamcast. The idea of a reference standard of certification for PCs built by outside manufacturers was also still on the table. Another approach stemmed from the fact that a lot of devices, such as a TiVo for recording video or a console system like PlayStation, were essentially just computers. If they had any interface, it was specific to that device's purpose, and not intended to serve in any other capacity. So why not consider a Microsoft-built PC with a Windows kernel, but nothing more? Such a machine could recognize a disc and start up a game from that disc without additional overhead or interface. It could cache some game assets to a hard drive to improve future loading of the game, save games in progress and provide other services, but it would still appear and function like a console—a Windows-based console. According to Bachus, they thought at the time that they could implement such a system and have it on the market by the end of 2000, when PlayStation 2 was expected to launch.

~6~
"Bill" Meetings

Between March and June 1999 several "Bill" meetings took place in which competing visions for Microsoft's game system strategy vied for Bill Gates' approval. In its way, each successive meeting was a go/no go situation—convincing Gates at each occasion that the ideas being put forth were at least worth pursuing further. The first of those meetings happened under somewhat false pretenses, or at least with a touch of bait-and-switch. The dates presented in the following section are sometimes approximate, based on the memories of some of the participants. In other cases, they are based on meeting documents I was able to attain. (*Many of the original "Bill" meeting slide decks are reproduced in the Online Appendix.*)

The First "Bill" Meeting

April 30, 1999: The xBox guys, still an unsanctioned and unfunded skunk-works group, decided that they had to have a meeting with Bill Gates, so Nat Brown pulled a few strings and suggested a meeting based on "important and timely" information about unified graphics architecture (UGA), which Brown knew was a hot button for Gates, along with unified text editing, unified file system, and unified whatever. They did talk about UGA, which Brown observes managed to upset a bunch of people who, according to protocol should have attended, but then they segued into a presentation of the business side of PlayStation: their sales volume, profitability from games, overall profitability, unit volume and software attach rate. "There was a four to five title attach rate for PlayStation. Bill easily did the math. There's 120 million units. That's more than a hundred million pieces of software at an average price of $60. Those are very attractive numbers. Those are 'Bill realm' numbers."

By the time the meeting ended, he had presented the idea of a controlled environment system that would rival console performance and be built by OEMs. Brown remembers, "It was kind of naughty. I had been in enough Bill reviews that I knew a bunch of his favorite hot buttons, and the fact that

PCs boot slowly and applications take forever to launch, that the file system gets corrupt, that applications shit on each other and prevent each other from loading and unloading and leave crap on your hard drive... I knew all of these hot buttons, and so I said, 'This is what a well-defined console should do. This is the kind of work that we should do in a controlled environment with some OEMs, or with a dedicated version of the OS, so that we can take what we learn about isolating apps and fast boot and fast launch and quick shut-off and fast hibernate and controlling graphics and controlling input devices and hot plug-and-play—things we were horrible at—perfect them in this system so that we can later put them in the rest of the system.'" The idea that the features Brown named could begin in this dedicated, console-like Windows machine, but eventually be applied to the wider range of PCs was exactly what Gates wanted to hear.

This first meeting with Gates did its job—perhaps too well as Brown recounts: "There was a lot of mail to folks in the DirectX group, who were managers and were above Otto, some who were tentatively above me... development managers and directors who sent us shit mail saying, 'What are you doing presenting about UGA and PC OEMS without including me?' And it's like, well, whatever. We just are. We really don't have time to talk to you about it. 'I want to see your slides. I want to review them next time, before you go in front of Bill.'" That's just classic Microsoft stuff. Whatever. The cat was out of the bag now, and Gates wanted to know more.

The Second "Bill" Meeting

May 5, 1999: The next "Bill" meeting included Berkes, Hase, Blackley, Bachus, and Brown, but also Craig Mundie and some of the WebTV and Windows CE developers. At the meeting, the WebTV group, who were all ex-3DO veterans, claimed to have been planning in secret to develop their own console solution, and the CE guys promoted their work with Sega as the first step in getting Microsoft into the console space. Mundie—a senior vice president—held the highest rank among the participants (other than Bill Gates of course) and became their champion.

Where the first meeting had been small, spontaneous, and productive, the next four were what Brown called "cage matches" while others dubbed them "beauty contests." Moreover, Gates picked Mundie to supervise the project strategy, which put him in charge of the agenda. It was immediately clear that there was going to be a battle over whose approach would be adopted. It was Mundie, with the WebTV unit and the Windows CE groups against who? An unofficial group of people from different divisions at Microsoft—DRG, DirectX, and Windows. Moreover, Mundie's guys were smart and already had experience in working with consoles.

In this second meeting, Mundie gave his opposition 20 minutes to present their ideas, and then said that the WebTV guys were going to pitch something called Dolphin. Battle lines were being drawn. According to Brown, "We didn't even realize that we were at the pitch stage. That was the first meeting, but once we had this kind of bake off/cage match meeting, we realized that we had to figure out how to shoot that thing in the head and be done with it."

(Another example and reminder of Brad Silverberg's statement previously quoted in *Game of X v.2*: "You have to be firm in your convictions, sound in your technical basis and be willing to withstand waves and waves and waves of conflicts. And what you have to learn about Microsoft is that people are relentless, and even if they lose a battle, they just keep coming after you and after you and after you… The only time you really know the decision sticks is when the product is on the shelf. Until then, it can still be overturned.")

The Third "Bill" Meeting

The third meeting probably took place on May 14, 1999.

In this meeting, Mundie's team argued the importance of the investment that had been made in Windows CE on Dreamcast, and how that was a promising direction that was already in motion. His team also made the point that they already had custom 3D hardware that had been developed in-house (Talisman). According to Brown, this second point was probably their undoing. "The fact that they had the Windows CE team, that they had a history of 3D graphics, all that was sort of playing in their favor. The fact that they were technologically five years behind the curve in terms of where NVidia was… that was the problem. You couldn't stand up technically and say, 'I've got 10 guys in the Bay Area who are currently pushing this many triangles, and they're going to push 10,000x or 100,000x in the next round… It didn't make any sense. You knew from the R&D budget of NVidia who was going to win that particular fight."

Still, the Dolphin group did have a few more advantages. They had a team already in the Bay Area, so there was no need to add head count, which translated into a huge financial advantage. Because employees meant more costly salaries; head count was a nearly perpetual issue at Microsoft. The other team also had experience with industrial design and consoles, and—a big one—Microsoft had already spent $425 million buying them. According to Brown, there were good arguments against them, too, including: inferior graphics technology, and "the Windows CE was a weak operating system with no developer momentum, and its tool chain was lousy."

Mundie countered that they had this underutilized asset that they'd spent $425 million to acquire (the ex-3DO team), that they had custom chip design people (Talisman), and an ongoing relationship with Sega (Dreamcast). His suggestion was to do custom hardware with Sega.

In reality, several of the members of the original xBox team showed little respect for Mundie and the groups he supported, and in typical DRG fashion, they saw the enemy's weaknesses and were determined to do what they believed would provide the best solution to solving the problems at hand. In addition to the inferiority of their graphics solution when compared with what was coming from companies like NVidia, they saw the Windows CE technology as being five years old and never the finest operating system in the first place. Brown expresses his team's sentiment, "The reality is that everyone had to face it, from Bill to Craig Mundie, and all the managers in that room who had worked on it, they needed to face the reality that their tools were broken, and their software was bad."

While having an ongoing battle with the WebTV and Windows CE contingent was immensely frustrating, especially with the PlayStation 2 launch looming, in some ways it was a blessing in disguise. After the "third" meeting, the xBox group refined their strategies and solidified their position. And they changed tactics. Much as Alex St. John had done during the battles between DirectX and Talisman, Brown now took on the political role, publically fighting the good fight against what they saw as a misguided adversary. Meanwhile, he told the others essentially, "Hey Otto, Seamus, and Kevin to some degree, why don't you... Go. Build. Stuff."

Along with a strategy of diversion and political infighting, they were actively seeking allies, talking to key people around the company, gaining their perspectives, addressing their concerns, and securing their support—people like Rick Rashid at Microsoft Research, Ed Fries, Robbie Bach, Stuart Moulder, and others. They also talked with video board manufacturers, like NVidia, 3Dfx, and ATI to get an idea about what they were working on and what the price points would be. Although people at Intel expressed skepticism about the project at the time, they, too, came through eventually.

Bachus even relates that they had found an original PlayStation emulator for Windows called Bleem!*, and contemplated the idea of building that into their system. Bachus states, "Every time we came back into the boardroom, we had delayed some damage from what they were doing, we had refined our strategy with criticism, we had discovered more little nuggets of things that Microsoft should be afraid of about Sony, and we had more and more kind of working prototypes of things."

*Bachus and Bob McBreen, a ten-year Microsoft veteran and the director of business development for Xbox, did go down to Los Angeles to meet with the Bleem! guys and offered them a sizeable amount of money for the technology. McBreen says, "I'm going to guess it was right around ten million dollars." But they counteroffered with a non-exclusive license and a prepaid one hundred million dollars of future royalties. "At that point, we just said, 'Thank you very much. We know what Sony's going to do to you without somebody like us.'" Bleem! was released commercially in 1999, and ran on both PCs and Dreamcast. It used DirectX and required a CD to provide copy protection. Two days after the product launched, Sony filed suit against them. Bleem! ultimately prevailed in court, but the company went out of business soon afterward, possibly from the weight of the legal costs.

Fast Boot in June

"They went and put together a demo for Bill Gates where they booted Windows NT in under three seconds, and that just blew everybody's minds. 'How did you do that?' Bill would ask. 'Well we hardwired a bunch of things and kicked the bios out…' And Bill just absolutely thought that was the sexiest thing on Earth. Which is super funny. He always loved a good demo. The ex-3DO guys did a much more business approach, saying here's how much the hardware could cost, here's all the different parts of the business model, and that kind of stuff."

-Rick Thompson

In one of the "Bill" meetings, probably on June 6 or 7, the xBox team arrived with two items. One was prototype of what a Microsoft console might look like.

An early Xbox prototype. Not necessarily the one used in the meeting.

It was created by the mouse team, which was between releases, with the support of their boss, Robbie Bach. As Brown remembers it, "The guys over on the mouse team, this is what they like to do. They like to sit there with some charcoal and sketch. So we just asked them to reimagine something and form it. And they're going, 'Oh, I don't know if I can use the former,'" and I'm saying, 'Charge Nat.' How much could it cost? Like $2000. Like who's gonna care? We don't care. Come on. Have fun with it. Stay late."

The prototype was a physical reminder of what they were discussing. Brown describes it as "a coated-foam prototype of the horizontal 'aerodynamic' xbox that looked similar to the vertical xbox. It was great for show-and-tell, and helped break up the monotony of endless slide decks, bullet points, and spread-sheets. It was tangible. For the first time, people were exposed to something that at least looked like a Microsoft console system. But it was the other item they brought that really closed the show.

It wasn't much to look at, just an ugly, small form-factor case, open-chassis PC with a small digital readout dangling out the top, sort of hot-glued to face forward and not fall over. "The readout initialized at 00:00:00 when you turned the machine on and stopped itself at 00:04:20 or 00:06:21 or various things like that when the BIOS made it past POST. We were using a super kludgy restore-from-hibernate."

As Brown remembers it, "The other group was saying, 'We only brought slides. It's not fair that you brought hardware.' And we're like, 'Why is that not fair? What are you talking about? It's just, we're kinda busy building stuff, and you guys are dorking around trying to derail us. We don't know why.' But we did know why. They wanted to remain relevant in the game space.

36

But it was really funny to come in this one time and to literally have them before the executive team in the room, complaining that we had made and brought hardware with us. And because we knew that Bill goes to 12 horrible board meetings a day in his boardroom—or used to—and the guy's a technology person. What he would like to do is see cool technology.

"So we came in and we had cool technology. And of course, no matter what the agenda was for the meeting, Bill was going to say, 'OK. What's with the computer with the clock on it?' And we said, 'We're not going to get to that yet... but we can if you want to.' And he said, 'Well, what is it?' And we said, 'Well, this shows you how fast we can boot a real PC to Windows 95. And here's a raw boot, and here's a hibernate boot, and here's how fast they are.' Not entirely intentionally on our part—we didn't want to derail the entire hour and a half that we had—but we did lose quite a bit of time where Bill was saying, 'What the fuck? You just booted a PC... like if my PC did this every day, you would save me an hour a day. Why can't we do this? What idiot here is not doing what they just did and making all the OEMs do it?'"

June 17, 1999: The Blue Book

The June 5th meeting with Gates resulted in the publication of three short—mostly technical—reports from June 6 and 7, and a longer one dated June 17, a bound tome they called the *Blue Book*. The *Blue Book* contained a printed version of a 65-slide PowerPoint presentation called *Game Console Follow-up*, which detailed the xBox current strategy and approach. Along with the main presentation, there were three attached reports: a report from International Data Corporation called *What to Play Next? IDC's Five-Year Forecast for the U.S. Electronic Gaming Industry*, an in-depth report about Sony and the PlayStation 2 by Merrill Lynch & Co., and a nine-page report titled, *XBOX: AMD Bill of Materials Estimate*, which detailed the costs of different hardware configurations and discussed the different options available. This report was based on the idea of working with AMD for the CPU.

The *Blue Book* offered a complete, official looking and up-to-date summary of the xBox design and strategy at the time, along with supporting documentation that helped make the case for a Windows game machine developed by outside hardware vendors. It was meant to influence Bill Gates at the mid-June meeting, and it succeeded.

In the June 17th slide deck, Slide 7 of the report introduces "the xBox," and the project definition reads:

- Create a new consumer platform—'xBox'
- This new platform is based on Windows technology and the PC architecture
- This new platform is designed specifically for the living room

The plan detailed in the report still postulated a combination of logo and certification programs, and offered comparisons and contrasts between its approach and those of both PS2 and Dolphin. Although many factors remained the same, one of the key assertions was that the xBox technology would be rapidly improved every two years, something that console systems could not match. They also suggested two kinds of software approaches from third parties:

- "xBox Logoed" encouraged existing PC game developers to repackage their existing titles and use distinctive packaging and logos as being compliant with the xBox requirements. To qualify, they would have to pass a strict evaluation, but would be eligible for co-marketing opportunities with Microsoft.
- "xBox Certified," required no evaluation, but did not allow developers to display the xBox distinctive packaging and logo. Otherwise, they had only to agree to application isolation, customer privacy, indemnity, and parental control. The plan would also allow for xBox content to run on "capable" PCs as well.

One of the advantages they saw was that the xBox machines could run both PC and console style games. The report mentioned that PC games were consistent award winners at prestigious game shows like E3, so having both would ultimately give them a content advantage. In addition, they anticipated a far more open business model that encouraged developers to make games for the xBox machines with familiar development tools that the developers already knew how to use, plus the ability to capitalize on improvements in hardware more quickly than regular consoles could. This xBox version was planned to be a sealed box, like a console, which simplified development considerably because developers didn't have to worry about multiple graphics and sound cards or input devices. However, new upgraded versions could be produced more frequently than consoles could match, using the best technology at the time for each upgrade. At $299, and with the addition of hard drive, Ethernet connection, and built-in DVD, they saw it as a competitive option to consoles like PlayStation 2 when it came out.

The promise of the xBox was that it would boot in under 10 seconds, use minimal UI with zero installation along with auto-play/stop. In addition, it must have parental controls and be open to emulation options. And how this worked? It would contain no Windows desktop, just a simple shell. It would run one application at a time, directly from CD and would evoke the installer when needed. There would be a UI for parental locks and for disk management and game removal, but not much more.

The report also included various marketing strategies and alternate year 2000 or 2001 launch dates, with advantages and risks associated with each. At the end of the presentation, they issued what was to be the first, but not the last, ultimatum. They promised that they could deliver this system, complete with OEMs and signed-up game developers for the year 2000, if it was approved within two weeks. On the other hand, they said, "If you say no, we go back to our day jobs building Millennium and Neptune."

For months, they had been heavily schmoozing game developers. Brown says, "Ted would fly them up. Or we would go to them. We would say, 'Look. We may get shot in the head, but this is what we're fighting for right now. Can you voice your support? Can you tell your Developer Relations, can you tell your favorite high-level person at Microsoft? Can you tell your favorite high-level person at Microsoft that you hate the 3DO team, that you hate Windows CE?' Ok. Not necessarily that they hate Windows CE, but that they didn't want to use Windows CE for games, that it made no sense, didn't match the Windows/DirectX APIs, wasn't a responsive or game-knowledgeable team. And they were like, 'Gladly. You don't even have to buy me dinner, but thanks for buying me dinner.'"

As is often the case with the passage of time, Kevin Bachus doesn't remember flying anybody up to Microsoft. "As I recall this was all done almost entirely through e-mail and we would circulate the e-mails like they were made of gold. These were people at very successful companies and we were dangling the prospect of a new game console in front of them. Their interest in supporting our plan came from our use of mature APIs and development tools and familiar hardware architectures. The WebTV/3DO/CE plan was to use a completely new and foreign hardware base with a limited and still-immature API/toolset."

Brown does specifically remember at least one dinner they put on with about 30-40 people at the Icon Grill in Seattle. He remembers Tim Sweeney and John Carmack attending because they were game programming heroes of his.

Interestingly, Bachus says that they ran into some resistance from one of the companies that had always been very supportive—Epic. "The biggest disagreement we had with Epic was that they really, really wanted us to do a mouse and keyboard, largely because that was what their games anticipated. And unlike where we ended up with Halo, they couldn't envision how an FPS would exist on a console without a mouse/keyboard. We on the other hand felt that a mouse and keyboard would forever establish our identity as a PC, and we were adamant that we not ship them because we were already fighting the assumption that Microsoft would, of course, deliver a living room PC not a console."

Overall, the response from developers was very supportive, and their advocacy finally paid off.

As the mid-June meeting came to an end, Gates told Craig Mundie that they were done with the bake-off, and that he should keep working with Sega, but stop trying to position Dolphin against the xBox. This sounded like a big fat yes, and it was. But there was a caveat. Gates told them that the amount of expenditures involved were high enough that he was not going to green light it without having Steve Ballmer involved. Gates also revealed his plan to transition from day-to-day operations as CEO to a new role as chairman, where he would concentrate more on software strategy. That meant that Ballmer* would soon take over the day-to-day reins of the company, another good reason to get him involved in what could turn out to be a multi-billion dollar decision.

*Bill Gates did step down as CEO in January of 2000, but remained active as chairman until June 2008, when he left Microsoft to concentrate on philanthropy through the Bill and Melinda Gates Foundation.

The Opposition Viewpoint

Mike Calligaro was the Dreamcast dev lead at the time and a member of the team arguing their case against the proto-xBox team. "We just assumed that because we'd already done a game system, we'd do the next one," he said. "So I won't say we didn't take it seriously.—you take a Bill presentation seriously—but I think they had more to prove and were more scrappy, and did their homework a little more."

Assuming that they had all the advantages, Mundie's team didn't expect a serious challenge from the other side. And though they didn't come in with such thoroughly researched pitch decks, they still had good arguments in their favor.

So what really turned the tide? According to Calligaro it was Windows and the promise of a faster boot-up. "We pitched whatever we pitched: We've done this. We know what we're doing. Let's do it again. And they said, "We're going to make Windows 95 boot in 5 seconds.' And Bill said, 'Why wouldn't I want that anyway? Even if I don't get a game system out of this, if you give me Windows 95 booting in 5 seconds, I win.'"

Calligaro remembers something that he thinks the president of Sega said to Gates when he was considering creating a game console. "All that happens with a game system is you lose a billion dollars, and all that does is get you the ability to lose another billion dollars." So Calligaro thinks he ultimately chose the xBox team because if he was going to lose billions of dollars on a game system, he could gain many more by significantly improving Windows, and that was, according to Calligaro, what ultimately determined the outcome.

PC vs. PlayStation

As part of their effective ongoing strategy to keep the pressure on and in their favor, the xBox group issued another report for the next meeting. The report, dated July 2nd 1999, was entitled, *xbox: a windows game console (and entertainment platform)* and was probably the one used at the upcoming meeting, the first that would include Ballmer.

The first section of this report was called "brief situational analysis," while the second section repeated the June 17th description of xBox. But it was the in the first part that arguably the most interesting material appeared: seven new slides that first ratcheted up fear of consoles, and then positioned Sony's architecture against that of the PC while looking at anticipated hardware trends.

Three slides carried the title: "#1: Is there a platform threat?" Three more were titled: "Is the PC architecture capable?" The final slide was called: "Sony Business Model."

The first slide displayed a graph and accompanying statistics, like the fact that, while 50% of retail consumer software revenues came from games, only 1 in 30 of the top-selling games (in 1998) were for PC. The slide also contended that, while this market was growing, PC was losing developers to consoles.

The next slide displayed graphs and statistics that showed how consoles had out-performed PCs in hardware units, software units and revenue. More scary facts and numbers.

Slide #6 included graphs that showed console gains in run-rate (essentially extrapolated sales trends) was catching up with PC, and that the original PlayStation was outselling the top five home PC OEMs combined.

The next two slides compared and contrasted the basic graphics architectures of the PC and the PlayStation 2, concluding that each was very capable, but that the PS2 had advantages based on bus and CPU speed that would allow for more novel and customized approaches by developers. Although one solution, which eventually did get adopted, was to add more computing capabilities to the graphics chips, this solution was not favored in the July report.

The conclusion at the end was that content, not hardware, would determine the winner, and that both the PC and the PS2 had advantages. In the subsequent xBox presentation, they promised to present some solutions, including "details on suggested ISV push that would assist us with a console as well." Was this an allusion to a Microsoft-built console?

There was one additional slide after the conclusions, which detailed Sony's business model, and among other things, claimed that profits from software accounted for 70% of PlayStation's overall profits (approximately $1.2 billion in 1990). The slide also showed a graph that predicted PS2 software volumes would far surpass those of the PlayStation at its peak.

On the next three pages I've included an ambitious and carefully worked out project plan for "xBox" and architecture sketch that were developed in June 1999 and was part of the team's upcoming pitch.

BILL MITTAL

xBox Project Milestones

June
- > preliminary platform specification
- > preliminary DXS graphics hardware spec
- > preliminary OS dev plan
- > functional UI/OOBE design
  - o persistent storage UI
  - o DVD/CD player
  - o pre-installed title selection
  - o overall functionality spec (turn-on/off, disk in/out, partial installation, etc.)
- > preliminary development budget
- > working demo prototype
- > billg demo

July
- > finalized OS dev plan
- > finalized development budget
- > OS team 60% staffed
- > preliminary platform logo requirement specification
- > investigative OS work complete
- > DX8 graphics hardware spec RC
- > preliminary OS modification specification
- > final UI/OOBE design
- >- preliminary test plan
- > Reference form factor available for review
- > **Develop names/positioning**
- > **Field research to test: brands, target, price points, features, etc.**
- > **Pick IHVs and begin scouting launch ISVs**

August
- > platform specification RC candidate
- > DX8 graphics hardware spec complete
- > preliminary title logo requirement
- > OS modification specification complete
- > final test plan
- > documentation staffed (+ 1)
  - o sample consumer documentation
  - o ISV documentation
- > **Sales/Marketing team calls on 5 accounts; Toys R Us, Wal-Mart, Best Buy, Electronics Boutique and Comp USA.**

September
- > OS team 100% staffed
- ;,. final platform logo requirement specification
  - o includes platform specifications, form factor requirements, subjective factors
- > complete demo system for external partners (OEMs)
- > Alpha ISV SOK for Windows PCs (new APIs, services on PCs)

October
November
- > preliminary documentation
- > OS alpha1
- > test development 100% staffed (+5)
- > **Pick merchandising vendor**
- > **Field research to test**
- > **Pick IHVs and begin scouting launch ISVs**

December

> final platform logo requirement
> includes test applications, license agreements, etc.
> Get Development systems out to first tier/launch ISVs
> Start heavy evangelizing to launch ISVs

January (2000)

> Platform prototype HW available to ISVs
> DX8 alpha
> OS alpha2
> Sales training - materials started - thru May

February

>- final title logo requirements
> o   includes license agreements, process description

March

> DX8 beta1, OS beta1

April

> launch title selection complete
> title qualification process started
> platform qualification process started

May

> test contractors 60% staffed
> First public display at E3, must have:
> Price point nailed down
> Mock hardware and software packaging
> Sales staff in place
> Merchandising units as prototypes
> At least 30 titles (in various stages of development) shown
>- Rough concepts of Ad campaign

June

> DX8, OS beta2
> Start early Buzz work through promo's and sponsorships

July

> test contractors 100% staffed (+6)
> DX8, OS RTM
> launch titles logo'd
> platforms logo'd
> Print campaign starts

August

> Some TV teasers

September

> final hardware ready for manufacture
> launch mid-month for back to school

November

> Holiday promotions, new ad creative and new titles introduced.

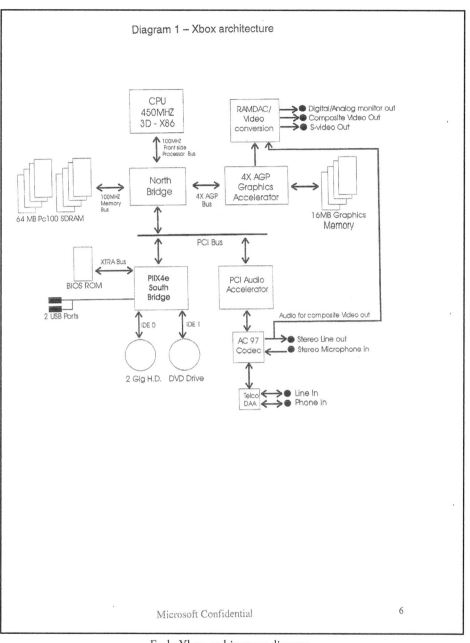

Early Xbox architecture diagram.

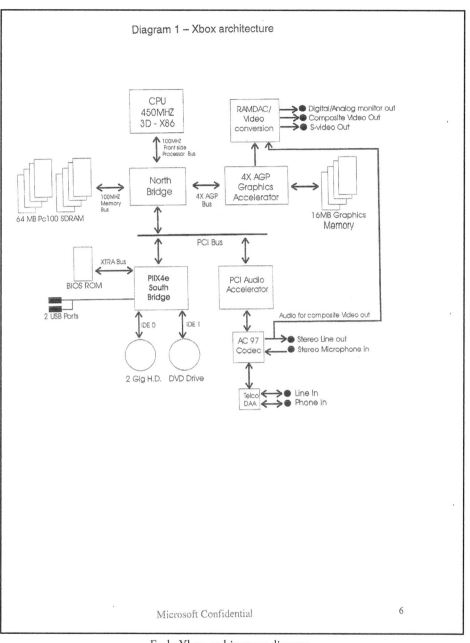

Early Xbox architecture diagram.

Meeting 1 with Bill and Steve

Early July, 1999: The first meeting with Gates and Ballmer was a tough one. In part, it was awkward to go over the entire plan for Ballmer with Gates present. As Brown puts it, "We felt as if we were repeating ourselves, and you try not to repeat yourself with Bill because he remembers everything you've said." And where they had ultimately sold Gates by emphasizing technology, Ballmer was all about the numbers—the financials and the business plan—and he quickly began asking the hard questions. "At that point, we had really been doing technology reviews and high-level bill of material analysis. All of us had enough knowledge to say we were in the right ballpark, but when you're talking with Steve, you can't be in the right ballpark. He wants the nickels and dimes. And I think that's a great skill he has, actually, because he also saw what we were trying to do, but he needed the specifics. And so we had to come up with a lot of backing for numbers that we had that we hadn't footnoted. That first meeting was weird because he ripped us a new one. We didn't have the numbers."

Brown also says, "When you go to a Bill review, you have ten slides and 50 pages of backup material. He asks a weird question and you say, 'Here's the short answer and page 37 has the backup.' And then, while you go on with your slide deck, he's turned to page 37 and he's reading that and absorbing it while he listens to you. He can kind of triple multitask. We didn't have any equivalently solid material to talk to Steve about. That was the mix of our team at that point. We didn't have enough number heads on it. And so we quickly put together a lot of numbers."

Ballmer was, in some ways, ahead of the xBox team when it came to the realities of OEMs, and he schooled them on the costs and margins associated with OEMs and their relationship with Windows. He knew the numbers down to the penny. By this time, the xBox team had more or less determined that Microsoft should make its own console, but Ballmer wanted to revisit the OEMs to see if anything could be worked out. According to Brown, "He said, 'I'm going to call up Michael Dell, and we're going to sit down and talk about if I actually spent $100 on a $95 purchase, whether that would make sense for him.' Which is weird, but that's how he thought about it, and he did understand the numbers at a deeper level."

Ballmer challenged them to firm up their numbers and their business model, and they started looking at other sources of revenue. "We had to dredge through and get a lot more of that data and talk a lot more about subscriptions and alternate revenue methods. And we also had to get real concrete about how much it would cost to market and how much it would cost to buy exclusive titles, because, unlike a lot of people, Steve really knew that one. That really, intuitively, resonated with him. 'What if you don't have a good title?' Because he knew that even a bad console, if it has a great title, it can really move a lot of units."

According to Bachus, they turned to the head of the hardware division, Rick Thompson, for advice. Rick was a business guy and a hardware guy, and he ran the most profitable division, per employee, at Microsoft. They even asked if he was interested in running the project. He offered advice, but he didn't volunteer to lead the project.

There was probably another meeting on July 14th, but I haven't found any specific details about that meeting, and it was probably a follow-up to clarify issues raised by Ballmer.

Bill Meeting: July 20, 1999

Convincing Gates had been the goal of the various competitive groups for months now, and later in July they met yet again, this time in an even bigger group. Like every meeting before it, this was a go/no go situation, and once again, it was a go—meaning "keep working on it," not "we're prepared to pour billions into it…" not yet.

Rick Thompson remembers the meeting well, and for good reason. "In July 1999 there was a meeting with 13 vice presidents in it, believe it or not, and Bill and all the rest, where the Windows guys basically asked permission to go ahead and start working on this project. And Bill said, yeah. Go for it. And the last thing that Nat Brown did, over the telephone because he was conference called in (from Hawaii), was to say, 'Hey, one last thing. We want Rick Thompson to run the project.' And I turned bright red and just about exploded, and my comment was, "I already have a job. I have a job running the hardware organization." But then, the next day, Steve Ballmer showed up in my office with a *baseball bat* in his hand, literally, and off I went to go work on the beginnings of the Xbox*. What he told me was that I could do both jobs. I could do the Xbox job, and I could do my hardware job."

* *From here on, we'll use this spelling for Xbox. All others became irrelevant at this point.*

Bob McBreen had been running the toy division under Thompson, and when the orders came down, McBreen had just licensed the toy division to Fischer-Price, meaning that Microsoft was not going to be manufacturing toys anymore and McBreen was ready for something new. So when Thompson asked him what he knew about the Xbox, he answered, "I know nothing." But after Thompson told him what it was about he said, "Ok. I'm in."

So both Thompson and McBreen began working on the Xbox project even though they retained their previous titles and were technically in the same jobs they had been in before. According to McBreen, Human Resources was not involved. They just shifted jobs while other people handled most of their previous responsibilities. McBreen didn't know if he would be working on the console project for a month or six months, or even if it would ever get made, but he started spending a lot of time on it.

There was one more "Bill" meeting to refine the ideas in September. (See ""Bill" Meeting: Sept 29, 1999" on page 343.) One more pitch deck before everything changed, and a new leader was chosen.

Under New Management

J Allard (right) with Nolan Bushnell (left)   *Cam Ferroni*

J Allard had gained considerable notoriety and respect at Microsoft as the guy who had clued Bill Gates into the importance of the internet, but after working on internet issues for years, Allard decided to leave on a long sabbatical.

Nat Brown had worked closely with Allard in the past. He had also worked with Allard's friend and work partner Cam Ferroni on Windows-related projects. He was certain that Allard would love what they were doing and would be a great asset to their project. However, Allard wasn't interested in coming back any time soon. As he puts it*, "i was on sabbatical after having been very focused on our internet efforts. my dream in the early 90's in coming to msft was to 'get my mom on the internet'. i realized in '99 that she was using the internet every week to talk to me and it had transformed her life - in essence the goal was complete. so, i pressed stop to think about what's next. took 3 months off and goofed around. got a beta version of tivo and satellite tv. bought a playstation. went to see toy story. ripped my cd collection and played around with early mp3 players. all of these things added up for me to one thing - that entertainment was going to become a software business."

Interviews with J Allard quoted in this book took place by email, and according to people familiar with Allard, this was how he communicated. I have left his written messages unedited for accuracy.

In spite of his realizations about entertainment and software, Allard still resisted coming back to work. Two additional factors were required. One was Nat Brown's "nagging and recruiting me while i was away." Brown even went so far as to take out a classified ad to entice Allard back. The second factor was sharing ideas with his friend and colleague Cam Ferroni. "We were essentially re-recruiting each other to 'do it again.'"

Ferroni says, "I was kicking around looking for something else to do. I had already worked on Windows NT and done 3 versions of IIS - it was time for something new. I knew Nat from his days in OLE and my days in Win32—he was clearly a smart guy and was excited about this opportunity. How could I pass it up?"

Allard returned to Microsoft in August 1999 and had lunch with Steve Ballmer. "i had lunch with steveb and we played 'you sell me' where he spent :30 minutes trying to pitch me on what he wanted me to do and i did :30 pitching him on what i wanted him to do. he said he had assigned rickt to build the biz plan (because rick was business minded and knew the hardware business better than any VP in the company) for xbox and to go spend time there. i told him that first order of business was to bring PURPOSE and VISION, not just opportunity to the thinking and that if we did, this would be a "B" plan - you see - the team was thinking in 'millions' but the opportunity was 'billions'."

At the end of lunch, Ballmer suggested that Allard go talk to Rick Thompson about the project he was now in charge of.

Thompson recalls his first meeting with Allard and Ferroni. "So the next interesting thing that happened after Steve put me on this project is that J Allard shows up at my door. He's on crutches. He's got a broken foot because he's been hit by a car on his bicycle or his skateboard. He's got peroxide blonde hair because he's dyed his hair white, effectively, what was left of it. And he just plowed his way into my office and he said, 'I want to work on this project.' And I'm like, 'Who are you?' The short version is that he hired himself onto the project, and I was very glad to have him once I got to know him, and he brought along Cam Ferroni. It was fun. The two of them were there and I asked them, 'Which one of you works for the other one?' And they both sort of hunched their shoulders and said, 'We don't really care.' They were very, very good guys, and those were the guys who did the heavy lifting, not me."

Green Light

While Thompson was in charge of hardware for the project, Gates tapped Allard as the overall project lead, which resulted in a complete restructuring of the project. "In the fall when this really started to get some organization around it, the DirectX group thought this should remain in the DirectX group, and so there became a massive schism right off the bat," says Brett Schnepf. "And then J got brought in as one of Bill's wonder boys—and justifiably so… J kicks ass. I love J. It became DirectX versus FOJ (Friends of J). That was one of one of the jokes. FOJ…. Friend of J. Can't do wrong, Friend of J."

Engineers Colin McCartney and Drew Bliss stayed on the project for another month, but they, too, exited as Allard took over and picked his own team, people he knew and trusted, the FOJ.

The first thing that Allard and Ferroni did was go buy a bunch of video games at Sears and lock themselves in an office that Allard describes as "like the boiler room in the office space movie… probably the worst office on campus, and we didn't care for a second." First they played video games, then they started filling up white boards with their ideas while recruiting people to the project. Their office was in the Microsoft Money area, and Allard says, "the money team thought we were nuts."

Allard and Ferroni were convinced that getting from millions to billions, as he had told Ballmer, required that Microsoft build the hardware themselves and collect royalties from the games. A major part of their vision was inspired by their early experiences with games that required social interaction. "we believed that gaming had transformed from something that was initially a social medium (pong and spacewars [sic] were both multiplayer-only games that lacked AI) - it was about using technology to bring people together into a shared context. atari as the first mainstream success started with 4 controller ports. pinball machines had 4 scoreboards. 90% of arcade games had 2 UP buttons (some, like joust had realtime multiplayer) and 4player collaborative games like gauntlet had lines waiting to play. over the years, 2 ports became the norm in consoles to save money and games like resident evil, tomb raider, diablo and mario 64 were the top sellers. arcades (the physical PLACE that brought people together around gaming) were over. gaming transformed in 20 years from a social medium to a solitary medium - a far cry from pong and combat on atari. it shifted from being designed for everyone to games being designed to address the 'most valuable segment' - 16-26 year old boys was the proxy that most people used."

Because of this perspective, they saw immediately that Microsoft's console strategy had to bring people together, and the growing interest in multiplayer, with LAN parties around games like Doom, helped justify that vision. "online/ live would initially be our strategic and brand differentiator, but in reality, it was the 'sun' of our solar system and the long-term play - it would become the platform that all sorts of different hardware orbited around eventually."

At the time they joined the project, however, their vision was not yet the official one, but they weren't the only ones with a vision. Behind the scenes, most of the original xBox team were also convinced that a Microsoft console system was the only way to go. Even as they wrote reports and created presentations that promoted OEM logo programs, they knew it wasn't going to work. What is most interesting about these presentations is the unspoken intention.

"Why was there so much 'multiple-oem' BS in the slides and in some of the models?" asks Nat Brown. "Because this was as much as upper management could absorb about the overall risk. It fit their view of the PC world. It fit into the types of phone calls they would make to big partners like Acer or Dell, and it fit into their relationships with other PC CEOs." It was about managing expectations and guiding the executives to the inevitable conclusion. "We always modeled the hardware costs in two ways, OEM-built or self-built. The difference in these two models amounted to less than one percent of total costs—just the OEM's 2-3% margin on hardware, since the fully-loaded BOM* was hardware plus distribution plus marketing, and the marketing and retail presence were significant. I always talked to this point, to make sure everybody started to understand that giving up a lot of control for <1% might not be worth it."

*Bill of Materials

It's Gotta Be a Console—Really!

A lot of people were now engaged in the search for solutions through research, while others were looking for answers outside the Microsoft campus.

Kevin Bachus and Rick Thompson were among those who traveled outside to meet with OEMs and game developers.

After taking over the project, Thompson still had concerns about the current OEM-based approach, and part of his initial research involved speaking with the people who would have to support the vision that Microsoft was currently favoring. "I started looking at it from the business side with my business manager, still trying to figure out what the P&L would look like, and where were the opportunities to make money. So the first thing I did was to go out and start talking to different companies. When Xbox was first envisioned, it was thought to be a version of Windows NT, and we would go to companies like Compaq, and HP, and Dell, and NEC, and like the PC market, we'd license them a copy of the Xbox Operating System. And I had a very good meeting with Michael Dell where he had the quote of quotes— this would be in August of '99. Michael Dell said, **'When you understand why my stock price goes down when I drop the price on a PC, and Sony's stock price goes up when they drop the price on a PlayStation*, you'll understand why I have absolutely no interest in your proposal.'** I got it instantly, but not until he said it, because I was sort of a Microsoft guy. So I wrote it down on a slide, and it was something we showed Gates and Ballmer at some point, and we all got a good laugh out of it."

*Because Dell depended on profits from the hardware alone, while Sony gained their profits from software, and a lower cost for the platform (PlayStation) meant higher sales and higher profits.

Thompson was also among those who traveled to some carefully chosen game companies to present their ideas and get feedback, where they met with some support, some curiosity, a bit of amazement, and a good deal of resistance. Electronic Arts was one of the toughest. Thompson comments: "Larry Probst is fantastic. He's going, 'Who are you, and why should I believe you that Microsoft is going to do this?' It was hard to get anyone to believe me that this was what we were working on."

In early September, Bachus visited various companies in the U.S., speaking under NDA with people like John Carmack from id and Tim Sweeney from Epic. Traveling to the European Computer Trade Show (ECTS) in London, he also met with European game developers, such as Jez San from Argonaut. Bachus often met with skepticism and received pointed feedback. Although developers tended to be positive about many of the tools that would be available, like the Win32/DirectX APIs, Visual Studio, performance analyzers, and profiling technology available for Windows games, they frequently commented that the proposed system didn't go far enough... it wasn't enough like a real console.

Finally convinced that the OEM program would not only be too expensive and hard to manage, but that developers were skeptical and outside manufacturers wouldn't be interested in the first place, the pressure was building to change the model. It was becoming more apparent that Microsoft should just create its own console system. Seeing an opportunity, the xBox team once again turned up the heat, providing even more facts and figures about Sony, and more reasons to fear them. According to Brown, "The way we shifted from the OEM model was that we began to get more and more Microsoft style paranoid about Sony, and the reason was: what their financials were, what their game titles were, and the profitability of that side of the business. This is very typical Microsoft that the more we studied a competitor, the more we became frightened of what they could judo that into."

Rick Thompson elaborates on how they went about building the paranoia: "One of the ways you convince a Microsoft exec staff person to do something is to give them a lot of fear, uncertainty, and doubt. So we got our hands on all sorts Sony presentations, and we'd show them to Gates. We'd show him how their vision of the future had multiple PlayStations and no PCs. That was like throwing raw meat to a tiger."

Much of Fall 1999 involved research and travel. Thompson spent time in Japan, speaking with various hardware contacts there, while Bachus and Blackley continued to speak with game developers and to seek their feedback. Blackley continued to work with prototypes, as well, refining what he called "the Silver X" model that would eventually be revealed to the public the next year.

Making the Silver X

All the early Xbox hardware demos used Windows 9x machines that booted straight into the front end using AMD chips and NVidia graphics cards in a normal PCI slot. According to engineer Drew Angeloff, there was a lot of experimentation going on. He says, "There was all sorts of fucked up hardware we had at the beginning. There were tons of all kinds of fucked-up weird beta hardware and alpha hardware and hacking process going on. The purpose was not to build an Xbox. The purpose was to get something in front of executives where they'd be like, 'I can see how that works.'"

They also needed something to show to developers and to the press. "As soon as you had to go talk to developers," says Angeloff, "it's like you needed a fuckload of machines. And if you had to go talk to people in the press, they needed a ton of machines. It became a real endeavor not only to have things that were fresh that we could show people about Xbox, but also be able to just show partners."

Angeloff says that one of their early ideas came from designer Horace Luke. "Originally what we would do is we'd haul around… It was like a PC or some cardboard box. It didn't look like a PC because Seamus didn't want it to look like a PC. It was like a cardboard box. It was some fucked up piece of hardware that we would carry around in our bags, and then we'd basically splay it out in front of a developer and get something running on it. A giant pain in the ass."

So they went back to Luke and he told them, "We're going to have an X, and it's going to be fucking awesome. We're going to have a green laser shooting out of it… A green laser is going to shine out of there. It's going to be so fucking bright. It's gonna have this acrylic lens, like you're peering into the soul of a fox…" and so on.

The idea of a X-shaped prototype sparked their imaginations, and Blackley went to the hardware guys in Red West and together they came up with a plan. The idea was to weld together some aluminum in the shape of an X and then stick a PC motherboard inside it. "Then we're going to stick a PC board in there," says Angeloff, "and we're going to have this crazy AGP connector. It's going to come out along one axis of the X, so the graphics card is in one part of the X and the other part of the X is going to be the main motherboard, and there's all this fucked-up wiring we had. We had to do custom power connectors. All of the power supply pieces of the X were outside of the actual X. It was just the processor on the inside."

When they showed the first model to Luke, he said the welding wasn't good enough and rejected it. "So what we ended up doing is we found this group of guys that wanted to make racecars. They were in Redmond, and they had enough money to buy a good amount of machine tools." And that's how they made the rest of the Silver X prototypes by taking a solid chunk of aluminum and routing it out to form a perfect, seamless X into which they stuffed a stripped down PC.

The Silver X chassis.

There were other visualizations of Xbox like this one that were never used.

When they set out to implement Seamus Blackley's vision of an eye-catching prototype, they stayed with that configuration. The problem was that Blackley's X-shaped concept didn't easily accommodate a regular motherboard. In order to accommodate the graphics card, they had to have a special PCI slot that would allow them to mount the boards parallel to the motherboard, at a 90-degree angle to their normal configuration.

Kevin Bachus describes the finished prototype: "It's functional," he says. Then, continuing, he goes into the specifics. "So basically you've got in one leg of the X, like one of the diagonals, we got the motherboard. It's got the CPU and the graphics chip and all that stuff on it. And then in another leg we got a DVD drive, so you can stick software in and in the other leg we got hard drive. And put the back on and there's like a flashlight that powers up and makes the jewel at the front of the X glow. It's awesome. People were blown away by it, but it's enormous, it weighs like 50 pounds and nobody thinks that it's going to be a real thing… but it's shiny and it's neat."

More views of the Silver X in development.

~8~
Changing Vision

While Bachus, Blackley and Thompson had been working to determine the project's direction, Allard had wasted little time, almost immediately rethinking the project from scratch. While Colin McCartney had stayed on the project, he had little contact with Allard. He continued his work, based on the original concepts. "There was a big focus on getting existing games to run, rather than writing new games. How can we get controllers to automatically work on these games? How do we get to zero install? How do we manage disk space? How to keep up with the hardware... How do we recover from any errors quickly?" But Allard wanted to go in a different direction. "They dropped the idea of running Windows 95-based OS wholesale, and started thinking about running just an NT kernel."

At this point, McCartney realized that he was part of the old project, and that Allard was heading in a different direction. "He wants to change the ideas, and we're tied to the old ideas. Rather than taking existing PC architecture, they were going to look more broadly to consumer electronics style architecture; they were going to change the manufacturing model. They dumped the requirement of running existing games; they were going to run new games only."

One difference that McCartney noted was that when Allard and Ferroni went out to purchase games at the local GameStop, they also looked at the customers. They began to think more in terms of the audience, and they came back and wrote a report about the project from the customer perspective. "It was a very different way of going about it than we'd been doing. We had been very—for good or bad—very engineering driven, and he had a bigger perspective. He was looking at the marketing and the customers and stuff. As an engineer I remember rolling my eyes at it, but you know... it was probably the right thing to do."

There were several reasons for McCartney's departure from the project, but one meeting in particular was pivotal. It was a large, all-hands meeting. Allard was spinning out his grand vision for the project, treating it like a startup. "And so he threw out this idea that he was going to cancel everybody's stock options and give people Xbox stock options instead. And that didn't sit too well. He didn't actually end up doing that, but this was one of the things he was spinning to us at the start. That was one seminal moment when I decided that I probably wouldn't stay about and see how it was going to play out."

In leaving the project, McCartney reminisces, saying, "We did some things that got Bill interested in the console. We showed him some stuff that could work—that this was important—and that got him to the point where he could say go, but when he said go, he put somebody in charge who went a different route."

The Allard Factor

One of the things that J, I think was a sort of a super power of his when we talk about his sort of spiritual approach, is that J had this philosophy always asking why rather than why not when it comes to features for consumer offerings.

—*Jeff Henshaw, project manager Xbox XDK*

Not everybody agreed with Allard. Not everybody necessarily liked him. But almost everybody agreed that he was smart, persuasive, connected, and the right man for the job. And for many of the people who worked with him, he was a remarkable leader and someone with the gift of inspiring others.

Of course, there was another side to the story. The original skunkworks team, started by Berkes and Hase, were not members of Allard's team. Some people felt that they had lost what was rightfully theirs. Blackley, in particular, was resentful and believed that Allard had more or less stolen the project out from under them. "There was a time of much hand wringing among management," he said. "It became incredibly frustrating, and we ended up depending on a bunch of proxies to deal with Bill, and one of the proxies we ended up with was this guy Allard, who was unbelievably opportunistic and a real climber. Instead of saying, 'Yeah, I'll help you guys out,' like others had, he wanted to take over and be the main man, even though he had only played console games* for a couple of weeks prior. It was interesting. Entertaining."

Animosity aside, Allard strongly disputes this assertion. "i Owned consoles from odyssey onward - 2600 intellivision colevovision vectrex sega nintendo game boy micro vision jaguar master system and all the modern ones."

Allard's philosophy avoids personal aggrandizement in favor of seeing everything as a team effort.* Referring to them as "directx," Allard is quick to differ with the perspective that anybody really lost. "dunno how directx 'lost' at all. it was the enabler for so much of the success of the effort. without that work, that team, that industry leadership, we'd never have had a shot at 1.0. there would be no nvidia 20 chip to select and tune for the box. there would be no pc-based dev kits. there would be none of the 15-20 superstars internally that we activated to get the program started and equip people like bungie to push the limits of what had been seen."

* In fact, Allard refused to cooperate with me until I convinced him that my book would attempt to tell stories from as many of the people involved as possible, and wouldn't focus unduly on him or other people who have traditionally gotten all the credit for Xbox.

Rob Wyatt, not necessarily a fan of Allard's, still recognizes his importance to the project, "Allard really knew the Microsoft way and we would never have made it without him. He was a critical component in getting it made and getting access to Bill and getting management's trust, but I know Seamus and I never saw eye to eye with him from the day we met him to the day we left."

Bob McBreen, remembers how Blackley had expected to run the project, but says that would never have happened. "Seamus and Kevin were great to put in front of the press and do demos. They were evangelists. But there was no way anybody else but J was going to take over. J was smart. J was driven. J was the right age. J had the relationships with senior Microsoft people. He got it. None of the other people could perform at that level."

Drew Angeloff, who also worked very closely with Seamus Blackley, says of Allard, "He's very, very smart. And the other piece is that he has a silver tongue. Like he has kissed that blarney stone quite well. His ability as a leader to speak to a crowd is practically at a magical level. I've seen him turn sentiment in a huge wide diverse crowd from skeptical to true believers, and it sticks with them. If you're Seamus you're probably internally rolling your eyes. You know that this is not necessarily true. If you're me, you're probably jaded anyway about pretty much everybody. But J has that knack; he knows how to craft a story."

One of several team photos that were taken during the early Xbox development, Front Row: Jeff Henshaw, Cam Ferroni. Middle Row: Todd Holmdahl, Seamus Blackley, and Don Coyner. Back Row: J Allard, Doug Hebenthal, Bob McBreen, and Gregg Daugherty

Jeff Henshaw, a 17-year Microsoft veteran was thinking about quitting and doing a startup. He had sent in his letter of resignation already. But Allard foiled his plans.

"So he says we're going to meet for beers before you do this. And so we wound up getting together for bagels instead of beer because morning time was the only thing we had free and we felt a little guilty having beers first thing in the morning. (I suppose there's something noble in making that decision.) But during this bagel breakfast, J pitched the concept of a game console, and the unique attributes of what it would take to be successful building that platform, in an effort to get me excited and sign up. But at the time, all I could say is, 'J, this sounds interesting, but knowing what I know of the game console space, this is probably a billion dollar investment, not something you and I can go do. I mean, between the two of us, we could probably scare up 25 million, but not a billion.' And that's when J disclosed that he wanted to take a run at doing it at Microsoft, with Microsoft's resources." And that's when Henshaw joined the team.

Don Coyner, who worked on marketing Xbox, also gives Allard a lot of credit for the success of the Xbox project. "It's kind of the miracle of Xbox, that it got done at all, and I credit a lot of that to J, for his ability to tell a convincing story and truly separate Xbox from the rest of the company. Many in the core company looked at it as, 'Oh, those stupid Xbox people. They're losing all this money, and they think they're so good. They can't be with the rest of us. They have to be down in a different campus, and blah, blah, blah…' And honestly, if Xbox had been sucked into the Borg at Microsoft, there's no chance it would have been the success it was."

Conyer tells another story Coyner that gives a glimpse into Allard's somewhat unique attitude about recognizing individual versus group achievements. "There's a picture of a group of us around the big metallic X thing that we made—J and Cam, myself, Seamus, Kevin, Todd… The person who did it just wanted to have J in the picture, and he was like, 'I'm not showing up. This is a team effort. We are not making this about me or any one human.' He was always so good at that, saying all this crap happens in a big place like this through a bunch of people coming together, and you can't attribute it to any one person."

Forming the Xbox OS Team

Jon Thomason was already a 10-year veteran Windows engineer by the time Allard tapped him to lead the operating system team for the new console. When I interviewed Thomason, he introduced himself by telling me, "So I'm the engineer in the story, if that makes any sense."

What Thomason observed in the early days of what we might call "the Allard takeover" was an uncomfortable transitional period during which he says that Otto and the others were "auditioning" for continuing roles in the project. "J knew that the guys they had were never going to be able to get it done. And the other guys had walked by then—Otto and the rest of the crew who had gotten it approved. So they started auditioning… I mean that word just like that. And I came in kind of cocky, saying, "I can do this" and I think that put them off a little bit at first (laughing). Maybe that wasn't the right approach, but eventually J asked me to come do it.

"My bosses in Windows land were very, very unhappy and thought that the whole thing was a ridiculous project and it would get cancelled soon, and I was making a huge career mistake… and so on. But I went over and did it. I

More on Allard's Arguments

1.　Fixed Performance vs. Growing Performance. Consoles are designed to provide the same performance over a number of years (fixed performance) while their costs drop over time. PCs are designed to increase performance over time while attempting to keep costs steady.

2.　Predictable Performance. Games put heavy performance demands on systems, which only increases when serving online play. The normal Windows operating system environment is designed for task switching and multitasking, which causes delays in memory reallocation and other background tasks. As Allard puts it, "When you want two 60 FPS games playing head-to-head across the country and trying to figure out 'who got the shot off first', the smallest 'hourglass' makes a huge difference."

3.　Windows Footprint. Because "stock Windows" is designed to be hardware independent, working with any graphics or sound card, any input device, any memory architecture, and so on, it was highly inefficient at conserving memory. What was required was to design for exactly one of every component—an OS for fixed-hardware, high-performance gaming applications.

4.　The Cost of Memory. "Cost is a primary consideration, and memory is a huge driver of cost. It is also the most important resource to make available to games for high-resolution graphics. With only 64MB of RAM, we wanted to give as much of the available memory to the games. So we counted every byte. Moreover, we allowed games to 'discard' components of the OS they didn't need. If they weren't going to be LIVE enabled they could dump networking, voice, leaderboard and live libraries. For instance, I believe Halo, which used every single library we shipped with on day 1, only gave up 720Kb of memory to the operating system. There are device drivers in Windows that take up more memory."

5.　Operating Systems. Where the Windows OS is designed for multiple applications, in reality, each specific game required only a spe-

brought two guys with me. One of them is still there on Xbox, Tracy Sharpe, the smartest developer I've ever worked with in my entire 30-year career and who has worked on every Xbox through Xbox One, and the other guy was Rich Pletcher, who has since retired."

During the winter of 1999, Thomason's team did the early design work on the OS. Sharpe did the majority of the coding while Thomason did a lot of recruiting and interviewing candidates for the team and leading whiteboard design sessions. Although the concept was coming along, the major development effort was still to come.

cific subset of features. By creating a small, custom OS that could ship on disk with the game, new versions could be developed over time, and the game developer could choose the version to ship with their game. In fact, this allowed for constant innovation without requiring any hardware changes. "We were constantly innovating, but when the developer needed to stabilize, they could choose the build they wanted to use and tailor it. No 18 months between releases and everyone on the same thing. Everyone could be different since the OS shipped with the game."

6.   Cross-Platform Compatibility. Knowing that many titles would be developed across different platforms, it was of no advantage to make developer tools that were radically different from those of competitors, forcing developers to devote extra development resources to restructure titles for a brand-new platform, which Allard called "catalog suicide".

7.   APP Support. "There was some early and lingering discussion around 'supporting windows apps' (like Office and Windows Media Player) which I never gave a lot of consideration for. I would remind everyone that we were shipping 'a really crappy PC' and that at TV resolutions there wasn't much point in spending all of the resources and making all of the compromises necessary so you could run Excel on your TV. If someone wanted to build an awesome 'TV PC', that was a different charter. It did come up repeatedly for the next decade, however, as a 'what if' by random executives."

No Windows

One pivotal meeting that occurred in the late fall involved only three people: J Allard, Rick Thompson, and Bill Gates. Thompson's version of the story goes like this: "J told Bill that we were not going to build this as a version of Windows, and that the business model was one where we had to have the hardware console… we couldn't just license the Xbox Operating System to third parties… that we would have to make it ourselves and the business model was a completely different one. And Gates basically went nuts, like literally spitting mad. That wasn't what he'd asked us to do. So J was very good. He was probably the only guy I knew who could stand up to that barrage. And by the way, I say that very respectfully. I think the world of Bill. He's a national treasure to me. The purity of what he wanted made sense. It just wasn't possible, and once he understood that and calmed down and stopped spitting, he gave us permission to go forward and do what we had to do. And J knew that it had to be that way, because he knew Bill was going to lose it, and he knew we just had to ride it out, and he didn't want Bill to have any more of an audience than he had to have."

Allard remembers what could have been that meeting or another that lasted about two hours in which he says, "i was a broken record on a couple of fronts

1) online-centric
2) game-developers first
3) gamers second
4) retailers, publishers, accessory mfgs, etc third
5) msft last"

In Allard's view, there was really very little real controversy. "in a world where we were shipping a 64Mb console when our desktop OS ate that kind of memory like potato chips it was clear to everyone that we needed to consider how to best adapt it. bill, and other execs, having no depth in the game market needed to be educated about the requirements and parameters we needed to apply to be successful… …bill and i can be colorful and hyperbolic and wind each other up a bit, so i'm sure you've heard some "drama", but there really wasn't much. in the end, the only thing we really disagreed on in gen 1 was modem vs. broadband and i'm glad we pushed forward the way we did (and was happy to work at a company to be empowered to disagree with the chairman and go forward with what i believed was the right thing to do)"

Early Visions of an Online Service

Another very early document that laid out the online philosophy was originally written by Jeff Henshaw back in April, 2000 with some minor updating just before it was shared with me for inclusion in my research. It's a very far-reaching document, particularly considering that it was written months before the launch of Xbox. You can see the document, "XBox Online & "XZone" Specification" *in the Online Appendix.*

.

~9~

Or We Could Just Buy Someone?

As we examine the Xbox story, we see a difficult, often contentious, but steady movement toward the concept of a Microsoft game console system. However, just because people were talking about and ultimately developing that console, doesn't mean that other options were being ignored. One such option that Bill Gates favored was somehow convincing Sony to use Windows technology to drive the PlayStation 2, and he did arrange meetings with Sony execs on several occasions. Of course, that didn't work. After all, why should Sony pay a percentage to Microsoft when they had already developed their own operating system? Another strategy that took a little longer to resolve was simply to purchase another company.

Buying Sega

One company that Microsoft almost purchased was Sega. According to longtime industry veteran Bernie Stolar*, the deal was already on the table. "Actually, I went to sell Sega to Microsoft, but Mr. Okawa screwed that up. Sega could have gotten sold to Microsoft—the deal was cut—but he went back again, twice, to get more money, and Gates finally said no."

*Bernie Stolar was president of Atari from 1990-1993. He was an executive vice president at Sony Computer of America from 1993-1996, and was president and COO of Sega of America from July 1996-August 1999. He was also president of Mattel from January 2000-December 2002. He held several other chairmanships after leaving Mattel and even spent a year and a half as a games evangelist for Google.

According to Bob McBreen, who was involved in this and other purchase negotiations, there was considerable tension between the two companies, aside from the purchase price. He recounts the story of a secret meeting at Microsoft that occurred in the midst of the negotiations. It was a Sunday, and the meeting began at Red West around 6pm. Part of the problem was that Microsoft had sold Sega on the idea of using Windows CE to create an operating system for their upcoming Dreamcast console. But once word of the Xbox became known, it soon became clear that Xbox would be a more powerful console. Their perspective, according to McBreen was, "They had just built their Dreamcast on this Windows CE reference design for gaming, and it was so underpowered compared with what we were doing with Xbox, they were basically paying Microsoft a per-unit royalty on CE for Microsoft to put them out of business."

Meeting with Bill and Okawa-san

Chris Phillips recounts a story about a special, and poignant meeting between Bill Gates and Sega's chairman, Isao Okawa, who was also the chairman of the Okawa Foundation, founded in 1986 and dedicated to providing grants and support for the promotion of information and telecommunications. "I was the only person in the room, I think, who knew that he was dying of cancer. He was the chairman and CEO of CSK, and he owned Sega. And that was one of the most surreal meetings in my life." Microsoft was already working on Xbox at the time, but the idea of acquiring Sega was still under consideration, if only to acquire their development teams. But Okawa's motivation was somewhat different.

"Okawa wanted to leave a legacy to Japan, and really wanted to keep making another mark, even posthumously, on technology and Japan. He wanted to build a Dreamcast 2 type thing with us, as an alternative idea to doing Xbox. It's kind of a crazy meeting to be in a room where people are throwing around billions of dollars like we're at Vegas and 'I'll put up X billions and you put X billions, and we build…' you know, the entertainment console of all entertainment consoles. And it was a surreal meeting. Here was a man that could see death, and was basically willing to put down monster bets, just throw it all on the table.

"At that time, Bill, I think, said 'I don't know how well we're going to do this [meaning Xbox]. We don't know what we don't know, but we're heading forward, and hopefully we won't totally screw this up.' Which was very Bill-ish. I mean, like there are times like that where I also could learn a lot just watching Bill and listening… You know, Bill could put a deal aside in an instant for business. Watching him do deals, or his behavior in listening to proposals just taught me a ton."

Buying Square Soft

Another company Microsoft tried to acquire was Square Soft. According to Rick Thompson, "We actually made a run at trying to buy Square. We were interested in buying Final Fantasy and make our own franchise. It went all the way to the point where Ballmer actually met with them, but the numbers they came up with… They wanted something like one and a half billion dollars for half of the company. So that never happened."

Bob McBreen was at the meetings with Square Soft in Tokyo. It was November 1999. There was a deal on the table and Steve Ballmer, who was in Japan on a sales tour, attended a celebratory dinner the night before the final meeting. The next day, everyone was gathered in a conference room, ready to sign papers. "Then Suzuki* stood up and said, 'Before we sign, our banker would like to say something.' And the banker got up and basically said, 'We want more money.' They just about doubled the price. I forget exactly what we were going to pay for them, but it was serious money. It was definitely in the billions. And their banker got up and said, 'After reviewing this deal, we realize that there are some errors in the numbers, and we'd like more money.' And we asked them, 'What did we miss when we did our due diligence?' And they basically came back and said, 'You missed that we're worth more money. We want more money,' and both sides walked away from the deal."

Hisashi Suzuki—president and CEO from 1995-2001

Buying Nintendo

Rick Thompson also relates another potential purchase—Nintendo. Even while he was working on the Xbox, Thompson was still looking for alternatives. "The Microsoft DNA is very much a DNA of 'let's build it ourselves, screw everybody else, we don't need any help…' that kind of mentality, but I kept looking at it and thinking the only company who is any good at this business is Nintendo. I loved Nintendo's model because they had Miyamoto, and they kept the game development business in-house, and they bullied the third-parties. Like when Zelda came out, everything else had to get out of the way. When Super Mario Bros. came out, everything else had to get out of the way. They understood the business deeply, and their first-party title business was remarkable. And they had that Japanese system where a guy like Miya-

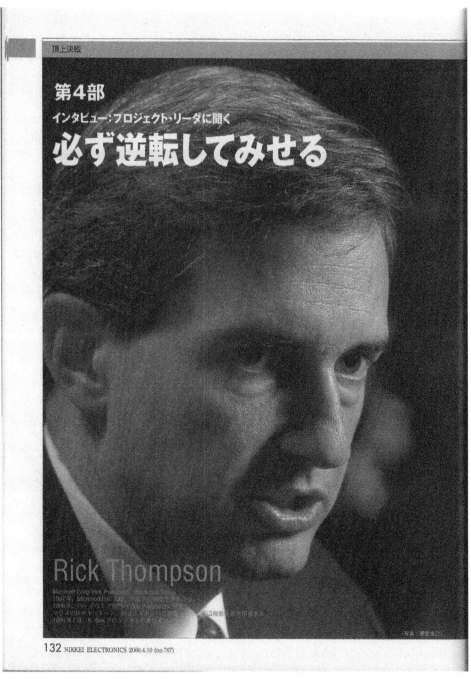

頂上決戦

第4部

インタビュー：プロジェクト・リーダに聞く

必ず逆転してみせる

Rick Thompson

Microsoft Corp Vice President, Hardware Div
1987年, Microsoft H K 入社
1996年, リバースエンジニアリング Vice President
マウスの開発からキーボード、他の周辺機器を作り出すす
1999年7月, 火 Box プロジェクトの責任に

（写真：栗原克己）

132 NIKKEI ELECTRONICS 2000.4.10 (no.767)

Rick Thompson visited Japan so often, that he was even featured in a story in a Japanese magazine

moto would never leave Nintendo. So I visited Nintendo seven times. Back then, the Nintendo of America offices were about 300 yards from my offices in Redmond at Red West, and I would literally walk across a dirt field to visit Howard Lincoln and the rest of the guys over at Nintendo. So between visits in Redmond and visits in Kyoto, I visited them seven times, and in my ugly American way, I just came right out and said, 'I want to buy you guys.' And they would say, 'We're not for sale.' So I got some of my Japanese buddies to do proper introductions to meet the guys in Japan, where I got instructed. The Nintendo company was started in 1889. They used to make playing cards—handmade playing cards. The guy who runs this thing, Yamaouchi, is 80-something years old and is the great grandson of the founder, and you're not going to buy this thing come hell or high water.

Don Coyner's comment about the trips to Kyoto is, 'Yeah, we went to Kyoto and had that conversation. I think they were just confused. 'Huh?'

"We did talk with a guy there, Takaeda-san," says Thompson, "who's still there making hardware for Nintendo. Takaeda came to Redmond a couple of times, and we talked about trying to build a joint box—basically their hardware design and our operating system. We got pretty far on it, but we could never quite get there because we both basically wanted to be in charge of the project.

"I used to drive the guys crazy because all they wanted to do was invent the future, you know, typical classic Microsoft guys, and I was kind of the anti-Christ going out to Nintendo and saying I'd rather buy them… In my mind we should have paid $25 billion for the company, rather than start this from scratch internally."

McBreen, who was also involved in negotiations with Nintendo, remembers several serious discussions. "We basically made the pitch to them that they weren't great at hardware. They were great at characters. And first we looked at buying them, and they said no." That might have been the end of the story, but apparently Nintendo was still interested in some kind of partnership. "I remember I was at the Red Robin in Redmond Town Center on a Friday night, and I got a phone call from my contact at Nintendo USA who told me that Mr Yamauchi wanted to start negotiations again. And so we negotiated with them for a little while. Rick actually went over to Kyoto.

"Later we disclosed the entire hardware design of Xbox to their engineers to see if it made sense to work with us. They spent three and a half days in Red West going through all the technical implementations of the design of Xbox. Xbox was no surprise to Nintendo. They knew when it was announced. I have faxes going back to Mr. Yamauchi about potential joint partnership between the two companies. So when Xbox was announced, they knew everything about the technical details. They had spent two and a half days in a conference room with their best engineers."

McBreen also remembers some specific elements of the negotiations. For instance, Microsoft was proposing that Nintendo would get out of the hardware business altogether and publish on Microsoft's hardware or through a joint venture. Nintendo could produce a certain number of royalty-free games per year, with the rest being at something like $9 per game. McBreen says, "It was very favorable to them, but in the end they basically came back and said—they were very Japanese about it—that no matter what the deal, how favorable it was to Nintendo, it would look like they had lost to Microsoft in a space where they had history and we had none. It was going to be a Microsoft product that would be endorsed by Nintendo. But the deal on the table was that they were going to get out of the hardware business, and Xbox was going to be the exclusive platform that Nintendo games played on."

~10~
The Hail Mary

"Hail Mary"

XB0X - 12-21-99

In December 1999, the Xbox team produced another report, which they titled "Hail Mary" (with the quotation marks.)* The report offered a close look at the alternative strategies and relative risks and rewards of the console strategy. It also contained what almost sounded like another ultimatum on one of the early slides.

In this slide deck there were two separate spellings of the console name: XBOX and Xbox. See the whole series of slides in the Online Appendix.

Reasons to Proceed

- The Gamer community is the right constituency to go after. Enthusiast Gamers = innovation
  - They are engaged and passionate
  - They can be relied upon to participate
  - They might be the only end user community with influence
- All other avenues to the home are encumbered by cable, phone and portal (?) companies
- XBOX is a chance to start our own independent asset base in the home

Reasons to Cut & Run

- It is unclear what the long term value of 43MM installed XBOXes will be
  - XBOX will not terminate a fat pipe connection
    - MS will have 3 boxes: XBOX, Dishplayer, STB
    - STB & TV-Pack is what ATT, Charter, et al license
    - However, cable modem and DSL suppliers will lock down (make proprietary) their fat pipe connections.
    - XBOX will be downstream from either a TV or a PC broadband connection
- The XBOX 8 year loss is $900MM
- XBOX performance is at parity with PS2

What Success Is / Isn't

- Goals:
  - Establish our brand and key standards in the living room through XBOX 1.0 (earn a seat at the table)
  - Develop long-term assets - content franchises, IP, and a profitable online gaming (and download) service
  - Ship 43MM consoles and 106MM+ games over 6 years (8 years)

- Non-Goals:
  - Uber-unification
  - Pushing productivity apps into console space
  - Fix PC Gaming fragility

Required Outcome & Recommendation:

- XBOX P&L:
  - Our decision: Whether to invest (lose) $900MM over 8 years to build a $4.6B/ year business with sub 5% RM
- We can only proceed if Console success is fundamental to CG's success
  - If un-modeled upside entices us (up-coming slide)
- Final, Final, Final decision needed
  - Unified "closed-ranks" if we proceed:
    - Nothing but support and personal commitment from you guys

> # What a "yes" today means:
>
> - Announce: CES / GDC
> - Financial Outlays:
>   - $1B for Hardware (same as 9/29)
>   - More headcount and / or ISV royalties
>   - Requested 110 incremental on just XBOX 9/29
>   - That number has increased to 315
>   - Total HC (with EBU) now 590 people
>   - $1B in content acquisition

One slide mentions un-modeled upsides, which included opportunities that might add revenue and/or popularity to the Xbox model, such as partnering on an MP3 player, getting $10/month subscriptions to Microsoft Game-Zone, a $49 browser/keyboard offer, and several more, including still offering the opportunity for OEMs to buy Xbox motherboards and build systems while paying the usual OS royalty. There was even the idea that these OEMs could produce a dual boot PC that, on the one hand would be a normal PC capable of running productivity software and on the other hand, operating as a dedicated game console.)

A "yes" would mean a commitment to announcing the Xbox at the upcoming CES (Consumer Electronics Show) and GDC (Game Developers Conference). In addition, it would require $1 billion to pay for hardware, another billion for content acquisition, and a head count of 315 for Xbox and, with the Entertainment Business Unit (Ed Fries' division), a total of 590 people. The hardware and content acquisition numbers were unchanged since late September, but the head count had increased by 205 people.

The report also included slides titled "Reasons to Proceed" and "Reasons to Cut & Run".

Reasons to proceed? Gamers are engaged, passionate, reliable, and possibly "the only end user community with influence;" other avenues into the home are already encumbered (cable, phone, etc.); Xbox could represent an "independent asset base in the home."

Reasons to cut and run? The long-term value of Xbox was unclear, even based on an installed base of their target—43 million units; Xbox losses of $900 million per year; Xbox is "at parity" with the PS2, meaning that it wasn't better, just equal.

It is interesting to see what they considered goals for success, versus those they weren't concerned with. For instance:

- getting a "seat at the table" in the living room by establishing the Xbox brand;
- developing long-term assets, such as game franchises, IP and a profitable online game and download service;
- shipping 44 million consoles and 106 million games over the life cycle of the console (6-8 years).

In other words, they weren't concerned about unifying gaming around the Xbox, including Office and other Microsoft productivity applications, or helping the PC game division become more robust.

There were several slides offering alternative strategies, such as putting $2 billion into Sega in exchange for equity and developing Xbox with them. Another idea, based on the concept that "it's all about content" was to create a new company in Japan (with majority ownership by Microsoft) to bring together game rock stars like Miyamoto, Yu Suzuki, Sakaguchi and others. Then have this "NewCo," as they referred to it, ship the Xbox. Other ideas centered around developing a strategy around Windows CE or abandoning the console altogether, for the moment at least, and concentrating on becoming a software powerhouse like EA.

The final slide in the main deck was called "Next Steps":

- This is a 5+ year decision / commitment
- "Grudging acquiescence" isn't good enough
- Create the XBOX—Games Division
- Get the organization decisions finished
- Move us—get us into one space

Another group of backup slides included some technical specs, justification for using Windows NT as the basis for the Xbox OS, suggested peripheral devices for Xbox, and strategy rundowns for both first party and third party titles.

There was no immediate Christmas present for the Xbox team, however. Although the Xbox concept remained technically alive at the change of the millennium, it was not yet fully approved and funded, meaning that it was still just an idea, but not a project—a noun, not a verb. More birthing pains were required, and labor really began a couple of months later in a contentious meeting on the day normally reserved for hearts and flowers—Valentine's Day 2000.

A Hard Decision

One of the issues that was sure to show up again in the next, and possibly definitive meeting was the inclusion of a hard drive in the console. No console manufacturer had previously used a hard drive in a console, but the idea of including one in Xbox was present from the beginning. The first mention of a hard drive that I could find was in a slide deck from April 1999, which was at the beginning of the "Bill" meetings.

The main area of contention was price. On a console that would retail somewhere in the neighborhood of $300, the hard drive at $50 dollars a pop was a massive extra cost. Besides price, the main argument against including a drive was that it wasn't necessary. After all, every previous console manufacturer had done quite well, first with cartridges and later with optical drives. Perhaps because Microsoft was at the time primarily PC focused, the idea of using a rewritable drive just made sense. Add to that the fact that back in April 99, when the proposed system was just as likely to have become a specialized Windows PC, a built-in hard drive was completely logical.

As the project trended toward a console instead of a Windows PC, the concept of the hard drive remained in the plan, but support for it was nowhere near unanimous. One of the problems pointed out by opponents of the idea was that, unlike other components of a console system like memory, graphics chips, and motherboards, hard drives do not reduce in cost over time. Part of the business of consoles depends on the fact that a lot of early components will get cheaper over time, meaning that over time the cost per unit goes down before the console's retail price is inevitably reduced. Not so with hard drives. For 50 bucks you could buy an 8-gig drive at wholesale this year. Next year, the drive will still cost you 50 bucks, but it might be a 16-gig drive. So you get more for your money, but you can't get a cheaper price per unit.

Another downside to the hard drive argument was that, even if you did add a higher-capacity drive for the same price, you couldn't get any benefit from it. For instance, suppose the initial system released with a 10-gig drive and the next year only 20-gig drives were available at the lowest price. You couldn't essentially reward later purchasers at the expense of your earliest customers, so the result is that every future drive, whether it was 20, 40, or 80 gigabytes, would have to be reduced functionally to 10.

Ed Fries and J Allard were big proponents of the hard drive. They saw the potential of having the drive—downloadable patches, better and more convenient storage of games and saved games, expansion packs—but ultimately the fixed price of the hard drive created a difficult tradeoff—a hard drive vs more RAM.

There were good reasons for increasing the RAM on the machine. According to Stuart Moulder, who sat in for Ed Fries at one of the more heated "Bill" meetings on the subject, they made the call to go with the hard drive, but in retrospect he realizes that Bungie—if they had been part of Microsoft at the time—would have opted for more RAM. "Limitations on RAM in the Xbox was a large part of why Halo looks the way it does. It was very repetitive in its look and feel because we had limited memory for textures and geometry. So the tradeoff was you could either have super-fast load times between segments by reusing assets that were already in memory, or you could have a wider variety of textures and so on, but you would have to hit the DVD for them with an impact throughout the game."

At the time, when Gates turned to him and said, "You're the games guy. You're going to make the software for this. Which would you prefer?" Moulder admits that he didn't have the definitive answer. At the time he did his best to enumerate the benefits of the drive.

Bob McBreen spent many hours trying to figure out how to manage costs on Xbox, and the hard drive was one of the big issues. "We had a spreadsheet that had Sony's costs in it, and then had our costs on it, and they didn't have a hard drive, and we did have a hard drive. We spent hundreds of hours in meetings trying to figure that out."

According to Mike Abrash, who was a staunch opponent of the hard drive, "I thought it was going to be a fifty dollar paperweight," the decision ultimately went in favor of the drive when Allard "wrote this very long treatise about all the things you could do with a hard disk, and that was kind of the end of that discussion." Abrash contends that, although Allard was very good at imagining things and very articulate as well, many of the things he envisioned in his treatise never came to be. Abrash also points out that for the Xbox 360 the hard drive was optional. On the other hand, he admits that customers liked the hard drive option in the 360, but still contends that it wasn't necessary.

Broadband

Another Xbox feature that had been proposed from the start, but that was controversial, was the inclusion of a broadband Ethernet connection. Some people favored a built-in modem, but proponents of the Ethernet connection argued that widespread broadband support was imminent. As previously noted, this was one of the major areas of contention between Allard and Gates. In many ways, ditching the modem in favor of an Ethernet port was a bet. The bet was that there would be large-scale broadband penetration into people's homes. It turned out to be a smart bet, but if the timing had been too far off the mark, it would have been a very bad one, and although they made the right choice, it didn't become clear how completely right it was until a year after Xbox launched, when Xbox Live started up.

Bandwidth Penetration and the 3 Bets

Robbie Bach says, "The interesting thing is that for Xbox the idea of an online game service was part of the original plan, but when we launched there was no online gaming. The only thing you could do… we had this very funny cable you could buy that would enable you to string Xboxes together. So people would have these Xbox parties where they'd bring TVs and Xboxes into a house and go and get some rooms and string cables together and then play multiplayer gaming that way. Particularly on Halo, people forget, the first version of Halo had no online service support."

Don Coyner was involved in these early modem versus broadband arguments, although he moved out of marketing soon after the Xbox launch. "Those were heated debates back and forth. There was a faction who looked at the numbers and said, 'So few people have Ethernet, how do we ever get traction when there's so little adoption of Ethernet at this point?' And certainly the games guys were all hardcore on it. 'There's no way you can have dial-up and have any kind of successful service.' And the idea of doing both was discussed for a while, but that was like, 'That's ridiculous. Now you're asking people to develop for two different things. That's impossible, and you'd have to build a service for two different things… that'll never work.'"

Meanwhile, the critics were correct to an extent, but in the end the Ethernet proponents won. Despite the fact that broadband access was still very limited at the time they were beginning to work on Xbox and Xbox Live, and the numbers they were seeing suggested that broadband penetration would not be sufficient to justify their risk, they saw some reason to hope by analyzing the trends in broadband adoption and changes in certain critical technologies. And so, Boyd Multerer, who later led the Xbox Live team, says, Microsoft made three "really big bets" on the future technology:

1. Bandwidth penetration was going to happen.

2. Data center bandwidth costs would fall.

3. Servers would improve so that they could handle the load.

Allard was adamant that broadband was the only way to go, and, certain that he would be able to convince Bill Gates of that fact, he made a $1000 bet with his friend and partner Cam Ferroni in October 1999 that he would succeed by December. He lost that bet, but not by much. Though it did take a little longer, ultimately Gates did come around.

Since large-scale broadband adoption had not yet occurred, there were a lot of unknowns, including what would happen if they succeeded. "We were worried about internet providers blocking our traffic because we knew we would make a lot of traffic, especially compared with most normal households," says Multerer. "And while we were worried about that, we also thought that ok, they actually want people to use a lot of traffic because that will push broadband adoption and give them all kinds of opportunities."

Of course, the inclusion of the Ethernet port at the time was about planning ahead, making bets, and moving forward. It was also clear that there was still work to be done just to get final approval for the console itself. At the time, nobody knew for certain that the the their bet on the Ethernet port would ever be fully realized, and without it the effort to create a true online service would not be feasible.

The "Hail Mary" did not result in approval, but it was only a matter of time, and a different holiday than Christmas.

~11~

The St. Valentine's Day Massacre Microsoft Style

The pressure was on to put up or shut up. Bill Gates was already signed up to deliver his first GDC keynote. Would it be the Xbox announcement or something about games and graphics? The meeting of February 14th, 2000 was convened at 4 pm to find the answer to that question, and many others, and to lead to a definitive decision.

On the night before and the morning of the meeting, J Allard wrote a pair of emails to Bill Gates and the senior management. The first email, (which you can read *in the Online Appendix*, described the technology of Xbox as they had it been planned. He started out the email writing, "goal of this mail is to be full-disclosure and to clarify technical points on xbox as there seems to be the serious confusion." The second email (viewable on page *page 381*) attempted to answer more questions about the vision and future expectations of Xbox.

The meeting was packed with executives, including Gates, Ballmer, Thompson, Allard, Ferroni, Bach, Fries, Mundie, Rick Belluzo*, Rick Rashid from Microsoft Research, and Todd Holmdahl. Allard was, by now, one of the chief advocates for Xbox. This was Team Xbox's moment of truth. According to Bachus, "We say, we're building it ourselves, we're marketing ourselves, it's going to cost billions of dollars to do, and it's the right thing to do. We think it can go successful, but it's going to take a while to succeed. And it was a massacre. I mean that was a very, very contentious meeting. It went on for a long time."

* Rich Belluzo came from 23 years at Hewlett-Packard and a brief stint as CEO of SGI, before spending 14 months as President and COO of Microsoft, leaving in 2002 to become CEO of Quantum Corp.

Fries remembers how the meeting began and, in particular, Gates' dramatic entrance. "Normally my boss, Robbie Bach, was good at doing what we called 'pre-disastering Bill,' but apparently we hadn't pre-disastered him. We're in the board room, it's full of vice-presidents—I mean, pretty high-up people in the company—and Bill walks in and throws the deck down on the table and says, basically, 'This is an insult to everything I have done at this company.' And that was the start. Sometimes he could be dramatic like that. We had seen stuff like that before, so we didn't give up hope, but we were kind of off to an interesting start to the meeting. And we all turned to J because we knew why Bill was mad. He was mad about Windows being gone, and we expected J to put up some fight.* But J was kind of caught off guard, didn't really say anything. So I tried to say something, and Bill just kind of shot me down, and then Robbie tried to say something, and he shot him down and, and then it just kind of went like that for a few hours."

*According to Allard, he had done the predisastering: "I had pre-mailed two long emails the day before that spelled out my posiition—(in the Online Appendix). Asked bill if he read it. Let him cool down. Made others uncomfort-able but hyperbolic "Hyperbole Gnip Gnop" wasn't going to advance the meeting. Bill knew the plan and the logic. He just needed to put his opinion on the record one last time. The plan was go/no-go and we weren't going to suddenly change our mind and try and stuff the full Windows OS into this gaming optimized 64Mb box."

The meeting focused on everything that had already been discussed and argued and beaten to death, and it dragged on and on. People argued the costs of the project, the business model of selling essentially a $500 hardware device for $300 and losing money on each sale, manufacturing and inventory risks, and so forth. Clearly, in the minds of some people, the plan had changed since September, when it was still based around OEM-built machines, to now, when it was clearly about Microsoft getting into the console manufacturing and marketing business. Of course, it was Gates and Ballmer who needed to be convinced, and so the attention was on them.

Everybody I've spoken to who was at that meeting agrees on several things:

1. It was incredibly contentious.
2. It dragged on for hours… and hours.
3. Almost everyone, at some time during the meeting, left the room to call a loved one and say they weren't going to celebrate Valentine's Day together.

However, there are different opinions about how the meeting eventually arrived at its resolution. What follows are the specific recollections of some of the main participants:

Allard says, "the one standout in my mind was rick belluzo who gets little attention in all of this. i think he pretty much put it over the top as i remember it. while it wasn't the 'final word', at some point steveb looked to rick and said "what do you want to do?" and rick said "i don't know a whole lot about the space, but i understand the plan and i believe in the team. i think we should bet on these guys". i don't remember it word for word, but it really stuck out that rick filtered the decision through PEOPLE whereas bill generally would orbit the TECH and steve the BIZ. so, it was a standout for me since i hadn't really seen an executive in the company make a call like that before."

Bachus believes that the point of decision coming might have come when Gates issued an ultimatum, something like "Here's the way that I see it: We need to have something like Xbox to build a cohesive consumer strategy. We either do Xbox or we get out of the consumer business altogether. Sell off the game division to Electronic Arts, sell off MSN, shut down the print productivity stuff, get out of the consumer business and basically go head-to-head with, let's say, Oracle on the business side." Nobody liked that option, and so the decision was made, and Xbox was approved. (*According to one participant, this might have been a different meeting.*)

Bach remembers saying to Gates and Ballmer,

"'If you guys don't think the strategy we're on is the right strategy, let's just stop.' I mean, I still had a job. I could go back and do my day job. Everybody else on the team could go back and do what they're doing before. Let's not get ourselves down the path on something we don't believe in."

Fries remembers the pivotal moment. "Then, at some point, Craig Mundie said basically, 'Well? What about the competition?' Meaning Sony, of course. And Bill and Steve looked at each other, and their expressions kind of changed, and Bill says, 'You know, we should do this.' Steve says, 'Yeah, we should do this.' And then they completely changed, you know, 180 degrees from where they were. They turned back to us and said, 'You know, we're going to give you guys everything you need, and we're going to let you go off and be your own part of the company. We'll give you all the resources that you're asking for, and we want you to go off and do this thing and make it be successful. And that part lasted about 5 minutes. And then the meeting was over."

"Steve said, 'This is what we're going to do, so we believe," adds Bach. "You're not going to get second guessed by us anymore. Go forth and prosper.' He didn't use exactly those words, but that's the videogame equivalent, and from that date forward, to their credit, Bill and Steve never doubted us."

"As Robbie and I walked out," says Fries, "I just remember turning to Robbie and saying, 'You know, that was the weirdest meeting I've been in during my fifteen years at Microsoft.'"

Cam Ferroni says, "We honestly thought they wouldn't go for it. When they did - we were elated… and scared."

During the meeting, Thompson says, "Stuff was flying around, hot and heavy. It's like being in your first fire fight to watch something like that. So we sat there all evening and sort of sang Kumbayah… Well, that's the wrong way of saying it. We sort of girded ourselves. 'We're going to do this. We're really going to do this.' That sort of thing. And then on March 10, 2000, I did the Tokyo announcement, Gates did the San Jose announcement, and J Allard did the London announcement. And we were off to the races."

In retrospect, the Valentine's Day meeting was the culmination of the many smaller go/no go decisions, and it would be fair to say that the project was approved several times leading up to that meeting. In fact, some people say, erroneously, that Xbox was approved back when Rick Thompson and J Allard were put in charge back around August/September. But this was it… the moment when it was full steam ahead.

One real irony is that the final project—the Xbox—was a dedicated game console, not the modified Windows box that Gates had wanted and that the Xbox team had initially proposed. Further irony was that the ex-3DO/WebTV/WinCE guys had wanted to do a console from the beginning, but it was ultimately the DirectXbox, which depended on the DirectX APIs, that prevailed. Whether, as some maintain, that was the Xbox team's plan all along, or whether the concept evolved out of the research the team had done to convince Gates and Ballmer, the end result was something that most people thought would never happen—and, perhaps, almost didn't: A Microsoft game console system.

-12-

Inconceivable

"When Cam and J and Jon Thomason came on board, the project hadn't gotten anywhere yet. I mean, it's also completely fair to say, those guys— Otto, Ted, Kevin, Seamus and Nat—were all on board before the project was approved. So, when you ask when did the Xbox begin, you know, you could say it was a gleam in Otto Berkes' eye. That's a fair statement. You could say Bill approved it in July because he said hey, there's some good product ideas here. You could say Bill and Steve approved it in December, which was a different outcome than what Bill was looking at in July, but still ok. And you could say, well it didn't really start until February because that's when they approved what we actually decided to do."

-Robbie Bach

When word of the console project began to spread, most people were dubious at best. A typical reaction was described by engineer Dave McCoy. "I remember when a lot of us first heard that Microsoft was going to build a console, our first reaction was to laugh because we thought it was such an untenable thing. I mean even inside the organization, it was like, 'Hey guess what? We're going to build a console.' 'What? Are you kidding? That's never going to work. That's preposterous. Microsoft doesn't know anything about this.'"

Even after McCoy had been absorbed into the team, he and many of his colleagues were still having a hard time believing in the project. "We thought it was preposterous, but here I was working in a small little group and it was all over the map in terms of what was this thing going to be. Was it going to be a device that just runs Windows and is it going to have a keyboard. Is it going to be this or is it going to be that? I remember seeing a version with a little C: prompt on it. Ok. That's cool… I guess."

Jon Thomason, who would lead the Xbox operating system team, said, "There was all this posturing. No code had been written; no hardware had been built—on either side. All the people posturing, wanting to do this. And all these sort of demos that Otto and Seamus and everybody did, there's nothing but smoke and mirrors there. And that's ok. That's what makes it a great story, because there were all these forces arrayed against each other with no substance and yet somebody won. And then a whole other team came in to build it. By the time I got on, my team... we didn't spend one second doing anything but real code. No demos. Any demos that happened came from the ATG team."

The Original Xbox Team When Approved

Corcoran, Elizabeth A.	Daugherty, Gregg R.
Booth, Jennifer A.	Holmdahl, Todd E.
Wilcox, Jon L.	Stewart, James R.
O'Rourke, John S.	Walker, Robert S.
Allard, J.	Hebenthal, Douglas C.
Ferroni, Cameron J. A.	McNulty, Mark J.
Spector, Barry J.	Mooney, Dennis
Del Castillo, Leonardo G.	Vingerelli, Enrico G.
Gibson, Greg S.	Friedrich, Bernd
Kwoka, Paul J.C.	Roshak, Todd G.
Liu, Dick C.K.	Thomason, Jonathan G.
Reents, Jeffery M.	Sharpe, Tracy C.
Blackley, Jonathan L.	de Leon, Juan Carlos
Dernis, Mitchell S.	Henshaw, Jeffrey D.
Engevik, Deborah L.	Bach, Robert J.
Ng, Brenda J.T.	Angeloff, Drew A.
Schnepf, Brett A.	Hufford, David E.
Coyner, Donald R.	

Chips for Xbox

With Bill Gates weeks away from taking the stage to announce the Xbox to the world at GDC, two of the most important Xbox components had still not been determined. The story behind the Xbox CPU involves two major players and some last-minute surprises while the Xbox GPU story involves one clear industry leader, an unlikely upstart, and some hardcore negotiating.

The Xbox CPU

The major contenders for Xbox CPU were Intel and AMD, although Rick Thompson says that Philips was also trying to pitch Microsoft on a custom CPU. Initially, Microsoft chose to use an AMD chip, in part because it had better performance than the current Intel chip and also because they couldn't come to agreement on the price with Intel. Both the original fast boot demos for Bill Gates and the infamous Silver X had been on modified Windows machines using AMD chips. According to Rob Wyatt, they had become comfortable working with AMD's ATX boards. They provided better performance for games than the Intel Pentium chips that were available at the time. At the hardware level, there was a lot of support for AMD. In addition, while Blackley and others were traveling around making their pitch for Xbox to developers, they were saying that Xbox would use AMD's CPU and NVidia's graphics processor, so that was the expectation.

Management wasn't quite as loyal to AMD as the engineers were, and Wyatt remembers getting an email from Steve Ballmer. "All it said was, 'Don't fuck up the Intel account.'"

Bob McBreen was directly involved in the negotiations with various chip manufacturers, both CPU and GPU chips. He visited both Intel and AMD to see who would offer the best terms. His first experience negotiating with AMD went very well. "They were great partners, fabulous negotiating." However, when he approached Intel, it was quite different. "Rick and I had a call with (Intel CEO) Pat Gelsinger and told him that we were doing this Xbox thing and that we had some very aggressive pricing that we wanted them to hit on chips, and in addition to that we needed them to develop chips with a faster front-side bus, and they basically told us, not interested. Not our business."

So with Intel off the table, discussions with AMD got serious. They met in Las Vegas with AMD's CEO, Jerry Sanders, and "a bunch of mucky mucks," but now AMD was asking for a very much more aggressive deal. They wanted Microsoft to take a $200 million equity position in the company and also pay aggressive rates for the chips. "We kind of choked. All we were trying to do was buy chips, and they were trying to leverage it. 'Wow, AMD is now a partner with Microsoft, and not only are they a partner, but they've taken an equity investment.' And we told them they were crazy. They thought they had us over a barrel because it had been quietly leaked to everyone that AMD was our partner. And they threw this thing, at the last minute, and stared us down."

McBreen says that it's possible that AMD knew that Intel had turned them down and figured they had the upper hand, but the Microsoft negotiators told AMD to take this proposal off the table and come up with a new proposal without the equity requirement, and they said no. The best they would offer is some adjustment to the pricing. As soon as they returned to Redmond, they called Intel again, and this time was different… they were interested in dealing. "And so, for a period of time, I was going back and forth with Intel and AMD, and AMD I don't think figured out that we had a backup plan. They thought that we were stuck, and so the negotiations with Intel picked up really dramatically."

Meanwhile, it was almost time for Bill Gates' big Xbox reveal at GDC, and they still didn't know what processor would be in the box. According to McBreen, Rick Thompson had already left for Japan to make the announcement there, and his slide deck said that the processor was going to made by XXX. McBreen was still going back and forth between the two companies and keeping Bill Gates updated.

The issue with Intel was that Microsoft wanted them to promise a more powerful chip, one that would equal or exceed the performance of AMD's chip. It came down to a dozen Intel negotiators with McBreen on the other side of the table. "And at the end, at the last minute they agreed. I sent the deal sheet over to Bill. Bill said, go with Intel. Got the information to Rick in Japan, and then all hell broke loose with AMD."

CEO Sanders called McBreen right after the announcement, "and just went crazy. Absolutely crazy. We tried to tell them what was going on. We tried negotiating with your people, and they kept coming back with this equity thing, and we kept telling them we don't want to deal with equity, and they kept coming back with it. And he was like, 'Why didn't you call me directly?' It was crazy. Then he ended up calling Bill, but by then it was too late. We'd already done the deal with Intel."

The Xbox GPU

From the beginning of the project, NVidia was expected to supply the Graphics Processor Unit (GPU) for Xbox. In part, the decision was based on

NVidia's quality and reputation as well as the relationship that some people at Microsoft had already established with them. Another reason was that it would lend credibility among third-party game developers that Xbox graphics would be powered by NVidia. And they needed those developers on board.

Negotiations began long before Microsoft had planned to reveal the project to the public, but word had leaked out somehow, and it made negotiations more difficult. McBreen was once again one of the principal negotiators for Microsoft. He says, "NVidia believed that there was no way we could ever choose anyone else for a graphics processor because it had already been leaked. They were at the top of the heap for gaming companies, and so if we came out and said we're going to do S3 or somebody, we would lose the 3rd party gaming companies. So trying to negotiate with (NVidia CEO) Jen-Hsun was next to impossible. He was very proud of his technology; he knew he had us over a barrel."

To complicate matters even more, the recently purchased WebTV team got involved. McBreen notes that the "honeymoon phase was still very strong... they were the darlings. They knew hardware. They were technology mavens, and so every decision we would make, Bill would say, 'Hey. What do the WebTV guys think about this?' Well, the WebTV guys did not think we were smart at all. They thought of themselves as silicon vendors, and they had this company that they had been talking to for doing graphics stuff on future versions of WebTV. It was called GigaPixel."

Gigapixel

George T. Haber is certainly not a major character in the Microsoft saga, but his story is worth telling, if only because Microsoft almost made him a multi-billionaire. Haber was a Romanian immigrant who came to America to follow his technological dreams. He came from the Transylvanian region on the border with Hungary. "All the Dracula movies and things that you read and hear about vampires, for some reason based in this mountainous place." Haber's history is remarkable. His mother was a survivor of Auschwitz, and his father had fought and been captured first by the Russians, then by the Germans, and then by the Russians again. He says, "I was brought up with this thinking that the only thing that matters in life is the thing that you can carry with you wherever you go, which is basically your brain and your education, and the persona you become by learning."

Haber was encouraged by his parents to explore art and learning, and at one point he picked up the guitar. "Back in Communist Europe, you could not build amplifiers or buy amplifiers because there were no materials. There was no guitar shop. There was no music shop. So me being passionate about music, I had to study electronics to figure out how do you actually build an electric guitar out of regular guitar by putting the coils to pick up the sound under the strings and then connecting them to transistors that will amplify, and then in the end, building a speaker out of paper coils and rubber from bicycle wheels. So, as it turns out, I probably was better at building these things than playing the guitar."

Because of some political negotiations between the communist government and the United States (that had nothing to do with Haber personally), he was able to go to Israel and study electrical engineering at Technion—the Israel Institute of Technology. In 1988 he made the decision to move to Silicon Valley and pursue his dreams of becoming a technology entrepreneur. He worked at a company called Daisy Systems, where he met Vinod Khosla, who would later become a famous and powerful venture capitalist. Following Khosla's lead, he took a job at Sun Microsystems. "I was employee number 100." Haber worked on floating point mathematics for Sun's RISC (Reduced Instruction Set Computing) processor and got a lot of experience in processor design. "Once I finished that job, I started looking around, and I saw all these colleagues that were working at Sun leaving and starting their own startups. So that bug bit me as well, and I decided to leave Sun and go and join a startup."

Haber heard through friends that Silicon Graphics Incorporated (SGI) was looking for an expert in floating-point processing to help in building a secret graphics engine. Working there, he met some of his future partners. Next, he created his first startup, CompCore, which specialized in video compression and decompression algorithms for use in both software and hardware.

CompCore released some very successful products, including SoftPEG and SoftDVD, which were licensed by PC manufacturers as part of the standard OS designed for playing back DVDs. They also started working closely with Intel, and Haber was invited to sit in the front row at a keynote by George Grove with Bill Gates and Michael Dell. "And I'm an inky-dinky guy from 'Eastern Europe nowhere' sitting here with the giants of Silicon Valley, in the same row, because I had the software to play back DVDs." Microsoft even invited Haber down and made what he called an obscene offer, "obscene in the sense that it was so low that it made me laugh, to buy the company, to the point where our annual sales were almost ten times bigger than what I was offered to sell the whole company." He says that Microsoft offered about a quarter of a million dollars when he was bringing in eight to nine million a year in revenues. Eventually he sold the company to Zoran for $80 million.

After selling CompCore, Haber was approached by two of his ex-SGI colleagues who had developed a 3D technology that was faster and more efficient than anything on the market. They had a small amount of funding from Andy Bechtolsheim, one of the founders of Sun Microsystem's, who was also one of the first investors in Google. In 1997 they agreed to create a new company. They called it GigaPixel, and very quickly found more investors and raised millions of dollars. Haber's business model was based on what he called "Haber's Law," which stated that "If it can be done in software, it will." He believed that, given enough horsepower on your system, you could do anything in software without having to build special-purpose hardware for the same purpose. And the unofficial corollary to Haber's Law was that if you could build it in software, you could license it instead of selling a product. This was the model he has used successfully at Comp-Core, and it was the model he envisioned for GigaPixel.

The GigaPixel technology was based on the idea of tiling. "Tiling was basically dividing the screen into rectangular tiles and rendering only the visible objects inside those tiles, and then you have enough memory and cache to bring all the textures and do the best rendering you can. After that, each and every tile is rendered separately. You reassemble the image like a puzzle, and it looks perfect. It requires a lot less memory; it's a lot more powerful." In many ways, GigaPixel's tiling technology was very similar to what Talisman did (see *Game of X v.2* pages 357 and 358), but it was independently conceived, designed, and developed and turned into a real product, whereas Talisman was never officially released and, more significantly, it would have required an ancillary graphics card.

Eventually Haber came up with the idea of offering his technology as an embedded system in computer chips, and he made his first deal with a graphics chip maker called NeoMagic. He was also in discussions with Intel and others at the time. When he heard about PlayStation, he decided to offer his technology to Sony. "I went to one of these conferences where Kutaragi-san was then the head of the PlayStation, gave a speech. I more or less followed

Kutaragi-san to everywhere he went, including the bathroom, to show him what we had, and in the end he yielded and came to one of the side rooms. We put up a small demo and we showed him GigaPixel technology." Kutaragi said that the technology was interesting, but it was too late to incorporate in their next project. He also said something about other companies possibly jumping on the bandwagon in response to Sony's success with PlayStation. "And that kind of gave me the hint that he knows that others are working on graphics technology, as well. So we started poking around. I called up friends at Microsoft and Intel, asking them who can be the big player, and very quickly it became clear to us that it is Microsoft, and that they are working with Intel and also working with AMD."

The next logical step was to go up to Microsoft and offer to do some presentations. "Microsoft really, really loved this concept of tiling and saving power, saving memory, making something that can be both hardware and software implemented, and they signed a deal with us, gave us some up-front payment and said, 'You guys are it. You're going to be part of the Xbox team, and they even moved us into the Microsoft building in Mt. View."

This sounds promising and simple. As it turned it, it was anything but.

Deals and Manipulations

In addition to the WebTV group, several chip makers also mentioned GigaPixel, and with NVidia's Jen-Hsun continuing to drive a hard bargain, interest in an alternative option grew. McBreen admits that they were bargaining hard with NVidia, too. "We were asking for things like, in addition to just buying chips from them, we needed to be able to say, 'What if we wanted to start our own fab <*fabrication facility*>' That we had the right to build our own chips and just pay them a royalty. Which is crazy, right? There's no way we're going to build our own fab, but the guys down in San Jose, the WebTV guys, were thinking that their hardware was going to take over the world, and that the next step was that we were going to get into the chip business. And we told Jen-Hsun that we could just pay him a royalty. So basically he had to transfer all of his IP to us, and GigaPixel was obviously willing to do all that because they had never built a chip before. And so when Jen-Hsun was being stubborn, we went and signed a deal with GigaPixel. We gave them five million dollars. And what that did was really bring Jen-Hsun to the bargaining table."

The GigaPixel deal forced Jen-Hsun's hand. He had already leaked information linking NVidia with Microsoft's new project, which had an immediate impact on NVidia's stock value. Also, word had gotten around Silicon Valley that Microsoft had rejected NVidia in favor of the upstart GigaPixel. "Why would Microsoft, that wants to make the best gaming platform, walk away from NVidia. What's wrong with NVidia? So when we signed the deal with GigaPixel, Jen-Hsun, as you can imagine, went ballistic. I remember this perfectly. It was a Saturday morning and my family was going to Sun Peaks for vacation, and almost the whole way there—my wife was driving—Jen-Hsun and I were talking about what we were going to have to do. He was concerned about his stock price, and so I told him, 'Real simple. Go buy GigaPixel. George will sell you the company. If you think the bottom is going to fall out on NVidia because Microsoft is going to do the deal with GigaPixel, go buy GigaPixel.' And for about two weeks all I told him was, 'Buy GigaPixel. Buy GigaPixel. Buy GigaPixel.' And he kind of went through the motions on that, but nothing seemed to be happening, "so I sent him a message. 'OK, Jen-Hsun, we're done dancing. We're getting ready to make the announcement here soon.' And then he came sent back, 'Send me a deal sheet. Send me a sheet that says all the things that I'd have to meet to get back in the game.'"

So they sent a deal sheet that stipulated everything they had previously demanded, as well as the right to extend their price of chips to OEMs, thinking at the time that other companies might put out entertainment boxes with built-in Xboxes—thinking of Xbox as a platform.

After both Thompson and McBreen had signed off on the contract, they informed Bill Gates that the deal had been signed. Later, while they were both coaching a Little League game, Thompson got a phone call from Gates saying, "All right. Go with NVidia if they'll really match the terms." The next morning Thompson and McBreen were on a plane. "We went down to NVidia, and we took the GigaPixel contract and everywhere where it said GigaPixel, we crossed it out and wrote NVidia. We were down there all day. We went through it. We signed it. We initialed it. And then it was done. No one knew about it, but we got everything that we wanted from it."

Jen-Hsun later initiated two lawsuits against Microsoft. One suit claimed that the contracts included sales forecasts, and that he wasn't obligated to meet the original pricing past those forecasted numbers. Then he tried to sue, saying that the original contract was for 15 million units and that after that Microsoft would have to renegotiate. These suits came later, however. At the time, the deal was done, and NVidia would power Xbox graphics.

So what about GigaPixel? Haber says they had a deal with five million up front and a fifteen million dollar investment in the company. They had come up to Microsoft and demonstrated their technology to several major 3rd party developers, including Square Soft, and everybody had been excited about using it in their games. And meanwhile, GDC and the public reveal of Xbox was just around the corner. They had given embargoed interviews to several news organizations. There were discussions with bankers to take the company public with a valuation of two billion dollars.

Expecting to do an IPO, Haber began discussions with S3, a high-volume, mid-to low-range chip producer, and 3Dfx, who were in the high range, but sold in low volume. So his pitch was that, with his $2 billion IPO, he would buy both companies for somewhere between $400 and $500 million. This was Haber's grand plan. "I actually get the world's best brand, which is 3Dfx with the best known and most dedicated developers group, and the world's most efficient high-volume 3D graphics engine provider, S3. And with our technology that is cheaper than what S3 had, and the significantly better performance than what 3Dfx had, we could take over the whole market." In his mind, NVidia would stay in the business, as well as ATI and other graphics card companies, "but I didn't see them having any chance of winning in the long run because we would have covered the high end and we would have had covered the low end, and come in with a technology that was cheaper and better than both."

Haber saw how it all was supposed to happen. "So the scenario was that Bill Gates talks about Microsoft's intention to become a leading player in gaming, and he introduces this unknown company that has the world's best 3D technology, because Microsoft always brings the world's best technology to consumers... that was the story. I go and shake his hand, and then a demo starts about our technology, I disappear and Bill continues his story. So it's all buttoned down. The script exists. The story exists. The PR agencies are in line."

And then he gets a call. Haber remembers that Robbie Bach called personally, but McBreen says categorically that it was not Bach. "On the day-to-day stuff,

Robbie didn't really pay a lot of attention. He probably didn't even remember the term GigaPixel. There's no way Robbie was there." According to McBreen, once the NVidia contract was signed and official, he went directly over to GigaPixel to deliver Microsoft's decision. "It was a very quick, 'We decided to go in a different direction' type meeting. Not a lot of details, other than hey, we decided to go in a different direction. There was a little bit of him trying to understand it. We weren't really in a position to disclose a lot of stuff."

Haber remembers that he was told the reason for the "different direction" was due to a lack of confidence in their ability to deliver the chips on time. There was some story about the chip maker, Flextronics, needing the components a couple of months earlier than originally thought. Stuff like that. McBreen doesn't remember precisely what was said, but says, "That's probably the party line that we gave him. Something like, 'We have an extremely tight schedule. If we miss the schedule we're not going to have credibility with the game developers that we're so highly dependent on." But McBreen says the real urgency was that they had already begun leaking the NVidia story to their game developers because the NVidia name gave them confidence and didn't require them to adapt to any new technologies.

Years later, you would think that Haber would be bitter, but as an entrepreneur, he's philosophical about it. "You can imagine I see the $2 billion disappearing. Today, after all these years of being an executive at running companies, I can tell you that I do understand them. From their perspective, like with any team, the weakest link is the one that breaks the chain. So they invested the billion dollars in Xbox on the software side, on the hardware side, on the PR, on supporting game developers, and they perceived us as potentially being the risky part, and if there is no graphics engine ready, then the whole launch is useless. How can you have an Xbox that doesn't have a graphics engine? And based on timelines, they felt that it was just too risky." Remember, his personal perspective on life was: "The only thing that matters in life is the thing that you can carry with you wherever you go, which is basically your brain and your education, and the persona you become by learning."

~13~
The GDC Reveal

Bill Gates personally revealed the Xbox to the world at the Game Developers Conference on March 10, 2000. This marked the first time Gates had appeared at GDC, which made a statement in itself. It meant that the top gun at Microsoft was into games. Well, he wasn't into games like Stephen Spielberg, who was an avid player, but for the first time game developers saw that Bill Gates understood their importance enough to step on stage and make this announcement.

Among those who joined Gates on stage was Seamus Blackley, who demoed the new machine, represented by the big Silver X. To Blackley it was a terrifying moment, the culmination of two years of dreaming and anxiety, meetings, conflict, and ultimate redemption. And this was the moment of truth. "We had one of them in the back, and I think Kevin was lying down behind it getting ready to switch it to another one if it crashed. He was lying under the stage with his hand on a switch. And I'm thinking that everyone I will ever work with, or will ever to get a job from or will ever get money from is watching right now."

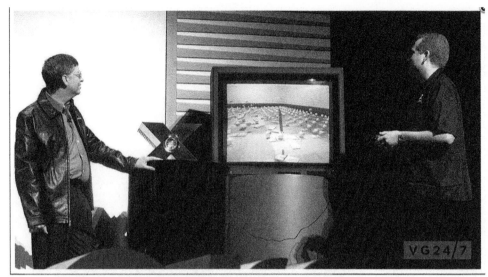

Bill Gates and Seamus Blackley demoing the Silver X prototype at GDC.

There was one big surprise for some of the developers. Not everybody had gotten the memo about the CPU. When Gates described the new system, Rob Wyatt was among many who had been working on the system who was completely (in recognition of Wyatt's Scottish background) gobsmacked. "The demo we showed on the GDC stage was our hardware on the AMD-based PCs. When Bill announced the Xbox, and he was like, 'These are the specs. It's an Intel Pentium processor, blah blah blah at this speed…' We're like, Fine… What? Tell them it's AMD.' That's when they switched it and we'd not been told." Of course, only a very select few people knew about the last-minute CPU switch; otherwise, the event continued without any obvious hitches.

Simultaneous events took place in London with J Allard and in Tokyo with Rick Thompson doing the unveiling.

London Launch with J

Marketing lead John O'Rourke was in London with Allard and tells a story that he says, "perhaps knocked four or five years of my life off." The night before the event they were in the Hemple Hotel in London, down in the basement, trying to rewire the Xbox prototype—the Silver X—with a soldering gun.

"J and I had done an afternoon of meetings, and we were going to do the pitch and the demo the next morning for a big press conference. I said let's meet after dinner and we'll walk through the pitch and the demo. He brought up the Xbox and plugged it in. We heard a little sound, and nothing went on. We quickly realized that J had not switched over the power from 110 volts to 220 volts. We'd fried the power supply.

"We quickly jumped on the phone, found a small PC shop that happened to have the right power supply or that we believed to have the right power supply—he had three or four different ones. We told him to bring all of them, and he came over at about nine o'clock that night.* We took two that we believed were going to work, and then had to find the tools and a soldering iron to connect this new power supply to the Xbox, which we did. We taped it all together, said a prayer that it was going to work, and it did. It was the only box we had. We didn't have a backup." At the time, there were only four Silver X prototypes. They had one, Gates had two in the States, and Thompson had one in Japan.

According to J Allard, the guy rode from Surrey to downtown London on a scooter to deliver the power supplies.

After the Reveal

Soon after the Xbox reveal at GDC, Microsoft consummated the deal to purchase Bungie Studios for $30 million. They continued the marketing of Xbox by showing at the Consumer Electronics Show and later, at E3 that year. At E3, they finally offered a release date and a price-point of $299. With a half a billion dollar advertising budget, they built demo kiosks, ran TV spots, and purchased print ads in the lead-up to the launch. They also began to show teasers of the early titles, such as Halo, Project Gotham Racing, Munch's Oddysey, Malice, and other games, while giving hints about online gaming to come.

Word travelled fast, as even the Des Moines Register
had a story about the Xbox reveal at GDC.

~14~
It's a Go! Now What?

Meanwhile, following the Valentine's Day "go forth and make a console" directive from Gates and Ballmer, the scramble to complete the project moved into high gear, but it soon lost one of its leaders.

Rick Thompson left the company 31 days after Xbox got the green light. "My basis for leaving was that I did not want to work on a project that never contemplated making money. My comment was, 'It's against my religion.' Nobody really held that against me. The separation was amicable, sort of like if you going to be a naysayer on this thing, and say I don't want to work for four years on Xbox and lose $1.2 billion, you have a good reason to be gone. So I left and I went to work for a dot com in Seattle."

With Thompson's exit, new leadership was needed. Robbie Bach was chosen to be the project's overall leader, Todd Holmdahl headed up the hardware division's efforts, J Allard remained focused on the software, and Ed Fries got busy shoring up their launch title lineup.

Building the Hardware

Building a brand-new, state-of-the-art game console system from scratch in less than two years is, as Holmdahl says, with classic understatement, "not a lot of time to build a piece of hardware." Certainly, the small Xbox hardware team, which numbered between 12 and 15 people, faced big challenges. For instance, they didn't have their GPU (Graphics Processor Unit) locked in until March 2000. "And then it was just a scramble to get it done with that group of people at the time."

They did get help. Intel and NVidia offered significant support for the motherboard design, and Flextronics helped with the mechanical design and did all the system testing. In fact, according to Holmdahl, the project went pretty smoothly, in stark contrast with the approval process that had preceded it.

The Xbox Hardware Team.

"We had Greg Gibson and Rick Vingerelli. There were three double Es (EE) on the team—me and Greg and Leo (Del Castillo). We were doing the system work, essentially putting everything together and architecting it. We had Harjeet Singh later on, and he helped quite a bit. Rick Vingerelli was in charge of manufacturing, so he worked to make sure the box was manufacturable and did a lot of the deals. Desmond Koval was a workhorse.

The learning curve was steep, but some elements of the project were less challenging than others. "The general architecture was pretty straightforward," says Holmdahl. "We were basically creating a computer that runs the best DirectX-based GPU that you could find at the time and just having it be dedicated to running video games." But a project of this magnitude is never easy, and there were numerous challenges, such as the sheer complexity of dealing with so many parts and component vendors.

Working on the custom GPU with NVidia presented its own set of challenges. "We got the first chip back, and it didn't work that well. We tried to get the best we could out of it. The second chip came back really late in the cycle. I think we replaced all the dev kits out there with these new kits so that the game developers had real hardware. It was super late in the cycle, and they were modifying their games with the new kits."

"I think the system engineering wasn't dramatic," says Holmdahl, "but the complexity of testing everything and bringing it all together was. We had never worked with anything like a DVD drive, and having that not work… you effectively had to brute force it. We had to apply as much time and energy… as many people as we had. And the top two people, Leo Del Castillo and myself, applied it to the DVD drive to try to get that fixed. So yeah, I learned a lot in a short period of time about getting systems together, getting people and a number of different companies together… organizing that and getting them to work together to meet a certain set of deliverables, and learned a lot about negotiating the deals that it takes to make something like this happen. And then I learned a lot about DVD drives and how they worked (laughs) and putting them together."

~15~
Xbox ATG

"We were a group of developers developing tools and code for other developers."

-Pete Isensee

Rob Wyatt remembers having lunch one day with Seamus Blackley. They were considering how they could still be part of the Xbox project, even if they had no role to play on J Allard's team. Wyatt had worked at other companies that had their own technology groups, and while Microsoft already had Microsoft Research (MSR), the Xbox division did not have something of that sort. The idea for an Xbox technology group was not to do pure research, but to become the world's experts on Xbox development so that they could help developers right out of the gate. "You can't make a console without having a bunch of guys who fundamentally understand everything about the console," says Wyatt. "So Seamus went to pull some strings. He went and did his schmoozing and it happened."

When Blackley created the Xbox Advanced Technology Group in mid-2000, he didn't cut corners. He went out and recruited some of the best technologists at Microsoft, including Mike Abrash, Rob Wyatt, Drew Angeloff, Mike Sartain, Chris Prince, Mike Dougherty, Mikey Wetzel, Michael Monier, Scott Posch, Mark Thomas, Pete Isensee and others. Together, they began to explore the Xbox operating system and hardware, creating sample code to share with developers and working directly with early developers to solve problems they encountered.

Shortly after forming the Xbox ATG, Blackley brought in Laura Fryer, a veteran Microsoft producer who was at the time completing the launch of Crimson Skies. While Blackley remained the ideological leader of the group, most members I've spoken with credit Fryer for being the practical leader and keeping everything together.

"She was one of the best managers I've ever had," said Pete Isensee, "and she was somebody who understood game developers because she had done that."

Technical artist Dave McCoy remembers being recruited into ATG because Xbox was going to have programmable shaders, which at the time were very new and advanced. After talking with Abrash about his work, he was encouraged to go talk to the ATG engineers. "There were about 16 people at the time in ATG, and the idea that you would bring in an artist or technical artist into this group seemed sort of exotic, but Seamus was like, 'Yeah, you know what? I think we should do that because we need to explore stuff. If we're going to build planes, we need a test pilot and we need somebody who can go talk to other pilots and go, hey, this is cool shit. You should be working on this.' So that's how I got involved."

Blackley had been trying to get audio engineer Chanel Summers to join ATG, but she was happy where she was, working with Ted Hase in the DirectX group. "I had a lot of free reign, a lot of power to create my own empire, and he was basically like, 'You run your whole thing. You set your strategy.' It's hard to leave that." But after holding out for some time and sticking with the DirectX team, she realized that it was a once-in-a-lifetime opportunity to work on a new console system. "And I thought, wow, a really great platform, then, is to do something great with audio within a console, and build a fantastic audio subsystem which was truly ahead of its time. So I saw this as a challenge." She was tired of all the focus being on graphics. "You have to think about the whole package. It's sound, it's music, it's design, it's story, it's character, it's art, it's graphics, and why is audio the bastard stepchild?" And so she went to Blackley and said, "Sign me up."

As excited as she was, leaving Hase's group was difficult. Blackley hadn't been subtle in his attempts to recruit Summers, and Hase, who highly valued loyalty, was upset when she left. She says, "He was one of the best bosses I ever had. Hands down. He would do anything for his team, and protect them, and empower them. But it was like, you've got to let baby bird fly from the nest."

ATG's Role

Pete Isensee joined ATG at the beginning of 2001. He was a game industry veteran and developer who one day decided to change direction by applying for a job at Microsoft. "I was thinking, well, maybe I could get a job at Microsoft making games at their Microsoft Game Studios, so I sent in a resume." Isensee ended up going through a rigorous screening process, "They gave you a lot of programming questions, and you had to write code, create graphs and do all kinds of things just to get in the door to get an interview." He did get interviewed, however, and was hired by Laura Fryer as an engineer for ATG.

Isensee says that he initially worked on "everything but graphics." Among his tasks was to help develop the certification process for Xbox games. He also developed a sample application that met all of Microsoft's requirements. The certification process demanded that developers adhere to a certain list of standards. For example, they didn't want developers to display the number of bytes that were required for saved games, but instead to use "concept blocks" to represent the amount of storage a game required.

Isensee observed that ATG was unlike most divisions in Microsoft. It didn't make a product, it wasn't directly building the Xbox, but they were definitely in the business of helping developers and competing against Sony and Nintendo while doing so. "We're here to help you make the game become the best it can be on Xbox. We're going to give you lots of source code that we've provided that helps get you up to speed. We're going to visit you, talk with you, and do events. That was the role of ATG."

ATG was in some ways, the first customer of the Xbox team. Any feature or component that was developed for Xbox was first given to ATG, which would test it and try to learn how best to use it. They would write minigames into which they would insert the code. "We would say, 'Yep, this is going to work well. This is the way the game developer would want it,' or say 'No, this is not going to work; this is not going to work if they want, for example, a poll model versus an event model.'"

Explaining his example, Isensee says, "Game developers are very different and they have very different expectations than a typical Windows developer. In an event model you get information coming to you in a queue of events—a window opened, somebody clicked here—and you grab the event that is at the top of the queue. In the poll model, you actually request what is happening right now, what button is being pressed on the controller right now. 'I don't want to wait for it to come through after I've processed a hundred other events because I don't want that latency.'"

In addition to testing components and features through minigames, ATG was writing the actual source code examples for the developer SDKs. In some cases, they would write side-by-side versions for how something might be done in Windows versus Xbox. "Another thing we would do is create a feature you can only do on Xbox and show the specific way to do it so that it is as fast as possible. It's more of a performance, highly tuned feature. Or maybe it was a new set of APIs, like Controller. Controller was brand new. There was no such thing on Windows. So, we had a sample that showed all the things you could do with a game controller. You'd see all the inputs coming in on the screen with the controller on the screen and the buttons getting pressed in real time. We were a group of developers developing tools and code for other developers."

In addition to developing and perfecting code, ATG's experts were providing technical support for developers all the time. They would tell developers, "If you have any questions at all—they could be technical, they could be business, they could be anything—send them to us." They were also diving into the hardware, working with companies like NVidia and Intel, debugging at the hardware level and writing low level code to determine if the hardware was working as it was supposed to work.

Rockstar

ATG support even extended in some cases to sending an engineer out into the field to help developers unravel sticky problems. ATG engineer and troubleshooter Mikey Wetzel, who had developed a reputation among developers for his superior DirectX sample code, such as a swimming dolphin that was a lot cooler than a spinning cube demo, tells the story of one of several exploits.

This story is about Grand Theft Auto 3, which was supposed to be a PlayStation 2 exclusive. "One of what we now call DAMs (Developer Account Managers) comes into my office and he shuts the door. He says, 'I need to tell you something, and nobody's allowed to know.' Like your boss is not allowed to know. Your boss's boss is not allowed to know.

"It turns out that Microsoft had made a deal for an Xbox version of GTA3, which is a big secret deal. The problem is that the Rockstar office in Vienna, Austria is having problems with the frame rate—severe problems, like it's running at 13 frames a second instead of 30 or even better, 60. They are paranoid as can be, so they won't send code over the internet or even mail disks. Worse, the game is supposed to reach the stores in a couple of months." So Wetzel is sent to Austria to fix the problem in a hurry, no time to pack or prepare. He can't tell his

A Touch of the Blarney Blackley: The KnowWonder Story

Drew Angeloff tells a story about the early days of the Xbox ATG. He begins his story saying, "Seamus has this whole thing planned out, of course, because it's Seamus."

Then he tells the story. "We end up having a discussion with the guys from KnowWonder, and they are like, 'Microsoft building a console? That's ridiculous.' But these guys had received their dev kits, and they were getting super excited about it. And Seamus says, 'You've got to start using developer support. We notice that you never send in any questions.

"And they're like, 'Ah, developer support is full of shit. We send questions to Sony and we get these half-assed answers back. We know better than they do. And it takes like a week to get things back.'

"And Seamus says, 'Oh yeah? Why don't you try asking developer support? Name a question.'

"And they figured out some technical question. 'OK. We'll ask this.'

"Seamus tells them, 'Send them an email.'

"Email goes out, and of course Seamus has partially prepped this, and over in Redmond there's somebody waiting for the email. The email comes in and they generate an answer to the question and they send it back ten minutes later. And the look on the devs' faces is like, 'Holy shit. Not only did they answer my email, instead of an automated response… it's an actual human being… but they gave me an actual technical answer I didn't know, and within a 15 or 20 minute window.'

"That was kind of the genius of Seamus. There's a little bit of carnival trickery going on here… everybody was prepped to do this. On the other hand, he really did deliver. There actually is a real answer, and he started building the trust pipeline between developers and Microsoft. They were getting real answers that would be useful for their development. And ATG built a huge pipeline of trust with the developers. ATG developed a reputation as one hell of an organization."

boss why he's not going to be at work. Microsoft is going to take care of his dog at home. That's it. He's on a plane within a couple of hours. At the other end he's picked up by a limo and someone asks him if he's a rock star or something. Irony.

At the Rockstar offices, he's given a computer and a quick rundown of procedures from an IT guy, but no contact with developers. He's able to get the frame rate to 60 fps, but then the developers are so excited that they keep adding features that they had previously disabled because while trying to fix the frame rate problem, like fog or real-time lighting, which slowed down the game again. Wetzel was able to fix the game again, and ultimately it shipped on time, and according to Wetzel, it was superior to the PS2 version.

Xfest

While DRG had hosted many developer events over the years, in the fall of 2000 ATG hosted their first of many Xfests, which brought Xbox developers face-to-face with the Xbox team to learn and share knowledge and ideas specifically for the upcoming console. The idea came from Blackley, but people credit Laura Fryer for actually running the original Xfests and several that followed.

According to Wetzel, the name for Xfest was inspired by a radio station event. "Seamus really wanted to call it XXX Hardcore, and he'd laugh. He's a funny guy," he says. But one day when he was driving to work, he was listening to a radio station he says was called The End. "It was at the end of the dial. 107.7 The End." The station was going to put on a festival with several bands, and they were calling it End Fest. Back at Microsoft, when Wetzel suggested the name Xfest, it caught on, and so XXX Hardcore became Xfest.

Xfest became a regular event that continues today, and many former ATG members believe that it was one of the reasons for the success of the Xbox. "One of the unique things about all the engineers at ATG was not just that they were great engineers, but that they knew how to communicate with other developers," says Isensee. "So they had this unique combination of understanding their stuff deeply and being able to talk with someone one-on-one or being able to go to a conference and share that information. Laura spearheading those Xfest events, making sure we had the right content, great speakers, professional execution... that's one of the biggest things that I give her credit for in addition to forming a great team. In the three or four years that she ran ATG, she hired some amazing people."

Three images from the first Xfest:
The setup
Registering for Xfest
And finally, socializing at Xfest

Announcement for Xfest London from 2001

UK: Microsoft has revealed full details on the European Xfest Unplugged event, a one-day conference for developers targetting the Xbox hardware.

The invite-only conference, Microsoft's first European event specifically for new developers, is targeted at producers, programmers, graphics and audio artists who are looking to develop current and future products for the Xbox hardware. The session will cover topics such as graphics programming, audio features, and online development as well as the latest technical information.

"European Xfest Unplugged is our response to the many developers who have contacted us, wanting to learn how best to maximise the transition to Xbox hardware and ultimately secure a development deal with a publisher," said Adrian Curry, account manager, Xbox developer programs. "Xbox is a system designed from the ground up to empower developers to achieve their wildest game fantasies. We are very committed to events such as Xfest Unplugged, which will help address the huge wave of interest in the development community about Xbox and maximise the creative and financial potential of projects in development."

The event will take place on Oct. 30 in central London. For registration details email Microsoft with "invite" in the subject line for more information. To this address... Xfest-EU@microsoft.com

Source: http://www.fgnonline.com/

Xfest Japan

Jon Thomason tells a story about the first Xfest that occurred in Japan. He was there with Laura Fryer and Seamus Blackley. Each of them gave a talk to the group, and then there was a reception.

Now it's pretty easy to mess up humor when dealing with different cultures, and Blackley managed to do just that. "Seamus gets up and he's trying to tell a joke," says Thomason, "and we'd been there for many hours in the room, and honestly, it did kind of stink in the room afterwards. So Seamus was trying to tell a joke, and he was trying to say that everyone must have been really good developers because it stunk really bad of body odor in there. And the translator looked at him really weird, like, 'Really? Am I supposed to translate that?' And so he's like, 'Yeah, yeah.' And so she translates it, and there was just silence. And Laura and I were just going, 'Oh. What did he just say?' We couldn't believe it. Obviously, that did not go over very well with a Japanese audience."

The Content Design Team

There have always been support teams for technical people, for program-mers. Never did anybody think about the content creators, and with the new Xbox, we really wanted to empower the people creating the content.

-Chanel Summers

Although Chanel Summers joined ATG as an audio expert, she was aware that there were many people involved in game development besides the core engineers. There were musicians, sound designers, artists—2D, 3D, graphic artists—and game designers. Just about anybody on a game development team who wasn't writing code or tools and wasn't in a purely managerial role, was a content creator, and Summers thought they also needed support to

"and make sure that they were taking full control over the capabilities of the Xbox, because we wanted the best damn games."

She approached Blackley and told him what she wanted to do, and he gave the thumbs up for the Xbox Content and Design Team, working as part of ATG. Summers brought in experts in all disciplines, like Scott Selfin from the DirectMusic team, and art expert Dave McCoy, and others from all of the content disciplines. Part of her purpose was to make sure that it wasn't only the programmers who knew how to get the most out of the system. "Programmers were kind of ruling the world,' she observed. So, by traveling the world and meeting with content developers to help them get the most out of creating for Xbox, they meant to shorten the learning curve that all consoles suffer, and bring out A+ games in the first generation.

"So it's really funny when people go, 'What games did you work on?' I'm like, 'Well I can definitely tell you that we had a hand in like pretty much all of those Xbox games that were coming out because we worked with all those content creators to do something special.'"

On the Road with Xbox

Special thanks to Kevin Bachus for supplying images from the Xbox road trip to Japan.

Once the Xbox was official because Bill Gates made it so, a serious effort to attract developers began, including road trips carrying the infamous silver X. Jon Thomason recalls these trips well. "We traveled internationally, and we had to wait for that Silver X all the time. It came through odd-sized baggage and stuff. And it would break occasionally. It was really fragile. But it was just a PC, and it was just running PC games. There was absolutely nothing there, but it was a concept and it was trying to get everybody psyched, and that was what Seamus was good at.

"The funny thing was—and Seamus won't remember it this way at all, and I know this is my biased perspective because it's the part that I was doing—but I really believe that the reason we got through all those talks was not just because we brought around the shiny X and because we tried to look cool, but because I and a few other people were telling a story about what we were really going to build."

Thomason asserts that they reached developers not just with flashy promises, but with a solid plan. It was something of an uphill battle, however. "In the first meetings we did, people just laughed us out of the place. They're like, 'It's going to take 3 minutes to boot. It's going to blue screen all the time.' When I presented in my PowerPoint, what we were actually doing, they were blown away. They couldn't believe that Microsoft would do this. What we were doing was completely radical for Microsoft."

The key to reaching the developers was to convince them that they were not just putting Windows in a box and calling it a console, but developing a lean, mean, from-the-ground-up operating system specifically for Xbox. "I told them how it was going to work, and how it was single process, and everything rebooted ran in kernel mode, and you rebooted between levels, and it could boot in a second, and it was going to have less than a megabyte memory footprint. We told game developers all this very early on, so I was not only committing it to the team that we were going to do it, I was also committing it externally as well." In Alex St. John terms, they were tar babying the OS and its features to Microsoft *(original reference in Game of X v.2 page 81122.* "We told them the actual project plan, probably even in advance of telling our execs. I mean, we were out telling everybody what we were going to do. Really early. I mean scarily early. It was another one of those risks. We were promising the world..." For the record, the actual boot time of the original Xbox exceeded their claims by booting in .85 seconds.

One of the radical ideas that Thomason's team had determined was that only the kernel actually resided in the Xbox, while the rest of the OS was statically linked into the game and would ship on the game disks themselves. "That was just unheard of for a Microsoft product. So, they laughed at us and mocked us when we first went in, and then I'd do my presentation and they would say, like, 'Well, if you guys can really do this, this will be awesome,' but they still didn't believe it. I don't think there was much real belief until the first Xfest where we showed real code working. They eventually did believe it, and we did ship it."

Entertaining Japanese Visitors

American and European developers were initially skeptical, but they could be won over. But how did you reach the Japanese, who rightly saw themselves as the leaders in the console business? Kevin Bachus tells one story in which the Xbox itself doesn't figure in at all. "We were really courting the Japanese. We'd met with them a bunch of times, and we were really trying to get them on board."

Bachus had the idea of putting on a party just for the Japanese visitors at E3, and he found a hostess bar that was similar to the bars he'd seen in Tokyo, but this one was in Torrence, less than an hour from the convention center. "So they showed up, they're having a great time and there're all these hostesses dressed in like elegant cocktail dresses, and they were sitting with the Japanese guys laughing at their jokes and making them feel, like, very friendly."

As the evening wore on, their guests started to get more and more carried away. "They started ordering all this expensive wine. Japanese folks love red wine. They're ordering basically every bottle of red wine in the place. Robbie (Bach) shows up, and they're stinkin' drunk. Robbie doesn't drink, so he basically comes and goes. 'Hey thanks so much, really looking forward to your support, we really hope you guys come on board, see you later.' And he is out like a flash." And after the party, Bachus got the bill. "I think it was like $26,000. I still have it, it's like itemized for all the wine that they drank."

The original Xbox ATG Team.

Kagemasa Kozuki, CEO of Konami, leads a toast at a sake ceremony following the XBox Partner Meeting, March 31, 2000. In the background, Sam Furukawa (President, Microsoft Japan), Kazumi Kitaue (EVP of Global Sales & Marketing, Konami), Pat Ohura, Robbie Bach. Below: More scenes from the Microsoft booth.

Linda Inagawa, Seamus Blackley, and Kevin Bachus posing with the Silver X at Sony's headquarters, and playing a prank by mounting the Xbox prototype on Sony's entry.

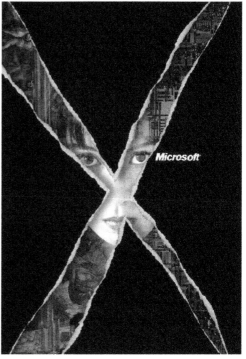

Hirohisa "Pat" Ohura, managing director of Microsoft Japan, head of the Xbox team in Japan, speaking at an Xbox partner meeting in 2000. Right: The crazy X background used at the event.

~16~
The Xbox OS

We had a tiny team. We were just a bunch of OS guys, and we managed to pull it off with just a ridiculous amount of risks. I'd never permit my guys to do that now.

-Jon Thomason

The OS team, led by Jon Thomason, Tracy Sharpe and Rich Pletcher was working concurrently with the hardware group. Of course, the team had grown, but still remained relatively small, having added a few junior programmers and some people cherry-picked from the Windows NT and Windows 9x teams.

Four Options

At the beginning of the project, the three leads sat down to determine their strategies, and they explored four options, which Thomason describes:

- Create something from scratch. "We quickly discounted that."
- Use the Win9x source base. "We thought about that seriously, just the Win386 part of Windows."
- Use WinCE. "We discounted that one pretty fast."
- Or use NT. "We decided to use NT. It was the most modern of the code bases. It was the biggest of the code bases that we looked at by far. But we thought it would have the best features. Ironically, Tracy was originally from the Win9x team, so he had a bunch of learning to do, but he's absolutely a genius, and he's really the hero of getting the software built. He's a Distinguished Engineer at Microsoft, which is the equivalent of a VP developer."

Note: While I was researching this book, I interviewed Boyd Multerer, who was at the time working on Xbox One. I asked him about Tracy Sharpe, who was also working on the project and he told me, "You really should interview Tracey. He's truly a genius. The problem is, Tracey doesn't talk much. You probably wouldn't get much if you tried." I decided to let his colleagues tell the story for him.

Quiet Team—No Name

Thomason refers to his group as "a very quiet team." In fact, they purposely didn't give the Xbox OS any kind of a fancy name. They just called it Xbox System Software. "We tried to keep it as bland as we could. In fact, my message for the whole team from day one, 'If anyone ever hears about us or if we ever do anything that calls attention to us, it's always going to be negative, because the only thing we can do is get in people's way. We need to be out of people's way. The only thing we want to be known for,' I told the team,' is to have the best development tools,' because we were in charge of the development tools, as well… 'the best development tools of any console in history, and we're going to be out of the way.' I set really tight goals about performance and time, and the whole goal was to be invisible. I don't know if we achieved that, but we certainly tried."

We Did It

Thomason talks about the success of the Xbox OS and how they won over developers. "The document literally said boot in a second, under a megabyte footprint," says Thomason. "We presented that to developers all around the world. I traveled a lot at that time, trying to persuade people that we weren't idiots, and it took a lot of persuading. Anyway, we built all that. We built the operating system we built all the stuff that plugged into Visual Studios, the debugger and everything. We had to build all the developer tools.

"At that same time, Seamus was hiring all these ATG folks, and had some really great game developers on his team. What they did was they wrote at least 200 samples by the time the first XDK came out. They did a fantastic job of writing samples. There have never been better samples than what those guys wrote.

The first Xbox XDK.

"My team did operating system and debugger interface and all that. And they did a great job of putting the samples in, and they we pulled the whole thing together as an XDK, and with their great game support and them putting on the Xfest developer conferences, we won over the development community, and that's not an easy thing to do. That's one of the things I'm really proud of. Nobody believed that we could do this. They really didn't. And I think that we showed that by putting the right people on it with the right goals, that we could build something they were happy with.

"On the other hand, I don't think we did a great job on Xbox UI. I think we did a much better job on Xbox 360. We put a lot more emphasis on the UI. We really only had one guy doing UI on the original Xbox. That wasn't a big success story. I think that was the worst part of Xbox system software."

Cowboy Coders—Rewriting Code

Even though Thomason's small team met, and even exceeded, their goals, how they did it is another of the many remarkable stories of how amazing things got done at Microsoft.

"We didn't have any program managers back then. We got our first program manager, Marc Whitten, who is now a VP over at Xbox. He was very junior at the time. So he was coming over trying to get some process into us, and we were total cowboys. I think that is probably pretty obvious from everything I've been saying, but 12 developers, all working in the same hallway, one meeting a week. You know, we were just writing code. We didn't have specs. We did have documentation… we had developer documentation, but it was all just a process that was super tightly geared toward doing stuff that game developers wanted. So basically, it was developer to developer. Developers would call us… they'd call me on the phone; they'd send me email. They'd talk to the ATG folks and talk to us, and we'd just slam the feature they wanted in. If we could fit it in that month, we'd get it in that month. Otherwise it would go in the next month. We were super developer centric.

"So eventually it was time to get some program managers, because it was getting a little unwieldy. The team was starting to grow later in the cycle. We were getting beyond our core 12 guys, and they wanted us to do more and more stuff, so we were hiring people. We started doing more UI and all those sorts of things where you needed to have some program managers. So Marc came in, and he was a good guy. He came from a Windows group where he'd been a developer, but he wanted to be a PM, and he did a great job.

Forking Windows

Jeff Henshaw says that there is still some animosity about what they did in creating the Xbox OS. "So the goal was to create the smallest, leanest, most efficient possible OS. We didn't want to start from scratch because it would be insane to ignore the deep body of OS legacy that Microsoft had." And Microsoft did have what they called WinMin (Minimum Windows), which they could have gotten, but, as Henshshaw points out, "It's four and a half megs, it's complex, it's huge, it's hard to build, it's not chipset portable, the driver model is complex, there's a ton of security stuff that is different from the security that we need." So what they did was to "fork" NT. And some people weren't happy about it once they found out.

Forking is when you copy the code and then begin active work on your copy that doesn't accrue back to the original place you copied from.

So Thomason turned to his ace programmer to solve the multiple problems Windows presented. "So the story I want to tell is that Tracy (Sharpe), our kernel architect, came to me right before Xfest. This would have been Xfest in the spring of 2001, so this is pretty late in the game, right? And I was getting ready to give my talk at Xfest, which I did every time, which was the talk on what was going to be available for game developers, and Tracy came and said, 'Hey, we've really got to rewrite the file system.' And I went, 'You've got to be kidding me. I mean, it's April, right?' We were supposed to have our first shippable libraries in June or July. And he said, 'Well, the kernel won't be done until August, right?' And I said, 'Yeah… but still…'

The NT file system consisted of 200K of code, and it was a proven and already well-used system. However, there was one problem. Working on PCs, not game machines, if the computer was turned off or rebooted without going through the shutdown process, it would have to go through a "clean process" and then run checkdisk. And it would display an error message about the file system. For the purposes of a game console, they needed to decide how to handle the situation, but the existing process was not acceptable.

"Of course we didn't show that error message, but we hadn't decided what to do if the hard disk was marked dirty. So Tracey had been trying to figure out a way around that, but there was just no way with our code. And so he came and said, 'We've got to rewrite it.' And I said, 'This is just nuts. This is completely insane.' And so I was too afraid to tell Marc that we were going to do it… I don't think 'afraid' is the right word, but I didn't tell him, anyway. So I just kind of, on the spur of the moment at Xfest, announced that we're also in the process of rewriting the file system. And so they were the first people to hear about it—the developers at Xfest. They were eating it up, though, because they could see that we were just cowboys, and were really trying to make a tight, fast, small system, and they loved it. And I got a huge applause.

"Tracy did rewrite the file system. He did it in about 3 weeks, if my memory serves, and instead of the 200K NT file system, his was 9K, and over the course of many years, I got to hear lots of RMA reports on Xboxes, because the service guys would give us reports on what was broken in the Xboxes that got returned. I never once… never in my entire time there, heard of a corrupt Xbox file system. Not even once. And he did this in about 3 weeks. And of course we tested over a course of a few months, and I think he fixed one or two bugs.

"The main thing about this story is how we just took tons of risks… unbelievable amounts of risks. Andrew (Goosen), on the graphics side, rewrote the driver completely from scratch. He kind of looked at some NVidia code, but they didn't even help us. There was this really bitter relationship, anyway, so he just wrote the driver himself, and he honestly didn't think he could do it when he started. And he just did it. He pulled it off. We just took risks everywhere.

"We had a tiny team, and were just a bunch of OS guys, and we managed to pull it off with just a ridiculous amount of risks. I'd never permit my guys to do that now. (laughs) But it really worked out. We made all the dates. We didn't make the hardware slip even a single day. We ended up with something that we're all really proud of. You can ask any of those original guys working on the OS, and I think they'll all tell you that they're proud of the code and proud of the way we got it done. It's not that common to look back on a project and not have huge regrets or 'I wish we'd done this' or 'I wish we'd done that.'"

At this point, I quoted Jason Jones from Bungee who once said, "We had the advantage 20 years ago of being really stupid. I mean, being really young, but that young is stupid." Thomason replied, "I think that describes us. We were all young and stupid. We really were, but we just did it."

Group picture of the Xbox ATG team.

~17~

Early Reveal

In advance of the upcoming CES event, John O'Rourke, who was the head of marketing for Xbox, says that they had been working on a "Behind the Xbox" exposé story—16-20-pages of pictures of the console, pictures of the proto-types, interviews with J Allard, Ed Fries and Robbie Bach. "Obviously we had a longer lead time, so we had a confidentiality agreement with them that they wouldn't put this on the newsstand until after we announce the name and what it looked like at CES. What we came to discover is that someone at the printer had pulled one of the copies off the run, scanned it, and posted it to the internet about four days before the CES event. So, David Hufford comes into my office and says, "I think we have a problem." He showed me the site, and you could see it coming up, page by page, full scans of everything. I'm thinking, "This is terrible! Our surprise is gone.

Bill Gates and "The Rock" presenting Xbox at CES.

"It turns out, that it was this incredible blessing because it ended up giving us about two or three news cycles around the announcement. This fed that frenzy of people that wanted to know what this thing was and what was happening at CES. We had to remain quiet because we were under embargo and we couldn't really comment on it, but others were talking about it left and right, taking different points of view on it. When Bill actually announced it at CES we got a whole other cycle of news, and that's when we got to come in on the conversation, also pulling in our third party partners to talk about it. It turned out to be one of the greatest marketing tactics that we ever fell into."

Gates and "The Rock"

Bill Gates took to the stage on January 6, 2001 at CES in Las Vegas. This time he was joined by professional wrestler and soon-to-be actor Dwayne Johnson—better known as The Rock—and they teamed up to unveil the real Xbox console for the first time. The previous year Gates had announced Xbox at GDC, but this was the first time the public saw the actual console, not the Silver X prototype. This time, it was the real thing.

In between some banter between Gates and The Rock (who was essentially on loan from THQ to help promote their upcoming WWF Raw game on Xbox), they managed to show some prerelease versions of Oddworld: Munch's Oddysee and Argonaut's Malice, while pitching WWF Raw* and another upcoming game, Tony Hawk Pro Skater 2x from Activision.

O'Rourke credits David Hufford, "a brilliant PR strategist," for organizing The Rock's appearance. "He was central to the launch of the announcement of Xbox at CES when we had The Rock there. He was incredibly young and always passionate about the gaming space, and he played a huge role in working with The Rock and the WWF to put together the script between the 6'4" The Rock and the 5'10" 150-pound Bill Gates."

O'Rourke notes that early feedback for Munch was very positive.

*WWF Raw was not a launch title, but came out in February 2002. Hufford later became the head of Xbox PR.

http://www.gamesfirst.com/articles/releases/xbox_unveiled_at_ces_2000.htm

Meanwhile, there were other deals in the works...

Behind the scenes, a rare look at what goes on behind the scenes.

~18~
Launch Titles

Even though they were new to the console market, Microsoft understood that console sales depended on the quality of games they could offer, and that strong launch titles would be critical to the new system's success, particularly when they were going up against far more entrenched competition from Sony and Nintendo. So, while the hardware team was building the console and the software team was creating the OS, Ed Fries was on the hunt for some first-party launch titles, and not just any launch titles, but games that would rock the world. He knew that his current first-party portfolio, which consisted of Flight Simulator, Age of Empires, the Links golf games from Access Software, and a few more small titles would not do the trick. Moreover, none of Microsoft's current studios had console development experience. They needed something big.

One of the first big steps Fries took was to contact Lorne Lanning at Oddworld Inhabitants. Oddworld's Abe's Oddysee had been a PlayStation hit, and Fries hoped to get him over to Xbox. "We had an opportunity to work with Lorne Lanning and we really saw that as a key deal because he had worked on PlayStation in the previous generation, and so to be able to take a developer away from Sony and have him working on our platform was good." Fries also approached Liverpool-based Bizarre Creations to adapt their Dreamcast title, Metropolis Street Racer for the Xbox, which became the launch title Project Gotham Racing. NFL Fever was another launch title developed by Microsoft Game Studios.

Oddworld

Oddworld was formed by two industry veterans, only their backgrounds were not in the game industry. Lorne Lanning was a technical artist who had worked in special effects and high-end animations, most recently at the prestigious Rhythm and Hues. (If you remember the famous Coca Cola bear commercial, that was from Rhythm and Hues.) Sherry McKenna was a Hol-

lywood veteran producer who had worked with some of the top animation and special effects people in the business, and at the time the two met, was working for Disney on theme park attractions.

Lanning had a grand vision for a five-game series (a quintology) based in a capitalistic nightmare world, initially featuring a truly odd character named Abe. He sold McKenna on the idea and together they started Oddworld Inhabitants. Their first game, Abe's Oddysee, was a big success on both PC and PlayStation.

While Oddworld's games were truly unique, so were their production values at the time, based on 1997 standards. They modeled and rendered every aspect of their games in cinematic quality 3D and then dropped them down to PC and console resolutions, and for the first two games, went from 3D to a 2D sidescroller. The second game in the quintology was Abe's Exoddus, which was released in 1998.

Although Oddworld was originally funded through investment from a private trust administered by the heirs to a billion dollar estate, they later made a deal with GT Interactive for a 49% stake in the company along with publishing rights. Although the relationship with GT went well enough for the first release, problems with the second release caused Lanning and McKenna to start thinking about getting out of the relationship.

Initially, when McKenna told GT that they were seeking a buyout partner, they were given the go-ahead. So in late 1998 McKenna began having secret meetings with Steve Schreck, who was a product planner for Microsoft. Although they were also speaking with another publisher, the meetings with Schreck were going very well, so well in fact, that they came to a verbal agreement that Microsoft would buy out GT's share and enter into a first-party publishing deal.

Sherry McKenna and Lorne Lanning

In the meantime, GT was experiencing its own problems and had decided to seek a buyer for their company. So when McKenna told them that she had found someone to buy out their shares, she was told no. GT was for sale, and they needed Oddworld as part of their portfolio. They would not approve of a buyout deal, and because GT was their publisher, Lanning and McKenna couldn't complete the deal with Microsoft. "Considering the playing field of business in Silicon Valley," says Lanning, 'who's going to buy a company that has a lawsuit going on with its current partner? And we were still a developer relying on a publishing deal, so we can stay fed month to month."

Consummate professional that she was, McKenna was mortified. "I pretty much told Steve that we were going to do a deal with him. And I didn't check with GT. I didn't think I had to… I had to call Steve, and it was really embarrassing. I had to say, 'Steve, I know you have every right not to forgive me, but GT won't let us go. And I'm so sorry, and you can't buy us.' And I felt like an idiot. I didn't think that GT needed us that badly to sell… whatever. And I blew it." According to McKenna, Schreck and the other Microsoft people, while they weren't happy, "they weren't mean about it."

But then Infogrames stepped in and purchased GT Interactive.

Life under Infogrames—their new 49% partners—wasn't any rosier than it had been under the original GT management. Ironically, it was McKenna's suggestion to GT that led to the Infogrames acquisition. After meeting a couple of Infogrames' people, she had gotten a very good impression of the company and made the suggestion that GT approach them. "I really liked them. I really believed them. And I thought it was a good idea. And then after I signed like a moron; I met Bruno [Bonnell]* and went, 'What have I done?'"

*Bruno Bonnell was one of the founders of Infogrames (later Atari after acquiring the name) and served as the company's CEO and chief creative officer from 1983 to 2007.

One main source of their concern with Infogrames in charge centered on a policy that Lanning heard about through the grapevine: That Infogrames was going to cut any of their titles with budgets above $3 million, a policy that would leave Oddworld out in the cold. They were working on Munch's Oddysee, but could not show any of it publicly because the PlayStation 2 developer contracts legally prevented them from showing any game footage that hadn't been approved by Sony. Lanning knew that Munch would be axed if he didn't do something.

Lanning performed what he called "a jujitsu." From his days working in the aerospace industry, he remembered that they often created "visualizations" of future products. So what Lanning did is have his crew pre-render game scenes from Munch. Because these scenes were not rendered in the PS2 devkit, but were simply "visualizations" of their product, it was perfectly legal for them to share them, which they did. They made about a hundred CDs with these game visualizations and sent them to major media contacts. They said, 'Hey, look at what we're working on. Here's the movie clips. Here's screenshots. Here's the story about Munch's Oddysee." And it worked. Pretty soon there was all kinds of buzz about Munch's Oddysee. "Infogrames is a public company," says Lanning. "And we just got blown up in the press as one of the early people that you should be watching for the PS2. Big Sony story, right? That got us into Forbes. That got us splashed all over because no one else had PS2 footage to show."

In *Game of X v.2* (page 118) there's a story about Alex St. John doing something similar, and as St. John described it, what Lanning did was to "tar baby" Munch to Infogrames. This not only saved Munch and Oddworld, but ultimately led to them regaining their shares, getting total control over their IP, and a new round of talks with Microsoft.

Once again McKenna and Schreck began discussions, this time to include Munch's Oddysee as a launch title for Xbox. From Oddworld's perspective, they wanted a publishing partner to help them complete the quintology. One embarrassing moment occurred at E3 when Bruno Bonnell walked into the room where McKenna was demonstrating Munch's Oddysee to Schreck. "It was a moment of embarrassment, but we pulled it off," says McKenna.

Eventually, they began speaking directly with Ed Fries who told them that he was very interested in working with them on a multigame deal. As McKenna remembers the conversations, "He said 'If we have Oddworld, we'll be able to attract a lot of other publishers.' And I said, 'Fair enough.' And he said 'We want to do casual games. And I'm sure you've heard this a million times, too.' And so… OK. Munch would be perfect. Munch is a casual game. That's exactly what we wanted to do."

The decision to go with Microsoft hinged primarily on the answer to one important, and currently unresolved, question. Were Bill Gates and Steve Ballmer going to greenlight Xbox? Even though they were hoping to go with Microsoft, there was at least one other company interested in them. The dilemma was that final meetings with Schreck and Fries took place in December of 1999, and Xbox had yet to be fully approved. Did they wait for Gates to make a decision, or take a deal that might not be available later?

When they learned that Gates was going to speak at the upcoming GDC, they were hoping that he would announce the console officially, but they weren't positive. "So we didn't know at the time and I think it was that Ballmer was hesitating or something, and we didn't know what the final decision was, and we had to wait until Bill got on the stage," says McKenna. "And I remember we were all sitting there terrified. Are they going to announce it or are they not going to announce it? Because if they don't announce it, that means we're not going with Microsoft, and that was a really scary moment. And they, thank god, did announce it."

An Artful Deal

Oddworld negotiated a very good deal for themselves. On the Microsoft side was the law firm owned by Bill Gates' father. On the Oddworld side was precedent. "Precedent is a big part of deal making," says Lanning. "So you can make demands. You can say, 'Well, these are our terms,' And then they'd say, 'Well, no one has terms like that.' And you can say, 'Well we do.'" And then they trotted out Exhibit A and Exhibit B: Two previous contracts that showed their previous deals. Precedent. The final deal didn't include any advances, but Microsoft took over development costs and treated the game as a first-party title at launch. Of course there were royalties, but that's another story.

The Traitors

When news got out that Oddworld was going to develop exclusively for Xbox, a lot of people freaked out. Sony wasn't happy, but they didn't have an exclusive deal, so there wasn't anything they could do about it. But the fans... Many of Oddworld's fans went a little crazy. There were even death threats aimed at Lanning. "Oh yeah. It was not funny," says McKenna. "'How could you do this?' 'How could you be a turncoat?' 'Abe would never do that.' 'How could you go with Microsoft? You're a traitor.' And I wanted to say, 'Wait guys. Sony is a Japanese company. Microsoft is an American company. What do you mean? Yeah we all have problems with some of the things that Microsoft does, but this is insane.'"

What the fans didn't know at the time was that work had begun on a PS2 version of Munch, and they were encountering problems. They weren't sure that the PS2 would be able to handle what they were attempting, and what they had seen of Xbox convinced them that it was more robust in certain important areas, and that they wouldn't have to compromise if they went with Microsoft.

Technical Issues

One of the reasons Oddworld had gone with Microsoft was because they didn't think they could do Munch on the PS2 without making compromises. "We were on a middleware engine," says Lanning. "It was complicating things, and our engineering was basically saying, 'Look, if we get on the Xbox devkit, all of these performance problems go away.' And then we get onto the Xbox and we were running at the same performance. So we had a big problem."

McKenna was no stranger to technology. Lanning notes that her experience working with Academy Award winning effects guys in Hollywood meant that she recognized a problem when she saw it, and wasn't going to let them miss their deadlines. "I don't play games," says McKenna, "and I have a reputation in Hollywood and a reputation everywhere of speaking my mind, and I don't like cover-ups." At one point Lanning recalls that she spoke directly with

Seamus Blackley and told him to come down and review the code himself, or send Mike Abrash. McKenna admits to being thoroughly embarrassed, "but I knew that I had to bite the bullet because we wouldn't be able to make the launch, and that is something we'd agreed to do."

She told them she needed someone immediately, "and sure as shit, they sent them down and they helped us." Blackley sent several people from ATG to help out and identify the problems they were facing, some of which were technical differences based on how Xbox handled graphics. ATG even helped Oddworld interview a new tech lead, who restructured their team and got them all up to speed on the technology Xbox was using. About ATG, McKenna raves. "They were great. They were just wonderful. I couldn't believe it. They just dove right in. It was really important for us. I mean we never could have gotten there from where we were. I mean, just no way."

Fixing the Brawl

One of the ATG people sent down to Oddworld was Mikey Wetzel. "Munch's Oddysee was ready to ship, but it had one lingering problem that was driving the developer crazy. In that game, fights could break out—in fact it was part of the strategy of the game. You could go up and you could slap a character and then start the equivalent of a barroom brawl, and all the enemies would start fighting, and that's one of the ways you'd solve some of the levels.

"The game boasted that up to 30 people could fight at a time. Well that was actually—I don't know if people appreciated it—but that was really impressive from a technology point of view, to have that many AIs running and doing different things at the same time. Well, what happened is that, whenever a fight broke out, the frame rate would go from 30 frames a second down to 3 or 4 frames a second. Obviously, they couldn't ship the game that way. Everything else in the game was ready to go. And I'm kind of a firefighter. I get called in at the very end. Fix this and we're good to go.

"I looked at the code, and the way the AI worked is that every character would look at all the people near him, and they had a variable called 'beatability'. Like beatable is that character? And so when they're in a fight, they're looking at all the characters around them, and the AI would assess which of the nearby NPCs was the least or greatest threat. Well, 30 characters looking at 30 other characters, that's 900 AI decisions going on every single frame. A thirtieth of a second later, they would go through all 900 permutations and look at who's closest to me, who's the easiest hit, and there were different AI criteria for how these characters would fight. Like a character would prefer to fight somebody who was less strong than him, another AI character would prefer to fight somebody who maybe didn't have a gun in their hand, who is closest to them… so forth, right? And I was thinking about it, and it was like, ok, if I was in a fight—a barroom fight—I'd probably have to pick a guy and just fight that person. I couldn't possibly be concerned with all 30 people around me at the same time. And so, my very simple fix was, once you make a decision to fight a guy, let's commit to that decision to fight the guy for, let's say, a second… like 30 frames. And rather than reconsidering that decision… it's not even realistic to think that you could change your mind 30 times a second on who you fight. And the developer took that fix and said, 'It's brilliant.' It was about two lines of code to fix it, and the game shipped. I was another pair of eyes, although I don't know why one of the other developers didn't think of the same solution."

About their experience working with Microsoft during the development phase Lanning says, "It was quite great, and the support was quite great. On the marketing front, leading up to launch, Ed Fries I think really had a lot to do with the vision at the time for software, and on one level you felt the energy of that group and its must-have success orientation and commitment; and those people worked hard. They were working round the clock. All of the people that I knew and was aware of at Microsoft at the time were running themselves really ragged. But they were excited still, so it was a really unique moment, and when they were at the studio, they were only helpful and productive. So that was a wonderful time."

Spielberg

Steven Spielberg was a gamer and had several times delved into creating games, such as The Dig for LucasArts. At the time that Fries was looking for hit titles, Microsoft was a major investor in Dreamworks, so it was natural that he and Spielberg would come together over an Xbox title based on his upcoming movie, *A.I.* "We actually had three games in development around this new movie," says Fries. "The movie was going to come out around the same time as Xbox and because it was from Steven Spielberg it was going to be this huge success and these games were going to ride on his coattails. So part of the launch of Xbox was going to have Steven Spielberg and these games."

Stuart Moulder was involved in the early planning stages of the *A.I.* game projects and took a trip down to the Amblin Films lot to meet with producer Kathleen Kennedy and Spielberg. "They led us through the entire story of the movie, because it was still in preproduction, so that we would have some material and know what kinds of thing we might want to build around it. Which was a fantastic experience. We walked out of that going, 'Wow. This is not *ET* 2. This is an adult, somewhat disturbing, very dark story. But it's hard to see how that could really be the lead IP for a new console.'"

Unfortunately for Spielberg and Xbox, *A.I.* flopped at the box office, and according to Fries, "We had to pull the plug on those games. It was a bit painful, but that's the game business." Moulder remembers that, after seeing what the movie was about, "we went a little ways further down the path with that before ultimately quietly paying them some money and walking away from it, and letting them take those rights back."

Bruce Lee

Jonathan Sposato was one of the first-party leads, and he remembers some of the more obscure titles that were considered. One in particular might have been quite interesting. It was based around Bruce Lee, and according to Sposato, "That was the one that a lot of us were hanging our hats on. We were working with the Bruce Lee estate, with his former wife and daughter, and we got face molds from Universal Studios from when he was a contract player on The Green Hornet." The game was going to be created by a team of ex-ILM (Industrial Light & Magic) employees who had broken away and created a game startup in the San Francisco Bay Area. Unfortunately, the game never materialized as the team missed deadline after deadline, forcing Microsoft ultimately to cancel the project.

Sposato also remembers working with Larry Holland, who was the developer of several popular games for LucasArts, including the very popular *Star Wars*: X-Wing and *Star Wars*: TIE Fighter games. According to Sposato, Holland's Xbox game, Archipelago, was released after the launch, but there seems to be no record of it.

Inside Job

No, Microsoft didn't release a dog or cat game at the Xbox launch, but they did include a game that was generally believed to be J Allard's pet project, *but there's more than one side to this story.*

It was called Azurik: Rise of Perathia from Adrenium Games, a company located in nearby Kirkland. According to Moulder, Allard had started the game with Adrenium (before they actually adopted that company name), and he had a pretty strong attachment to it, despite the fact that other people at Microsoft did not like it. And because Allard was involved, it became a first-party title. "They basically were forced to give the game to us. It was terrible. It was terrible because J didn't want to give it up because it was his personal love and passion. It was terrible for us because we didn't want it. But we were told we had to take it, because to just kill it would piss J off and he'd quit, basically." Moulder goes on to explain that he was sympathetic to Allard's position. He had started it, sponsored it, believed in it. He was forced to hand it over to the first-party team, only to watch them kill it. "So J's point of view was understandable, but it was just the worst possible situation. We don't have any love for this thing, but we're told we have to keep it alive."

Moulder's story may represent what many people at Microsoft believed, but Allard contends that the situation was quite different. He says that the game was started by some superstar employees from Rick Thompson's hardware group. "the goal was for the platform team to have a customer 'in the building' to test everything we produced and said to developers." When Thompson left, Allard took over the team. He admits that they weren't "game guys," but says that the two leads, Matt Stipes and Russ Sanchez, were perfect for the task. As far as it being his presence on the project that more or less forced first-party to adopt it, Allard says, "1st party insisted on taking it over and managing it like all other titles they were working on. I really had nothing to do with it other than being someone interested in learning what we could from them, advising and helping how i could and then sticking up for them when rick left."

Azurik did eventually get published, either at launch or shortly afterward. It didn't do well and got mediocre reviews, although it may have broken even. But as Ed Fries would say... again, "That's the game business."

Bungie

Bungie was one of the top developers of games for Macintosh. They were a small, independent group led by Alex Seropian and Jason Jones, who had met in college at the University of Chicago in 1991 and discovered a mutual fascination with video games. Their original offices were in the not-so-classy South Side of Chicago, which was described by various team members as smelling like a frat house after a long weekend or "something out of Silent Hill." (Silent Hill was a sinister and dark game from Konami).

Bungie released several games over the next few years, including Pathways into Darkness and their first shooter and hit game, Marathon. Their next significant offering was a departure, a strategy game called Myth: The Fallen Lords, which was released in 1997 on the Mac, and for the first time, also on Windows 95. Life as an independent game developer and self-publisher was not easy, and it became even harder when they released Myth II: Soulblighter with an install bug that completely nuked people's systems. Bailing themselves out by recalling 500,000 copies of the game and reissuing it was, in the words of Bungie's music composer Marty O'Donnell, "A million dollar mistake."

The Soulblighter debacle put Bungie in a hole, but they had an ace up their sleeve. It was a new and ambitious first-person shooter game in development. To raise some operating cash, they approached Take Two Interactive and showed them the new project. Take Two was impressed and ending up funding Bungie in exchange for 19.9% of the company, promising to distribute the new game as well as another Bungie project, an animated game called

139

Oni, which was being started in a satellite studio in San Jose, California. They had some operating capital, but it wasn't enough to keep going for long, and they were still in the market for a better offer.

That's when Microsoft showed up. Peter Tamte, who was an executive vice president and Bungie's head of business development, recalls a meeting at Take Two's New York offices that was attended by Rockstar Games' founders, Dan Hauser and Terry Donovan, Bungie's Tamte and Alex Seropian, and some Microsoft people, including Kevin Bachus and possibly Brett Schnepf. Bachus remembers that this meeting was part of a technical briefing tour that took them to San Francisco, Los Angeles, New York and London during January and February of 2000. Tamte later observed, "In this one meeting in New York were sitting the guys who end up defining the future of the Play-Station 2 with Grand Theft Auto 3, and Bungie who went off and defined the future of the Xbox with Halo." Of course, nobody knew the future at the time, and it was one of many meetings they all had participated in. Ordinarily, it would have been forgotten, but the situation was not ordinary. It sparked a fateful idea.

Following the meeting at Take Two, and a subsequent dinner with the Microsoft team, Tamte and Seropian talked about the implications of working with Microsoft. "They're going to need a game that can help define this platform, and we were thinking, 'Wow. Wouldn't that be amazing if our team—our amazing game—could have that kind of impact on the next console generation?'"

They believed in Halo, and they believed it could be the very product that Microsoft was looking for. But they were also looking for a partner, or a buyer. So the next day, Tamte called Ed Fries. Fries had previously met Tamte at an industry event, but other than that, "he was just somebody in my Rolodex." Bungie, Tamte told him, was in financial trouble. Bungie was looking for a buyer. He said they already had one potential buyer, "but as long as they were going to sell it, would we also be interested in bidding on the company?" Tamte recalls that Fries answered, "You know, Peter? That's a really interesting idea."

Fries was already a fan of Bungie's games, having played several of them. Even if nothing in Bungie's previous portfolio would necessarily translate to a console, Fries was interested in the team for its creativity and experience as

140

developers. At the time of the call, Fries says he didn't know about Halo, even though it had been announced at a Macworld event and previewed at E3, but he looked into it. The first video of Halo he saw, he says, "had these little animals that ran across the field and stuff, but it had the core elements of Halo."

According to some people, Jon Kimmich, who was working for Moulder to help locate potential first-party developers, had visited Bungie and talked with them about developing for Xbox, but according to Tamte, Kimmich did come to meet with the Bungie team, but a couple of weeks after his phone call with Fries. Moulder confirms that there had been some discussion about having Bungie produce first-party content, but not with him, and Fries says that the call from Tamte was his first direct involvement with the company. It's a little uncertain, based on different reports, who made first contact and when, but there is no confusion about how the deal got started.

Tamte says that they were impressed by the Microsoft contingent that came to visit. "It was clear that the guys that Ed had sent out were hardcore gamers." The first thing Tamte remembers them doing when they got there was to play a team death match on an early PC version of Halo.

Meanwhile, Fries and Tamte started working on the deal. The first major problem Fries faced was how to deal with Take Two, so he got on the phone with the company's founder, Ryan Brant, and together they worked it out. Fries was mostly interested in the team, and Halo, although very promising, was far from being a serious product at the time. The deal Fries brokered was that Take Two could have all the back-catalogue rights and that Microsoft would fund the completion of Oni for Take Two to publish. "I would just take all the developers and this new Halo property."

Making a deal with Take Two was one thing, but it wasn't the main thing. They still had to convince Bungie to become part of Microsoft. That was going to take some convincing, and one of the people charged with that task was Stuart Moulder. "I flew out to Chicago to basically convince Alex and Jason and the rest of the team that becoming part of Microsoft and moving to Seattle was actually a cool thing instead of a stupid and scary thing to do." According to Moulder, "Being mostly a Mac shop, they thought Apple were the good guys and we were the bad guys."

"In reality, I didn't think they were the Evil Empire," says Seropian, "but I needed a lot of convincing that they were serious." Because Bungie had already developed for the Windows architecture, and Xbox was planned to be based on that architecture, he thought that they could develop games for the new platform. "Prior to talking specifically about the acquisition, we talked a lot about Xbox together, and how they were going to try to make it a success, what they thought they were good at and what they thought they weren't good at. And I think those conversations made us realize that they were serious. We were certainly convinced that they didn't just want to buy the IP, or buy the product... or even just buy the team. They wanted us to play a strategic role in a new platform that they were going to put half a billion dollars into in the first couple of years. That right there is the reason we ultimately went ahead with it. You could say, 'money talks, bullshit walks.'"

Jordan Weisman, who had joined Microsoft with the FASA acquisition (*see Absorbing FASA pg. "Absorbing FASA" on page 6*), was another one of the people called in to help convince Bungie. "I think it was Ed, or Ed and Robbie, who said 'Hey, we're talking to Bungie about buying them and we want you to sit down with Alex and Jason and tell them how well the integration of FASA Studio has gone.' And I was like, 'What planet are you on?' At that point, I was acting as creative director for the whole org, but I had seen what happened to that poor studio and the challenges it had gone through in trying to maintain its development culture, which frankly, it lost. It went through an absorption process into Microsoft development culture, and the result was that the game we were working on when we were acquired was a year later still not done."

With Bungie, Weisman was honest, but also persuasive. "I shared some of the reality of what had happened to us and kind of laid out the good and the bad. I told him what I believed to be the truth, which was that these guys had a unique opportunity to show their work on the largest stage they were ever going to have a shot at." Jones seems to have understood what Weisman said and is quoted as saying, "Microsoft is holding the biggest cannon in the world, and they're pointing it right at Sony, and we can be a bullet in that cannon."

Learning from their mistakes and becoming more aware of the idiosyncrasies of game development, Microsoft sought to allow Bungie to keep a more autonomous studio culture. Moulder echoes what Weisman said: "Previously, what Microsoft would do is you'd buy a company—like we bought FASA—and then they would reorganize and just fit in a Microsoft organizational structure. Which it turns out is a stupid thing to do, because you destroy the corporate culture that you acquired and presumably valued. So we said we weren't going to make that mistake again."

They told Seropian that it was his studio, and it was his decision how to run it. Among the commitments believed to have been offered was that their compensation would ultimately include royalties, something Microsoft had never offered before to in-house studios. (*Ed Fries denies this. "I never offered this. No internal groups got royalties at that time.")* Also very important was that Microsoft recognized another key difference. In Microsoft, people had their own offices, and any other arrangement was inconceivable. "Back then Microsoft had all these perks, incentives to go there as a developer," says Fries. "You got your own private office and you got free soda pop and stuff like that."

In fact, the original location they had set up for Bungie was a very nice suite of offices in their own wing of one of the buildings on Union Hill Road. From a Microsoft point of view, it was very generous and prestigious. There was just one problem. Bungie had an open, bullpen approach to game development. So when they saw the offices they said no, and had them all torn out to create a big open space in which they could work. They even had their own separate security doors, and only a few employees were granted access. Fries even joked at one point that they didn't even allow him in.

According to Moulder, there were people within MGS who resented Bungie's exclusivity and "special" treatment, but Moulder saw it from another perspective. "I personally thought that if they weren't treated that way, you don't get the results that they got. I would say the keyword is passion more than work cheap. A studio that's comprised of a bunch of really expensive people is an odd studio, but what you really care about is, do they have passion? And do they have a culture—a creative culture, and a gaming culture—that's unique and that informs how they do things—what they do—and that energizes and inspires everyone in the studio. And you can tell the ones that have it, and you can pretty easily tell the ones that don't. Bungie had it. Ensemble had it."

Steve Jobs

In November, 1999, shortly before Microsoft's acquisition of Bungie, Steve Jobs had personally introduced Jason Jones and the Halo preview on stage at MacWorld. Tamte takes credit for bringing the game to Jobs' attention. He had previously worked at Apple, as senior director of worldwide consumer marketing and had reported directly to Jobs. Within weeks of joining Bungie, he contacted his former boss. "I called Steve and said it would be really cool if you would introduce this game, because I think you would be interested in it." And so Jobs invited Jason Jones and Joe Staten to give him a personal demo of Halo. It must have gone quite well because at the next Macworld Expo in New York, there was Jobs on stage introducing Jason Jones and Halo. "That's a personal endorsement," says Tamte. "He would never do something like that unless he personally had a very deep interest in the product."

This was a rare moment for Jobs, who almost never showed much public support for computer games, and never in a keynote. So when Microsoft more or less scooped up Bungie, including of course Jones and Halo, Jobs was not pleased. According to Moulder, he called up Steve Ballmer, furious, and gave him an earful. Ballmer then took the problem to Ed Fries. As Moulder recalls the story, essentially what Ballmer said was, "Look. I just want to make sure this is worth it. I back you. We're going forward. I'm not going to let Steve Jobs tell me what we're going to do, but they are an important partner. We sell a billion dollars' worth of software on their platforms, so I just want to make sure this is worth doing. Worth the pain it's going to cause us." Of course, Jobs not being a big "game guy," a reasonable assumption might be that he was just embarrassed and felt outmaneuvered, but would get over it. "It really just turned into Steve Jobs is mad at us for a little while."

However, Tamte provides a more nuanced view of Jobs' interest in games, indicating that Jobs was more receptive to games than most people know. For one thing, when he personally hired Tamte, it was because of his experience running MacSoft, which sold 45% of all Mac games at the time. So why did he have a reputation of disinterest in games? "I think it was just a matter of time. I mean, he's rebuilding Apple and also running Pixar, so this is a very busy time for him. But the conversations that I had with Steve indicated that even though he may not have spent a lot of time on video games, there was an instinct that he understood about video games and their importance. What was valuable? What was not valuable? How that fit together with Apple."

Tamte also relates a story about the first iMac, which was going to use a Rage processor, but Tamte and others urged him to go with the Rage Pro* for one reason. "There was nothing else that needed it other than games," says

Tamte. And Jobs listened to them and made the change. He also spent time personally in meetings with a games advisory group, and as Tamte observes, "Steve did not spend time on things that he was not interested in."

The original iMac shipped in August 1988 and featured a 266 mhz G3 processor and an ATI Rage Pro Turbo graphics card with 6 megabytes of SGRAM. It also came in five (healthy) colors—tangerine, lime, strawberry, blueberry, and grape.

Maybe Steve Jobs had a little more interest in games that most people think, but there's no doubt that he was more than a little bent about Microsoft's essentially stealing Halo after he'd obviously become personally involved with it. But, as Moulder observes, he didn't stay mad for long, and Ed Fries can explain why. After the acquisition became known, says Fries, Ballmer emailed him. Ballmer's email essentially said, "Jobs is mad about us buying Bungie. Here's his phone number. Call him." And Fries found himself thinking with a combination of awe and dread, "Ok. I'm going to call Steve Jobs now."

Fortunately, Fries came up with a plan. During the acquisition of Bungie, they realized that they had jobs for everybody except Peter Tamte, the guy who initiated the deal in the first place. "We didn't really need another biz dev guy," says Fries. However, Tamte turned out to be the perfect chess piece to play in this situation. Tamte had expressed an interest in starting a company of his own, a company that, among other things, would port Windows games to the Mac. "I think both the Apple people and the Microsoft people trusted me," says Tamte.

Having formulated a plan, Fries made the call. He began by apologizing for the situation, mentioned that he was personally a Mac fan and had even worked on Mac Office, and then said that he would be happy to see PC games ported to the Mac, including Halo. "So what I would like is to do a deal with you guys and a third party where we help set up a Macintosh publisher to port our games to the Mac," he told Jobs. "And I know just the guy to do it. His name is Peter Tampte." Of course, knowing Tamte well, Jobs was mollified and put Fries in contact with people at Apple who would help move the idea forward. And that was it. "I thought it was a real win-win because I got Ballmer and Jobs off my back, and I got a job for Peter Tampte—because without him I don't think we would have had Halo—and I got Apple to fund it, not me. And we were going to get more licensing revenue because we were going to get money for licensing our games on the Mac. So to me it was a deal that worked out really well."

Jobs had added only one additional condition: That Fries and Seropian appear on stage with him at an upcoming Macworld in New York to announce the deal.

And so, a few months later, Fries and Seropian flew to New York, arriving the day before the event and expecting to participate in a dress rehearsal. While in a cab on the way to the venue, Fries received a phone call from one of Jobs' handlers:

"We don't want you guys to come in."

"What do you mean? We need to do the rehearsal for this."

"Well, it's really not going well. Steve Jobs is not happy. Just go to your hotel and I'll call you later."

Later they were told just to show up in the morning, which they did.

Although Fries and Seropian had no clue what was going on, Tamte is able to shed some light on the situation. "When Steve was doing his practices, even the union guys could not be inside the place. There would be two or three people. Steve would always announce something really, really big, and if word of that got out before then, it could affect the stock. Even back then the rumor mill for Apple stuff was out of control crazy. So if Steve was not ready the night before, things would get pushed back. That would be the reason why. And Steve would practice, and they would change things, and there'd be just a small number of people who were allowed to be in the room when that was happening. A very small number of people."

On the morning of the presentation, Jobs was still too busy to see them. "Finally, it seemed like ten minutes before the show was going to start," says Fries, "Steve Jobs comes up to me, and he says, 'Here's what's going to happen. At this section of the show I'm going to introduce you two. You guys come up on stage, shake my hand, you guys talk for 30 seconds, shake my hand again, you're off stage. You're all done.' And he was very nice about it. Very matter-of-fact, and Alex and I were just like, 'OK. That's what we'll do.' And that's what we did. We went on stage and we did our bit. We announced that Microsoft was going to be bringing a bunch of games to the Macintosh, including Halo, and then we walked off stage. And that was the end of that."

Fries adds that this was the one and only time he ever met Jobs, but that it was memorable in part because he got a front row seat at the event. "I tell you, he did a great job. I sat there in the front row and watched him do his spiel, and he was really impressive. I mean, his reality distortion field* was in full effect."

*Steve Jobs was famous for being able to convince anybody of just about anything. He was very persuasive, and people would claim that he had the ability to change reality to fit his needs—a reality distortion field.

And from Tamte's point of view, "I had the weird deal of having my new company announced publicly for the first time by a vice president of Microsoft during a Steve Jobs Macworld Expo keynote."

Gaining Trust

As creative director of MGS, Jordan Weisman worked closely with Bungie during the transition. One of the things he did was to help organize the Halo project. "My team came in and worked with them on writing all the original world bibles for the Halo universe." Weisman's team also put together contracts for novels and novellas based on the Halo property and even found a novelist for the job, Eric Nylund, who also happened to be a member of the game studio.

Trust did not come immediately, but was built over time. For instance, Fries tells the story of the testing team who were part of that trust building process. Bungie, like many game studios, thought of testers as "a bunch of high school kids to just play the game and beat on it" according to Fries. But at Microsoft, testers were professionals and an integral part of the development process, whether it was games or office products. Based on their preconceptions, however, when Fries told the guys at Bungie that he was assigning them a test team, they said no way. They didn't want them. "We went back and forth and finally I said fine, if I can't put them inside, I'm going to put them right outside your door. So I gave them all the offices right outside the doors to Bungie's area."

What happened next was that the test team became a huge asset to Bungie. "They didn't just beat on the game. They did things like build a system to speed up the rendering of the lighting by a huge amount so that they could turn the builds around really quickly. They also developed lot of data collection systems that Bungie has become famous for, around where people die on maps and how to optimize maps for better multiplayer play and things like that." After Halo: Combat Evolved shipped, "they knocked down that wall and the test team became an official part of Bungie. They basically moved the wall that had the card key access farther down." The test team leader was Harold Ryan, who ultimately joined Bungie and became the studio manager.

The Big Push

As Bungie began settling into their new offices, the work of creating Halo restarted with a new goal—creating a kick-ass first-person shooter for a brand-new console system. Previous to Halo, there had only been one successful FPS for consoles—GoldenEye 007. And, although there were plenty of challenges, "It was preordained that it was going to be Halo," says Weisman.

One main challenge was learning how to develop for a console system and its main input mechanism—the controller. They knew that if they failed to map the gameplay successfully to the buttons and triggers of the controller, the game would suck, and even worse, it would fail. In the end, they not only succeeded, but established a controller model that has since become the basic standard for console systems.

Bungie also looked more deeply into the game, not just from the action and gameplay perspective, but into the story they were telling. They created a classic conflict and backstory, two very memorable characters—Master Chief and Cortana—and equally memorable enemies—Covenant and the Flood. What is quite possibly the single most influential aspect of Halo: Combat Evolved was almost cut at the end, however. More on that later…

Crisis at Gamestock

Jonathan Sposato had spent years in the games industry, and at the time was a manager for Xbox first-party titles. In that capacity, he worked closely with companies like Bungie. As the Gamestock event approached in February 2000, Jason Jones came to Sposato in something of a panic.

Gamestock was an important yearly event created by Senior Marketing Director Beth Featherstone's division to showcase works in progress, and most Xbox developers attended, along with a press corps contingent. Gamestock always took place in February, says Featherstone, "because that was the optimum time for retailers, and allowed you to build the right amount of buzz for the press going into E3, and it didn't conflict with GDC in March."

According to Sposato, Jones came to him and said, "'Jonathan, February at Gamestock this year ain't gonna work. I can tell you right now that we're not going to have anything good to show.' At this point, Sposato had not worked directly with Jones all that much. Perhaps he was just being too much of a perfectionist. "Maybe it's good. Good enough for Gamestock," he said. But Jones was adamant. "*Nonono* Jonathan. You've got to get the date changed."

So Sposato went to Featherstone and lobbied on behalf of Jones. "I worked on Beth for weeks, but she was like, 'No. You're effing crazy. These guys are just being whiners. There's no way. What they'll have is great. I'm sure what they'll have will be better than 90 percent of the other games at Gamestock.'" Sposato was persistent, and eventually Featherstone began to take him seriously. Then Jones wrote an email—thoughtful, passionate, sometimes impolite, but persuasive.

Featherstone finally agreed to take the unprecedented step of delaying Gamestock for a month—into March and much closer to GDC. "A lot of times the producers on the different games, or the developers themselves, were very emotional, and they're not capable of giving you rational business reasons why something has to be different than how it is," she says. "Jonathan was always the opposite of that. He's capable of separating the emotions from what the reality is… you know, the facts. He was able to come and convince me that, yeah, this isn't just them being perfectionists and them being really difficult. They really are saying that we're not going to have a quality product, and we're going to embarrass ourselves."

Of course moving the date for Gamestock was a major headache, to say the least. Gamestock that year would host up to a thousand non-Microsoft attendees. There were a lot of details to change, emails, phone calls… and then there was the press. "When you're talking to the press you don't necessarily want to say we're not ready. Then it looks like you don't have your act together. I think then, too, at some point you're just honest and go, 'Hey look. Our flagship product… we don't want to drag you all up here to Seattle and not have anything substantial to show you. We're trying to be respectful of your time. And there are a lot of places you guys could be and things you could cover, and we don't want to waste your time.'"

For Halo fans: a special treat on these two pages.

Very early screens from Halo, courtesey of Peter Tampte.

Sposato, who has since created several very successful businesses, gives major credit to Featherstone. "To this day I look at it and I think, 'Wow. How remarkable to see good senior managers who can admit when they're wrong and come back, and not be passive aggressive about it, but say, 'You know, Jonathan. I heard you. I'm capable of change. We will move Gamestock this year.'"

Halo at E3

Of course, there was still a lot of work to do and not much time before the launch of Xbox and the game. One of the milestones they had to meet was a preview of the game at the E3 show in May, 2001. Featherstone says that from her point of view, they knew Halo was going to be the franchise. "It was just a matter of getting Bungie to meet the timelines that we needed to have to sync up with the hardware." Syncing up was easy to say, but not so easy to achieve, and Bungie worked the way Bungie worked.

"When you look at developers on the perfection scale, from 1 to 10, they're an 11," says Featherstone. "They can be very difficult to work with, but they are also utter perfectionists in terms of what they're doing. They're the type of developer that doesn't want to show anything before they think it's perfect and ready and meets all their expectations. But from a business point of view, sometimes you can't do that because it doesn't line up with the market cycle."

There were meetings. According to Featherstone, lots of meetings. E3 was approaching, and they needed something to show, but Jones was complaining that it wasn't ready and wouldn't be ready. "I can remember having a lot of conversations with COO Pete Parsons at the time, and just saying, 'Pete, I don't care if it's smoke and mirrors, but you have to come up with something that is going to wow the public at E3.'"

Halo did have its launch preview at E3. Featherstone considered it a success, but Bungie didn't, and neither did a lot of people who viewed the demo. According to Robbie Bach, "Ironically they showed the networking version of Halo. It was a multiplayer level and the graphics weren't quite right. Who knows what hardware we were running at that point? It certainly wasn't real hardware."

Fries answers Bach's question about what hardware was being used, and perhaps offers a reasonable explanation for Halo's less-than stellar performance at E3. "The dev kit Xboxes we had at E3 used a much slower graphics card in them, and so the framerate was about half at E3 what it was going to be."

Whatever the reason, many people were disappointed with Halo's debut at E3. Fries points out that it got mediocre reviews, while Bach said it confirmed the skeptical view that "shooters can't be successful on a console." And so, according to Bach, "After that event and the feedback we got, Ed basically told people we could no longer show Halo. Until it's done, nobody gets to see it." The decision to cloister Halo wasn't out of lack of confidence in the product, however. "I think Ed was confident from the start, but that's just because Ed's Ed."

Bach, on the other hand, was not Ed, and he did have his reservations. "I mean, here you have a game which was clearly started as a game on the Mac, then went to the PC. It's clearly a first-person shooting game that should have great online gameplay. And we're going to launch it on a game console with no online support. You know, it's not the easiest bet to see."

The Death March

After the E3 preview, it was clear that there was work still to do, and anxiety was building among some people at Microsoft. But at Bungie, it was more of a nose-to-the grindstone attitude, or, as many people called it, a "death march" to completion. Andrew Walker, who helped with bug testing says, "Everyone was panicking because Halo had to do a complete rejigging of all of their graphics, like four months before launch."

Featherstone describes the anxiety many people were feeling: "They worked 24 hours a day, I think, to get it done. It was insane. On the marketing side, it's sort of like jumping off a cliff, like tandem jumping, and you just kind of close your eyes and hope you land when you're supposed to. That's just kind of the nature of that business. I could go through too many examples in the gaming business where these developers come out and puff out their chests and tell you how great everything going to be, and three years later they still haven't shipped their game. So you hope you put your eggs in the right basket. They knew what the deadlines were, and to their credit they got it done."

Bungie did get it done, more or less by the skin of their proverbial teeth. They had a lot of trials, technical and graphical glitches, and features to consider—drop it?/keep it?—but they did complete the project on time. Part of their eventual success might be attributable to Jason Jones' remarkable creativity and ability to swoop in and solve problems. Highly creative and individualistic, Jones could hold the game's vision and articulate it clearly. According to Jon Grande, "Jones is kind of a savant who can touch all the parts of the organization and every piece that he dives into just somewhat miraculously begins to work. That happened with Halo."

One of the features, the one I mentioned before that was critical to Halo's success—and almost didn't happen— was the multiplayer capability of the game. As time was running out, some people were in favor of dropping multiplayer. It wasn't working right and they weren't sure they could fix it. Some people were questioning its feasibility, since it required people to lug their consoles and TVs to a central place to play together. But, as Pete Parsons says, "some people" were not Bungie. "Everybody was pushing to keep multiplayer in, but none of us knew just what it would mean."

"Marketing's job at that point is to manage expectations and stuff and get the buzz out," says Featherstone. "That was obviously before Twitter and Facebook and all that stuff, so we had little fan groups and that we were cultivating to try to get the hardcore to carry the buzz. So by the time we got to launch, it was actually not that hard. And the game really did sell itself in a lot of ways."

Despite coming out a year before the launch of Xbox Live, Halo's multiplayer was hugely important, and various LAN parties sprang up all over so that players could play together on their Xboxes, even though they had to haul them from place to place, with all the necessary equipment. But even though Microsoft was a year away from launching a real networking solution, they did what they could to support Halo's multiplayer capabilities. Boyd Multerer, who later would lead development of Xbox Live says, "We went to great lengths to make sure Halo worked with System Link*, which in a way was the precursor to Live. We wanted people to be comfortable playing online with consoles and to prepare them for it."

*System Link was a direct, console to console linking system that worked over Ethernet cables on local area networks (LANs). In Halo: Combat Evolved, up to 16 players could connect and play together on four different Xboxes, which were displaying the action on split screens.

By all definitions, Halo: Combat Evolved was a mega-success, and it became the flagship title for Xbox, launching not just the console, but a franchise that has continued to this day. Bungie left Microsoft in October 2007 and became an independent developer again. Microsoft has continued to develop new games in the Halo franchise while Bungie turned its attention to developing a huge new project—their massive multiplayer title, Destiny.

What Happened to Munch?

The emergence of Halo as the showpiece game for Xbox appeared to change the marketing focus. Whether Munch's Oddysee was ever the best showpiece product is doubtful, and even though it was a quality game from a quality developer, it was dramatically overshadowed by Halo. "Halo totally deserved its success," says Lanning, and McKenna adds, "Halo is a once-in-a-lifetime fabulous game…" She remembers going to Gamestock, where all the developers were showing their products. "I'm thinking, 'Our game is good. It's good,' and then they show Halo and I'm going 'Holy shit! That's not what we had been talking about. That's not a casual game.'"

At that point McKenna started talking to Pete Parsons from Microsoft marketing (who later became Bungie's COO). She told him they weren't ready to compete with that, and that they needed more time. Perhaps it should be released after the launch. But Parsons and the other people at Microsoft were still encouraging her. "No, no. We love your game. We're behind it."

McKenna understood what Halo meant to the console player demographic. "Now I'm a girl, and so I don't look at games the way that most guys do. Because you say to a guy—to a gamer—you go, 'Ok guys, so what you need to do is, you need to shoot everything up, and then you need to blow everything up. You've got to kill everything, and that's how you win.' And the guy goes, 'Awesome!' You say that to a girl and she goes, 'Why?' And I knew Munch is not the kind of game that was going to go over the way a Halo would. And Halo kicked our ass."

~19~

Third-Party Titles

There was a time when video game consoles relied entirely on first-party games, but those days are long gone. Early systems in the first wave of consoles, such as the Atari VCS, Mattel's Intellivision, and Coleco's ColecoVision relied primarily on titles created in-house. It wasn't until some Atari developers rebelled and formed Activision to create products for the VCS that the industry saw original third-party games for console systems. Even in the next generation of consoles, like the Nintendo Entertainment System, Sega's Master System, and Turbografx—a collaboration between Hudson Soft and NEC—many of the most important titles were still first-party.

By the time Xbox was being developed, third party titles were an essential part of any console's strategy. Where once console makers very jealously defended their console titles and put up walls against third-party titles, in the late 1990s the entire outlook had changed, and now it was the more the merrier. As John O'Rourke puts it, "The hardware in many ways was nothing without the games."

First-party titles definitely provided important benefits. All profits went to the console maker. They helped strengthen the brand. They were completely under the control of the manufacturer. They also had some down sides. For instance, developing triple-A titles was expensive, and it got more and more expensive year by year. It was also difficult to create enough titles to feed the hungry appetites of gamers, who now numbered in the millions when only a few years before, the reliable game audience had been estimated at about 800,000, with only major hits reaching larger audiences.

In any case, the people behind Xbox understood the need to attract third-party developers and gain their support for the new system. After all, DOS and Windows had relied almost entirely on third-party developers, and these developers had been extensively supported and recruited by the Developer Relations Group. But games for DOS and Windows had never represented the operating system's core business model, whereas for a console, obviously games were what it was all about, and a new group of developers was needed. The job of gaining their support wasn't going to be a cakewalk.

Don Coyner remembers the skepticism that many people felt when they found out that Microsoft was going to try to challenge the big console makers, especially Sony and Nintendo. "They would say, 'Is there room? I mean, you guys are really going to come in and take on Sony and Nintendo? What the hell do you guys know about this stuff? You guys make Office and SQL Server.'"

Coyner says that a big part of the skepticism was essentially a challenge to Microsoft's resolve. How serious were they? "And that's where the credibility of, 'Here's what's going to be our brand story; here's how we're going to market this thing. It's going to be about the games; it's not about the hardware. It's not a technology story, even though that was a powerful underpinning— it's a powerful system to go after the hardcore gamers…'"

Establishing credibility was one issue. Making deals was another, and there were a lot of discussions about what kind of deal Microsoft was offering. "Those were some hard discussions, particularly with EA. People were playing hardball, for sure, because they knew we needed them desperately if we were going to succeed, and so they kind of had the upper hand."

Jennifer Booth had been part of the marketing team that launched the original PlayStation, and she was recruited by Microsoft originally to join the hardware division's marketing team as a planner with Don Coyner, who was doing marketing.

Early in the Xbox project, Booth and Coyner were working in Hardware under Rick Thompson, but with previous console experience—Coyner from Nintendo and Booth from Sony—Booth says that they were both viewed as possible assets by the Xbox team. "Somehow it came to their attention that we both had backgrounds in the console business," she says, "so Seamus and Kevin took us over and showed us their plan. I think it was a marketing plan, like, 'Here's what we're going to do with third party,' etc. etc. So they just kept coming over and we kept giving them documents. Like I remember giving them some game data because they wanted sales data. So we were acting as advisors. We were kind of doing this at night. Once we got approval from Gates, then Don and I came over full time on it. I think it was a couple of months going back and forth and kind of moonlighting and helping them."

It was actually quite logical that several key members of the Xbox marketing team—Beth Featherstone, Don Coyner, and Jennifer Booth—came out of the Hardware division. After all, the Hardware division was the only unit at Microsoft that had successfully marketed a product to the gamer audience. Moreover, Xbox was fundamentally a piece of hardware that would be designed and built by the hardware division and marketed to the same audience that they had successfully engaged with SideWinder. Logical or not, Rick Thompson eventually had to put his foot down, telling Bachus, "Ok listen. You cannot continue to poach people from our group."

Head Nods

Both Coyner and Booth played roles, albeit mostly silent ones, in the ultimate decision to go forward with Xbox as a console. Booth remembers going to two of the "Bill" meetings that occurred prior to the decision to go with the console. "There were two different plans put forth to him. Should we do the Kevin/Seamus plan or should we do the DirectX plan? Kevin/Seamus were wanting a more typical console style business. I think it was at a breakfast… They <the DirectX team> were promoting that we do something a little bit different, more along the lines of what we had done with Windows … more of a Windows model. So they put Don and me in the back so they could say, look, we've got people who have actually done this before. We were there for kind of a head nod. Like in one of the meetings they were saying, 'You don't need to launch with certain titles. You don't need to launch with sports. Sony didn't.' It was typical of the bluster around the table, and we had to say, 'Well actually, they did.' So that was our role."

Booth saw one of the advantages Microsoft had with third-party developers was that many of them had unsatisfactory relationships with Sony and/or Nintendo. One thing that Microsoft promised (and delivered) was good development tools. "Many people found working with Sony's development tools frustrating and difficult. Since Xbox was based around Windows technology, it promised to be easier to work with. And with the incredible support they were offered by the Xbox Advanced Technology Group, third-party goodwill grew over time. Once they got a developer on board they encouraged the third-party developers to help them with Xbox marketing simply by talking about Xbox."

Third-Party Agreements

As Booth points out, third-party developers complained about was how they were treated by Sony and Nintendo. In Sony's case, there was a great disparity in the kinds of deals they offered. Some people got far more generous deals than others, such as how much the made per unit sold. Developers didn't like the perception of the haves and the have nots. In Nintendo's case, they often treated third-party developers with a degree of contempt, the message being that they were fortunate to have the opportunity to publish on the platform Nintendo had built. They were also very picky and selective and often created barriers and challenges to getting published, but offered what seemed like poor per-unit payments.

Microsoft adopted a goal of consistency. Their deals were flat. Everybody got the same deal, although there were some variable marketing incentives—money offered specifically for the purpose of promoting their Xbox games. According to Kevin Bachus, some of the bigger publishers hated this egalitarian approach, especially the Japanese publishers who were used to getting preferential treatment, from Sony especially. But the toughest nut was Electronic Arts.

EA was the big cheese in the industry at the time. One of the Xbox team dubbed them "Snow White" with the rest of the game companies being the Seven Dwarfs. CEO Larry Probst had expressed some early skepticism about Microsoft's entry into the console market, and he drove a hard bargain when it came time to support Xbox. According to Bachus, EA negotiated a far more complex deal that read more like a partnership agreement. Although some people have said that there were stipulations preventing Microsoft from competing with their sports franchises, Ed Fries says, "This is completely false (and would probably be illegal). It makes no sense because we launched a competing football game at launch and many other sports games after that." Later, when negotiating over support for Xbox Live, they had more concerns, but in the end EA and Microsoft did come to terms on a deal with stipulations specific to EA.

A Good Story

In part, it was because the media loves a good horserace, and with Sega fading, Microsoft's entry into the race made a good story. And, well… it was Microsoft, after all. Booth says, "I think the story in and of itself that Microsoft was actually getting in the console business was so big with many journalists that the story mostly wrote itself. It was so interesting to them that we were doing something new and getting into the consumer business in such a big way, that we got a lot… a lot of interest."

Beth Featherstone also saw the press as their ally—for the most part, anyway. "It was a really interesting dynamic, and I think a lot of the journalists didn't strictly like Sony either because they weren't any nicer to the press than they were to third party developers. So they really wanted us to do well." She credits J Allard with some of their success with the media. "J was a great spokesperson to have out there on the platform side. They were convinced that we got it, that we weren't just out there being Microsoft, you know… late to the game and we're going to suck all the air in the room out because we have the most money. We couldn't do that with Xbox. We had to put people out there like J and convince the gaming press that we meant business and that could do it, and that we understood the mentality of the console gamer." She also pointed out how the press loved a "three-horse race" and wanted them to succeed, if only to make things more interesting and to have more to write about. "That made things a little bit easier," she says, "but working on all of that was very stressful."

Third-Party Japan

Japan was the home to many of the top console developers in the world, and Microsoft wanted to sign them up for Xbox, all the while knowing that it would be no easy task. However, there were potential openings.

Resident Evil

Kevin Bachus was out there recruiting in November 2000, and he remembers meeting with Resident Evil creator Shinji Mikami from Capcom. "We heard that Mikami-san was trying to decide what he was going to do with Resident Evil 4. He hated Playstation 2. He thought it was very difficult to develop for. He was going to move it to Gamecube… or to Xbox."

Mikami met with Bachus and a member of Microsoft's Japan division, and told them that he's impressed with the tech, but he needs to have something to tell his team…to tell them why he choose Xbox over one of the Japanese console options. Of course, the conversation is in Japanese, so Bachus isn't sure what they're saying, but from what he can tell, the conversation isn't going well. "I say, 'Well? What's he talking about?'" Somehow Bachus' message didn't get through and Mikami left the meeting.

Afterward, his translator told him that Mikami wanted to know how Microsoft viewed the game industry. "He says games are entertainment. Nintendo says that games are toys. And I said, games are are art. Games are art!! We've always said we want to elevate games to a higher art form, we want to allow creators to focus on the art of game making rather that having to deal with the complexity of the hardware. And he goes, 'Oh. That would have been great!'"

Bachus tried to go through somebody else at Capcom, but it was too late. Mikami had already committed to Nintendo. "So that was why we lost Resident Evil," says Bachus.

Tecmo Story

Not everything was as frustrating as the Resident Evil story. With Tecmo, Bachus had developed a good relationship, and the game everybody wanted was Dead or Alive. "I went in and said, screw Dead or Alive, I hear that you're making a new version of Ninja Gaiden. I want Ninja Gaiden to be exclusive to Xbox. They loved that. It was like everybody was coming in and begging for the beautiful daughter rather than the younger daughter, who was going to be even more beautiful later. So like that we got on really really well with Itagaki-san. He and Seamus got along really well, they went to hostess bars together and hung out. In fact, Seamus wanted to suggest that he do a Ninja Gaiden beach volley ball game, which he later actually did do."

In the end, Dead or Alive 3 ended up being an Xbox launch title while Ninja Gaiden, which was not ready at the time, was published later.

Namco

Bachus and his group met with Konami, Capcom, Namco, and Sega on the same trip, and they were hearing stories about how a representative from Microsoft Japan had been approaching companies. For instance, with Namco this guy would come in and say "I want Tekken. I want this. I want that." So when Bachus paid a visit to Namco and met with executive director Youichi Haraguchi, they had this conversation:

"Well Namco has been in the business for a while."

"Yeah."

"We've been pretty successful."

"Yeah, you're like one of the top."

"Well, why is it that your guy keeps coming in saying I want Tekken, I want this, I want that and we thought you'd want to be partners with us. Your sales people would be asking our sales people for advice, your marketing people would be asking our marketing people for advice. Instead you basically make demands. You need to tell your people that they don't work for you, that they work for me. You just pay their salary."

Bachus says it was ironic that this was what he always said. "It's almost word for word what I had told the people that work for me in the US and Europe. I said look, if you're an account manager working on Xbox, you actually work for your publishers. Right? It's your job to understand what they need and to advocate for them and and and basically be their voice on the inside."

So he was getting a lesson from Haraguchi, and it was time to act on it. "To hear this guy at Namco saying this... We made a change, like the next day. We brought in somebody new to replace the previous guy who had the really difficult conversation with Mikami and was going around throwing all these demands around." He says that the new guy, Hiyashi, worked out great. He had the right attitude.

Even though working with the Japanese developers was difficult for any number of reasons, in the end their efforts paid off and, even though they lost Resident Evil, they ended up signing third-party deals with all of the companies they wanted, with the exception of Square Soft who remained with Sony.

~20~
Marketing Xbox

Even before the final approval was given, the research and market planning for Xbox had begun. Consumer marketing at Microsoft was comparatively new. Microsoft had experience marketing to corporate accounts, but less experience with marketing to individual consumer demographics, and almost none at marketing for the video game crowd. In fact, according to Beth Featherstone, prior to Ed Fries games marketing was actually achieving a net negative. "Prior to Ed taking over Games, the group was run by someone who managed to piss off all the influential press at the time. He took the typical we're Microsoft and we can shove our weight around attitude, which did not go over well with the press."

Early Marketing Success

Beth Featherstone had joined Microsoft in 1991 as an international product manager in the hardware division. She was later promoted to worldwide group marketing manager. In 1996, with nothing but Flight Simulator and some simple Windows games, there wasn't much for Microsoft to market on the game side, and the majority of gamers didn't even consider Flight Simulator a game. Featherstone states that it was hardware, not games that finally broke through to the gaming market—specifically the SideWinder joystick, which was launched alongside Duke Nukem and became a favorite peripheral among shooter fans. She says that the ergonomic Microsoft Natural Keyboard also became popular among gamers. Featherstone credits David Hufford*, a young PR guy who worked for Waggoner-Edstrom, with turning things around. "David literally had to beg and call in favors to get the editors to meet with us on the joystick launch. We took a very humble approach and were able to convince them that the Hardware group really did 'get gaming'".

*As noted earlier, David Hufford later joined Microsoft's public relations department, and at the time of this writing is senior director of Xbox public relations.

Shortly after Ed Fries took over the games group, Microsoft "removed" their head of consumer marketing and did not replace him for another six months. Featherstone, having grown bored in the hardware group and unhappy with its direction at the time, decided to seek the empty marketing position. "I was looking for a new challenge and they were looking for someone who understood the games market but could also navigate the Microsoft political and bureaucratic machine. My email name was "Bethfe," and one of the hardware developers christened me 'Iron Beth.' I had a reputation as being fair but tough as nails. I was a good fit and took the job."

Featherstone became a group marketing manager for PC games just before the launch of Age of Empires, and quickly discovered that the group she was taking over was sorely in need of supervision—and a good deal of reorganization. "Truthfully, going to that group was a bit like trying to manage a very large group of kindergarteners without any supervision. There was a lot of bad, immature behavior. Half my team needed replacing as they were in the wrong jobs. The other half needed support and political air cover to be able to perform well." Over time, working with Fries and his senior staff, she was able to create a strong and effective team.

Initially, Featherstone had to face down an organization that did not understand the gaming market. One of her first challenges came when a new product manager, who had just relocated from France, was exasperated by Microsoft's insistence that the game packaging be part of the Microsoft Home brand, and in addition, that they would not let the sword on the cover of Age of Empires overlay the branding bar. Featherstone had to take the case all the way to the top. "Battle number one," she says, "get corporate marketing to understand that games were not going to sell under the Microsoft brand or Home brand. Not easy, but we won, and I had to go all the way to Bob Herbold, who at the time was the COO of Microsoft, to get the OK. Thank god Bob came from P&G* and was very savvy about consumer branding."

*Procter and Gamble

Xbox, From 100,000 Feet

John O'Rourke had years of consumer marketing at Microsoft, having joined the company as an intern before the launch of Windows 3.1 and worked on the marketing efforts of consumer-oriented products like Publisher, Works, and

Money. He also worked in the Microsoft Office division with Robbie Bach. When Bach took over the lead role in the consumer division, he recruited O'Rourke, who ended up in charge of all consumer marketing, which included PC games, but also Encarta/Bookshelf, the kids game division, mapping products, and eventually Microsoft Money. During the early, pre-approval phase of Xbox, O'Rourke also led some of the initial marketing research.

O'Rourke was looking at the marketing requirements of the proposed console "from a 100,000-foot view." He was still working at what he calls a "thin, very conceptual level," considering how much it would cost, what channel commitments would be necessary, and, in his words, "What does the go-to-market look like?"

One of the interesting perspectives O'Rourke describes is how to "t-shirt size" the marketing commitment required. In other words, was it going to be small, medium, or large? The questions he asked were:

• Is this going to be fifty million dollars or two hundred and fifty million dollars?

• How many people we are talking about here?

• What are the parts of the marketing mix that are going to be required to launch this?

• What will the teams look like? Regionally focused or one global team?

Of course, this was all pre-approval. Once the project was approved, his job title changed to Senior Director/Xbox North America (while Bach became Senior Vice President/"Chief Xbox Officer"), and his focus shifted entirely to Xbox. At that point he says, "…it really came down to taking it from the conceptual level into the real specifics of the marketing plan, the brand strategy, PR and media perspective, and the hype strategy to get the word out there, building excitement and anticipation for this great new thing."

Marketing Challenges

Competitive analysis suggested that the effort to market a brand-new Microsoft game console system was going to be challenging, largely because of public perception of Microsoft. "We absolutely had to get a deep understanding of our gaming customer" says O'Rourke. "My point of view was very much about getting focused on what it was going to take to shift and to build the positive perceptions around what this Xbox thing could be, as well as understand the space and the consumer hearts and minds for where we had the opportunity to go. We learned that, as Microsoft, it was going to be a real challenge because people didn't think of us as an entertainment company. They didn't think of us as a consumer company. They thought of us as a business productivity and operating system company. As a result of this, there was very strong discussion and debate from a naming and branding perspective as to whether this console, at that point code-named Xbox, was going to be a Microsoft product or branded under another name."

When Nintendo veteran Don Coyner, transferred from Hardware to work for O'Rourke, he took over the marketing and branding research. He went on the road early on to speak with retailers, seeking answers to some pressing questions. What would Microsoft have to do to be an effective competitor in the video game market? Did the Microsoft brand add value or did it detract? What would people expect from Microsoft if they released a video game console?

Of course, having spent years at Nintendo, Coyner already knew a lot about video game marketing, and shared his knowledge with the company, not always meeting with a receptive audience at the beginning. "I remember a presentation I did for Bill about who makes the decision to buy a console, and I was saying it's really the kids' decisions, and mom and dad basically take the order because they don't want the kid to be disappointed on Christmas Day when they open the box and realize that they got the wrong console. And he was like, 'That's crazy. I don't believe that at all. Aaarrrrg.' And I was like, 'No. That's just the way it works.' And he's like, 'That's the stupidest research I've ever heard in my life.' It's not even research. It's just a fact. And his best comment was that I was the dumbest person who'd ever been in his office."

Nintendo: An Inside Look

For those who might be interested in getting a glimpse into how Nintendo worked, Don Coyner offers some insights based on his years there.

"When I worked at Nintendo, one of the things I never fully understood was that Miyamoto wanted to look at every package we ever did for his games—the packaging design—and he gave us feedback. When it came to

TV advertising, they wanted to see commercials after we were done with them. We'd send them over. We cut about 130 TV commercials in my seven years there, and I think I only heard from Japan one time on a commercial they didn't like. I had a $50-$60 million media budget and another $10 million for production, and their real passion was around the packaging, and not around the things that we were spending all this money on. I think that's just the way stuff is built in Japan, that the package is much more important. I remember talking with Miyamoto, talking about the style guide for Mario because Mario was inconsistent in the early days. Sometimes he had four fingers; sometimes he had five. So I said, 'Look, if we're going to do a merchandising program, Mario needs to look the same. He can't sometimes have a blue shirt and red coveralls and sometimes have blue coveralls and a red shirt. We have to lock it down for the style guide.' I remember taking him through this, and he's like, 'OK. I guess that makes sense.'

"I still can't believe Nintendo doesn't license their content for other platforms. We pitched that to Arakawa back in '93. Like, 'We should make games for Sega.' And they were like, 'Absolutely not!' And today, if they opened up that library to other platforms, they could be rollin' in dough, but they are so determined that they need to stay in the hardware business.

"You never really knew how things happened. At NOA, when I was there, they were really very shut out of what was really going on. I mean Arakawa would talk for hours every night with them, but he was their main point of contact. So decisions would get made and you never quite understood. Is this because it's a Japanese company? Is it because it's a family business? Or a combination of both? You could never really tell what the real story was."

Surveys

Coyner's team did several distinctly different surveys. In one, they never mentioned Microsoft, but, after asking some standard demographic and game usage questions, described a new potential console called the "Apollo." They directly compared Apollo to Sony's PS2, Nintendo 2000 (which possibly referred to Nintendo 64), and Sega Dreamcast, and then asked a series of questions. Of course, the stats and qualities they ascribed to Apollo were actually all about Xbox. They did three different versions of the survey, changing key numbers to see how strongly potential consumers reacted to various elements

169

of the systems. Apollo and PS2 were the strongest two systems, and in the results of this survey, they came out pretty close to each other, but far ahead of the other two systems.

In other surveys, they specifically asked people how they felt about the idea of Microsoft creating a video game console. Coyner remembers one of the most memorable responses. "Well, if Microsoft made a video game console it would blue screen all the time; it would take three minutes to boot up, and the best game they would have would be Flight Sim." On the other hand, some people were more positive and believed that Microsoft would do well with "anything online," that they would be good with the technology, and, possibly in reference to Sega abandoning their console division, that Microsoft had enough money not to bail on the project. On the negative side, was the question of whether Microsoft could provide compelling content.

This feedback was largely used to determine just how prominently they should feature the Microsoft name in the branding of Xbox. The decision was yes. Use the Microsoft name, but minimally.

In other types of surveys, participants would be given paragraphs of information and instructed to cross out the parts they didn't like and underline material that they liked.

What's the Silver Bullet?

From the beginning, people from outside the game and Xbox divisions tried to define Xbox in terms of what they knew, and what they knew was everything but games. Bill Gates wanted it to run Windows and thought it could do be used as a sort of Windows PC replacement that, oh, also played games. Kevin Bachus talks about how executives were always coming and asking, "What is the silver bullet?" In other words, what will Xbox have that PlayStation doesn't? Bachus would tell them, "Our games are going to be better because we have better tools, we have better technology, we're releasing this a year later. The games are going to look better, play better, sound better, and that's why people buy consoles." And they're like, 'Non-ono. Everybody has games. That's not a silver bullet. Like does it do photo editing? Bill Gates is a big fan of the idea, so maybe it can do photo editing. Like what about Internet Explorer? Like, do you run Office on the television set?"

Don Coyner also had issues with people's visions of Xbox, and in this case he was dealing directly with Bill Gates. "When Gates said, 'We need to put Windows on Xbox,' I was like, 'Are you kidding me?' So my first job in planning was, 'OK. Would you figure out if there's a customer for this, and what they would do with Windows on Xbox? How would it work, and what would their expectations be? So we did a bunch of research, and I had to share that with Bill, too, and he didn't take kindly to some of the feedback we'd gotten on that subject. But we killed it, so that was good."

Bob McBreen remembers one of Coyner's observations in the early days that helped shut people down who wanted to add unnecessary pet features to the console. "Don was a genius in the fact that he very early on targeted that our customers were angry young men. Any time we looked at any particular technology or feature, we quickly said, 'Does this allow us to deliver the best product for angry young men?' And so, what had originally been pitched as a Windows box quickly got thrown out the window as we said, 'We don't need this feature. We don't need this feature. We need this, we need this, we need to improve that.' And one of the biggest challenges we had internally was fighting people who would argue, 'Oh yeah yeah yeah. It's going to be a gaming machine, but it also has to be able to edit digital photos.' And so, using Don Coyner's target market of angry young men, we were able to quickly define the product features and technology."

Coyner eventually left the marketing team to work directly under J Allard. "The engineering team was being asked to build a lot of derivative products for Xbox, like 'put Windows in Xbox,' or 'turn it into a DVR,' and things like that. They realized that they had no idea what consumers would think of that, so I went over to J's team to be a product planner and help the engineering team prioritize and decide whether we should do some of that stuff or not."

Branding the Console

Naming Xbox

How do you name your new console? The precedent for consoles wasn't too inspiring. The Atari VCS—Video Computer System. ColecoVision. Intellivision. Nintendo Entertainment System. Sega Master System. Sega Genesis. Sony PlayStation... Sega's Saturn and Dreamcast were imaginative, but there was a lot of precedent for boring names and not much history of highly suc-

cessful consoles with clever names. However, calling it the Microsoft Entertainment System would definitely not cut it.

It's very common for major systems in development to have code names. Windows 95 was called "Chicago". The Atari VCS was "Stella" (named after Joe Decuir's bicycle). Nintendo 64 was "Project Reality" and Sega's Dreamcast was "Katana". Microsoft's first console was xbox, Xbox, X-Box, xBox or Xbox, depending on how people spelled it in the earliest days of its conception, but almost never does a codename become the final product name. So naturally Microsoft had to find a real name—the right name—for the thing they were building.

At first, they did a lot of conventional research. "We had a big list of potential names," says O'Rourke. They did surveys targeted at hardcore gamers. "We tested different names against different associations for the console itself, and we did it in such a way that our testers couldn't determine if we were Microsoft researchers or Sony researchers. They just knew that we were from the gaming industry and we were doing studies. As a team, we looked at every one of those big decisions because we knew we had to get this right. We knew we only had once chance. We wanted to make sure all voices could offer their points of view on that and, where possible, that we could have good market feedback and input into that, whether it came from the gamers, our partners, or the channel, or all three."

GAMES WILL NEVER BE THE SAME

Eventually, the naming team decided to hire what Bachus described as "a very very expensive naming company." Naming pros. "They asked us things like, if it was a car, what kind of car would it be? Or, describe it like you would describe a person… that kind of stuff. So we answered all these questions, and they came back with a list of names and they were all terrible. They all actually sound like car names. The Allterra, the Lanca and that kind of stuff."

They told the agency that the names didn't work, and after some more specific feedback, the agency went back and worked on it some more. "So they come back, and they're going to have a big presentation. (Actually, we got on a conference call.) And they say, 'Ok, this name is going to knock your socks off. We've tested and tested and everybody loves it. So Microsoft 11X."

At this point Brett Schnepf, who was on the call says, "I put the phone on mute, and I looked at Don and I said, 'If they use the Spinal Tap analogy, we just fire them.'" And sure enough, the next thing the presenters said was, "It's a great Spinal Tap analogy… It sounds futuristic; it's like that whole Spinal Tap thing: it goes to 11. The X is mysterious."

And that was when Bachus turned to Coyner and said, "Yeah I'll get working on the Xbox trademark."

Xbox was already a trademark of a NASDAQ-listed company called XBOX Technologies, but they were going out of business anyway. "We gave them a little bit of money, not much, but they were thrilled to get anything," says Bachus. Apparently there was also a German porn sight, xbox.com, and a few other Xbox-related issues to clear up. Then there was the matter of marketing in Japan. "Xbox was a controversial name to some extent, because in Japan the letter "X" means "bad," but we figured they'd get over that, and so Xbox was the name. Then we just had to figure out, was it X dash box, or do we capitalise the "b" versus lower case and all that kind of stuff had to be figured out. And then we were designing the actual device itself."

Even after all the research, when Coyner took the decision to Robbie Bach and said, "I want to use Xbox. That's the name we're ought to go with," Bach's initial response was something like," Nooo. Really? No, I don't like that name. It's so uhhh…?" Coyner explained the process they had gone through. "We've got names where people think we're trying too hard; we're trying to be too hip. I mean, look. We're Microsoft. People know it's Microsoft, so we have to do something that isn't so out there, and we also can't do something that's really mundane. And when we talk to people about the name, X connoted mystery." At the time, X-Files was very popular, and Coyner worried that they might be seen as copycats, "but really, when we gave that name to people, their reactions were, 'That's interesting because it's X, and that can mean all kinds of things.' And it is a box. And it's short, and nobody thought we were trying too hard or trying to be too hip. So we're saying, 'Robbie. This is the right name.' And he's, 'Well OK. If you say so.'"

For some insight into the methodology used to determine customer reactions, see "Microsoft Video Game System Name Evaluation" on page 308. And to see some of the actual names suggested by one particular agency, on page 400.

Picking the Logo

Anyone who has ever tried to design a logo for their business knows that it's a challenging process. You may go through dozens, or even hundreds of designs trying to get it just right. At Microsoft, the logo decision was as critical as finding the right name.

One major decision involved how to use the Microsoft brand. Research had suggested that it was important, but should not be dominant. There were also

One Small Step for Microsoft...

remaining opinions about whether the Microsoft logo should even be on the box at all, or if it Xbox should be a brand of its own, or released under a completely different brand. "There were strong debates on both sides," says O'Rourke, "and the decision we made was that there was tremendous value to having the Microsoft name on the box, particularly in the first holiday, for many parents that might be buying this thing. It added legitimacy that this isn't a fly-by-night company that put out a console and is going to be out of business a year later."

Once it was decided that the Microsoft logo should be present on the box, the next question was, how big? O'Rourke answers the question. "You can see the weighting of the Xbox logo was twenty times the size of the Microsoft logo, but it was there."

Then there was the logo itself. There is a popular story that a creative guy named Horace Luke designed the Xbox logo, and that the color he chose—green—was just an accident. Don Coyner recounts the version of the story that is often told. "So the color green that we chose, his version of the story is that he was in a meeting with a design firm, working on logo stuff, and the only pen he had in his pocket was green, and that's how we ended up with green."

Coyner finds the story amusing, but inaccurate. "It sounds so, sort of hip to say it that way, but the reality of it was that we didn't just randomly choose the color. That was my job." First off, look at the competition. Nintendo used red and Sony used blue, so what other color would distinguish them? What color could they own for Xbox? "Green is a great color," says Coyner. "So what would be a great color of green that would stand out at retail? And we did some work where we created some signs in different colors of green, and we put them 30 feet away in a retail-like environment, and the color we chose was chosen because it popped. You'd see it from 30 feet away. It's a powerful color. It wasn't as simple as, 'I had a green pen in my pocket, and the rest is history.'

"My job was to decide brand name, decide logo type, decide colors, fonts, decide how Xbox would be written. If it's capital X capital B, cap X small B. All that stuff. And the logo we ended up with, it was breaking through. It's this idea of an X that's breaking through the surface. And again, we were talking about raw power, and we did some shots where we showed this where it broke through and there was a noise sort of like an earthquake to try to connote the power. So that whole X and the way we treated it and the way it's designed it was all about that vision."

When asked about the legacy of DirectX and their branding, he said, "They may well have had things that looked the same. Alex St. John may believe that it came from DirectX, but having been the person who decided all that stuff, I can say that wasn't true."*

*Although the name Xbox was derived from DirectX initially.

Xbox Marketing Strategies

According to Robbie Bach, marketing concentrated on the hardcore game market. They were aware that people's perception of Microsoft was a company with plenty of money, but not necessarily one that could deliver what gamers wanted. "That is why we focused so much on Xbox as a brand and on hardcore games, performance, and online as key attributes. Our strategy was to build that credibility with serious gamers and then expand from there over time."

Beth Featherstone elaborates saying, "Halo was going to be the flagship game. We had to win the hearts and the minds of the hardcore gamers. We started out saying that this was not initially going to be a platform for the casual gamer. We don't want to be Nintendo. We're perfectly fine to let Nintendo have that space. They do it really well. We're not going to go there initially. We're going to concentrate on the hardcore gamers that are the early adopters that are going to drive the opinions… they're the opinion leaders."

Although not technically a marketing directive, Featherstone notes that another of the ways they would make the Xbox platform successful was to capitalize on Sony's poor relationship with developers. "They were not nice to the game developers. They kind of shoved their weight around." In addition to their unequal third-party deal making, they were very autocratic about game approval. She mentions one particular guy who was in charge of third-party development who would regularly kill any game he didn't like. "We took the approach that we were going to be good partners with the game developers and that was going to help endear us to the opinion leaders and the hardcore network, and then the waves would ripple outward and we'd be able to get the more casual gamers."

Who Controls the Message?

One specific area in which Coyner played a major role was in retaining a great degree of control over the Xbox message. Initially the Central Marketing Group at Microsoft told him to use Microsoft's outside agency, McCann Erickson in San Francisco. Coyner didn't believe that McCann Erickson understood the game market well enough and wanted to have more control over the agency they used. So took his case up the ladder, directly to COO Bob Herbold. "I asked if we could handle management of advertising, in particular, ourselves. He agreed and we did an agency search and went back with recommendations."

According to John O'Rourke, "Don had short listed a number of more 'boutique' agencies that 'understood gaming.' We were going to go with one of them when we were pressured by CMG (the Central Marketing Group) to at least have McCann give a pitch for the business. We agreed to listen to a pitch—and surprisingly they did a GREAT job on the pitch. We ultimately chose them over the others based on their ideas/strategy and NOT because we were pressured to do so." Coyner clarifies that they chose to work with the New York office of McCann Erickson, "and we got our own staff at the agency. I also did all agency management and direction (except media which continued to go through the central Microsoft media person)."

Doubts?

Xbox was a big step for Microsoft, and everybody involved knew it. For the marketing people involved, it might have seemed daunting, but the enthusiasm throughout the Xbox division was infectious, and the optimism was high. There were difficult moments, but they never succumbed to fatalism. O'Rourke remembers going home every day and waking up excited the next morning. It was at the same time the most difficult and the most exciting job he had ever had. "Most of it was because we were having to break many of the rules and go through these barriers for the first time. We had to be at our smartest and our sharpest. When we fell down, we had to get back up quickly. Having the intestinal fortitude, the drive, and the commitment to make it happen is what carried us from day to day. We never found ourselves in that navel gazing problem where you go into analysis paralysis. We had a bias for action." He adds that it was a big help to have a great technology platform to support.

Marketing in Japan

Coyner had the unenviable job of trying to promote Xbox in Japan. He oversaw focus tests with simultaneous translation and talked with people about console design, attitudes, the concept of Xbox… "We spent a ton of money. We built out a huge team, relative to the size of the country. We didn't have Square, which was a huge gap in the games lineup, and that was a major problem." Coyner says that the reasons the focus group participants would give for not wanting to buy an Xbox would change based on the various criteria they were offered. For instance, "Initially, it was, 'They don't have Final Fantasy. I have to have that game.' And then once we had it, it was like, 'Well, they're an American company. This is a Japanese thing. They will never understand the video game business. They just won't.'" Coyner concluded that there was definitely a bias against an American-made console and a belief that an American company like Microsoft probably would never figure it out.

"It was very frustrating. Man, the amount of time we spent over there trying different things, and the amount of investment we made, how hard we worked with the team over there, with retailers over there." One of the big questions was whether they could be successful if they couldn't win over the

Japanese market. "It was a real question. Also, the content is quite different—the stuff that really appeals to them. We didn't excel at that stuff. We had content issues, no doubt."

Coyner also visited third party companies talking about how they were positioning the console, and having worked for Nintendo for years, he was aware of the response he was getting. He said that somebody without experience with Japanese culture might have walked out of these meetings thinking that the meeting went really well, "but I'd walk out going, 'Well, that was a disaster.' And others are saying, 'No. They said good things.' I answer, 'They said good things; they didn't mean good things.' When you hear a lot of the sssssss… the sucking sound, you know you've got trouble. Having spent a lot of time with Arakawa over the years, who I adore, and a lot of other folks who would come over from Japan and talk to us, I could tell them that they thought we were crazy."

According to Coyner, he heard a lot of excuses and criticisms. "They also said that the original console was too big. They hated the fact that it had a curved top because you couldn't pile things on top of it. One of the reasons that we made the Xbox so you could stand it up as well as lay it flat was for Japan, because over there, they live in tiny apartments. They would frequently put the game console away when they were done with it. And they'd drag it out. The idea that it could stand on the floor… it was important that things could be vertical over there, and that you could stack on it. And Xbox design had the concave top, but you can still pile things on top of it. They had all kinds of excuses of why we wouldn't be successful."

On the following page are several examples of original artwork that J Allard commissioned from one of his favorite artists—Mark Kostabi—after the Xbox logo was finalized. Allard had them displayed in different areas of the Xbox offices.

~21~
Hardware—A Rocky Finish

While marketing was refining its strategies, production of the Xbox was nearing completion and the last-minutes of the development and manufacture process were underway. "Every component on that thing had to be negotiated," says Holmdahl. "Everybody was taking any job… doing what needed to be done, and I ended up negotiating a bunch of these deals. I remember all the different characters from that, from the Micron deals to the Micro Chip deals, to Conexant video encoders, to the GPU and CPU deals. It was a lot of work to get all that in place with the number of people we had available."

Then there was the optical drive. The problems started in the summer of 2001 and persisted. The console was only months from its release date. They were working against time now. "We had lots of problems with the ODD drive that we were pitching at the last moment," says Holmdahl. "I think Leo and I met for 60 days in a row with Thompson Manufacturing in order to try to address the problems we were having. We were literally working day and night on that one. There were a number of things… they had to detect a CD-R, they had to detect a CD-A, had to detect two or three different disk formats, and it had a hard time detecting them, and once it detected them, it didn't read. We started working on that around July or August of 2001. Not having a DVD drive that read disks was a problem, so we worked long and hard on that." Eventually, they did resolve that problem but with little time to spare.

The actual Xboxes were being assembled by teams in Guadalajara, Mexico and in Hungary, and plans were in place to ship them and test them in time for the launch. "Rick Vingerelli and Desmond Koval were the guys who got both Guadalajara and Hungary set up, and that was a monumental task. They were living in Hungary and Guadalajara. This was before we ever moved to China. They have stories of sleeping head-to-toe in beds in Hungary that was the last room they could get."

9/11

Having finally wrestled the optical drive into compliance, Holmdahl says that the rest of the box came together pretty well. Then the attack on the Trade Towers in New York happened. 9/11/2001. "We had units being built in Guadalajara at that time, and basically they shut down flying things for three or four days, and we were under such time pressure that we chartered a jet to fly from Guadalajara to Redmond. So we got all the units in, and I remember it was a Saturday, and we unloaded them in the parking lot of Millennium D for people on the team to take them home that weekend and test them out. We had an instruction sheet for everybody to use in testing them out. People were sticking in DVDs and playing games, playing with the dash and trying the controller out all through the weekend. We were using that to gather information in order to make a decision and assess the viability of the product."

The 9/11 attacks also affected other members of the Xbox team. Robbie Bach remembers that day vividly. He was on an Xbox press tour, along with J Allard and Seamus Blackley. "I flew into New York City the morning of 9/11, and J Allard was flying to the east coast as well. He ended up in Canada, I think… or Buffalo or some place. And I had already landed in New York. I took the red eye and was doing a press tour that afternoon and went to the hotel to sleep. I woke up to a phone call from someone in our PR agency, who's a lawyer. It's like, now why is a lawyer from the PR agency calling me? And he says 'Look, my office is across the street from the hotel. If there is anything I can do to help, let me know. Sorry your press tour has been messed up.' I said, 'What are you talking about?' He said, 'Turn on the TV.' So, of course I turn on the TV, and I'm watching the towers burn. There were two other Microsoft people from my team with me, as well as a friend of mine from our local church who happened to be there on business. We got together, and the next day we were able to rent a Ford Taurus, which we drove home to Seattle. It took us 55 hours with very little sleep."

In South Dakota, at the Mount Rushmore Mall, they stopped to buy some pillows at a Target and grab a quick meal when they noticed a nearby Software, Etc., which was displaying Xbox promotional material. This was three months before the product launched. They had a good talk with the assistant manager of the store, took some photos, and moved on. "It was 8:30 at night and the mall was basically closing. We're eating bad Chinese

Robbie Bach at Software Etc. on the way back to Seattle after 9/11

food across from Software Etc. and that's my first exposure to Xbox at retail." Bach relates that he has exchanged emails with that assistant manager each year since.

Blackley was also on a flight to New York that night and ended up in Buffalo, NY. His adventure was a lot less harrowing, however. According to Bachus, "He made his way over the border to stay with a friend of ours who's one of the singers for Bare Naked Ladies." Blackley was able to get a flight to Vancouver Canada, and Bachus drove up and brought him back to Seattle.

Direct Impacts from 9/11

Ed Fries says that the 9/11 attacks did affect one of their launch titles directly.

"We were building Project Gotham Racing, and the 'Gotham' in Project Gotham Racing comes from New York City. You could race through downtown New York and the Twin Towers were in our game, and so there was a lot of debate whether they should remain in the game. Ultimately, we took them out. It was pretty late in the process. By September we were pretty much finishing things up for a November launch."

Fries mentions other factor that did not affect Xbox, but did affect people at Microsoft. "We were the ones building Flight Simulator, not for Xbox, but it was our product and, something that came out in the early days was that the terrorists had trained on it."

Various versions of Xbox

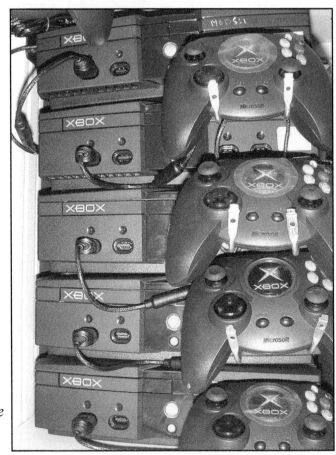

*Images of testing and
duplication setups here
and on the next page.*

Xbox boxes open and ready to receive. Spider-Man approves.

~22~
Pre-Launch

Contest

A couple of weeks before the Xbox launch, Microsoft ran a 24-hour gaming contest in New York. "We hired out a restaurant on 5th Avenue," says O'Rourke, "and set up a bunch of Xbox consoles for a contest among hardcore gamers. Among the games were Madden, Tony Hawk, and Project Gotham Racing. It was essentially an Ultimate Xbox Gamer contest with the winner being the one that had the most points after all that time. We got a lot of attention paid because of it, saying the console was ready for prime time, and those were on very early production units coming off of the line." In addition to J Allard and other Microsoft people and an MTV crew, Gavin Rossdale of Bush attended and performed an acoustic set during one of the breaks, which, according to O'Rourke "very un-Microsoft in many ways."

Pre-Launch Anxieties

Anxieties were high as the day of the launch approached. The whole process had felt rushed—and it was—and there had been many surprises and peaks and valleys during the production process, both on the hardware side and the software side. O'Rourke remembers the anxiety he felt over the final months leading up to the launch. "In the early days, we thought Munch's Oddysee was going to be a big hit because it was one of the earlier titles that we could actually show. It was ready enough to actually demo. Gotham demoed incredibly well, also. We didn't have titles to demo until late summer when we could truly show off the games that we had. If there was any time that we were concerned or scared, it was in those months leading up when we were worried that weren't going to have any titles that we could show."

By launch day, most of those worries had subsided. Their launch titles were strong, and most important of all, Halo was ready to rock and roll.

The Big Leagues

Sometimes all it takes to make someone anxious is to realize suddenly that, figuratively speaking, they aren't in Kansas anymore. Or they are suddenly thrust into the major leagues. For Beth Featherstone the Xbox experience was like that. She, like Ed Fries was when he first took over the Games group, had been happy in her former, low stress position in the Hardware division. When she took over the game marketing, that, too, seemed comfortable. Even Xbox, at first, was an interesting and exciting challenge. But then it became a different, bigger… no, massive event. A story visible to the whole world and a multi-billion dollar responsibility. "I liked being in the hardware group and then the little games group where we could do our thing and make money and not have to impact the P&L of the company. And all of a sudden, we were in that position. Imagine you're a baseball player. It was sort of like going from triple A to the major leagues—in a second."

Skepticism and No Mario?

Ed Fries was concerned as Launch Day approached. There was a lot of skepticism about the platform, he says, and especially about Halo. Despite the fact that people were very excited about it, there were those in the press who were still not convinced, and they were finding ways to pick it apart. "Halo was seen by a lot of traditional console press as a PC game. Even if I pointed out that another first-person shooter, GoldenEye, had been done and was pretty fun on a console, they're like, 'Yeah, but that was Rare. You guys aren't Rare.' Within my own team people were concerned with the way Halo looked. Somebody did color palette analysis. They said Halo was built using PC colors, not console colors. The colors weren't bright and cartoony enough, like console games. There were a lot questions, including from Bill. 'Where's your Mario?' I heard that a lot as the head of the 1st-party group. 'Where's your Mario?'"

There's a First Time for Everything

Part of the pressure people felt had to do with the realities of retail sales in the game industry. They were planning on launching during the most important time of the year for game and system sales; it was the logical time to launch.

And Microsoft wasn't dipping its toe into the water to test the temperature. They were diving into the deep end of the Christmas buying/selling season, and based on their experience in the field, or to be more precise, their lack of it, they were swimming in completely uncharted waters. When Sony launched its original PlayStation, it not only had decades of experience with consumer electronics, but they had worked previously with Nintendo, and Ken Kutaragi, the leader of the PlayStation team, had even controversially moonlighted with Nintendo while still working at Sony.

In Microsoft's case, other than Coyner and Booth, they had nobody on the team in marketing or in development who had previous console experience. They had very limited experience with hardware and had never produced a successful consumer device other than joysticks, keyboards and mice. Even their number one game had been developed by a company that had never produced a console title before, which was the case for many of their developers.

Add to that the impact of 9/11, and it was clear that they were coming to the end of a long, complicated, and improbable yearlong sprint, and, with both excitement and trepidation, they could see the finish line approaching quickly.

Retail Realities

Featherstone points out that movies are not generally released before all shooting and editing is done. "Well, the reality is that in the video game business and in the console business, 80% of your sales occur between Thanksgiving and Christmas, and so yeah you can say it's your marketing people who are driving the deadlines and everything, but the reality is that's really the marketplace, and it's retailers like Walmart, and Best Buy and Target and Game Stop… That's who's driving those dates."

"A video game is not a toy," she adds, "but it has a sort of similar life cycle as a toy product because it winds up being a huge holiday gift item. And so they can sit there and complain, 'Well Beth, I'm not going to be ready.' And I'm like 'OK, do you want to go in and tell the buyer at Walmart why you can't meet their deadlines? Because if they don't pick up your product, you're dead. If you miss the holiday season, you have no product. We fail.'

And in launching a new console, it's even more important to be on time. You only get one chance to make that all-important first impression. And to be sure, some games can launch successfully at any time of the year. (Maxis famously launched some of their hit games, like SimCity, outside the holiday window on purpose because the market was less crowded at that time.) And arguably games destined to major hits, like Halo and Grand Theft Auto 3 could ship at any time of the year. But the same can't be said for a console, which is not a single product, but a consumer platform.

"A lot of the developers are focused on their product and getting it to be the best it can be, and they're not necessarily thinking about the big picture," observes Featherstone. "Bungie had never done a console game before, either. They were a Mac developer primarily. When we bought them, they were planning on developing it for the PC and the Mac. It was not intended to be a console game, and part of what messed up their schedule and made things take longer was that they had to do some reengineering work to make it a console-friendly game." The job of marketing, she says, is to work with the developers and producers to understand the realities of the business. "It's not your evil product manager plotting against you in the marketing wing of the building. This is the reality. And this situation was unique. That's the marketing side of it."

-23-

Bill Gates hands over the first Xbox video game system ever sold to Edward Glucksman of Keansburg, New Jersey, at the Toys "R" Us store in New York City shortly after midnight, November 15, 2001.

Midnight Madness

The Xbox North American launch occurred at a Toys"R"Us on Times Square on November 15, 2001. At midnight. By January, 2002, they had sold all of the 1.5 million units they had shipped, while their flagship, first-party launch title, Halo, was setting sales records.

http://usatoday30.usatoday.com/life/cyber/tech/review/games/2001-11-15-xbox-launch.htm#more

By some act of serendipity or excellent planning, the international flagship Toys"R"Us store was brand-new and had yet to open its doors to the public. It was right on Times Square—the world-famous central hub of New York—and Microsoft was able to convince them to open the store ahead of schedule—at

Scene of the Midnight Madness event in a quiet moment.

midnight—and stay open all night selling Xbox and its accessories. Microsoft took over all the giant electronic billboards in Times Square, and Bill Gates personally gave away the first Xbox midnight. And the event was called, somewhat appropriately, Midnight Madness.

Also starting sales at midnight or soon after were Electronic Boutique stores in Redmond (the home of Microsoft) and San Francisco.

The whole of Times Square was lit green, and a big launch party was taking place at the WWE/WWF cafe across the street with The Rock in attendance. And there was BillG playing his favorite Xbox game, Fusion Frenzy, the bright lights of the Billboards showing clips of Xbox games, and thousands of eager Xbox buyers. And there was plenty going on behind the scenes.

Before Bill Gates walked out to present the first Xbox at midnight, he was given a little Xbox lesson in a hotel room by John O'Rourke. Even though Gates was familiar with the Xbox and how it worked, he hadn't had much time to play it, and the plan was for him to give the first Xbox to someone and then play a game with that person. "I got the TV and put the Xbox next to it," says O'Rourke, "but the hotel TV didn't have any type of inputs other than a coaxial cable connector. I had to run down to Best Buy on 47th and buy the cheapest CRT I could find to set it up in his hotel room so he could practice the game we had set up."

When Gates arrived, they started practicing. "He was like a kid in a candy store. I taught him how to play Halo, Project Gotham Racing, and some other games. He had this huge grin on his face and was having the time of his life. For me it was the highlight of the overall experience. I'm sitting there with the CEO and chairman of Microsoft, with the Xbox controller in his hand in a little hotel room in NYC playing on this 15-inch screen."

Many people who have known Gates have commented on his sense of humor and willingness to do fun things. He participated in several goofy stunts with Alex St. John. But he rarely had the time for what most people would call fun. Even if he was the head of a corporation making big moves in the field of video games, his usual games were of another type. But O'Rourke gives us a glimpse of what drove them to do what they did—even Bill Gates, one of the wealthiest men in the world. "We were so counter to what so many people's perceptions were of what Microsoft was all about—so corporate… arrogant. We weren't like that at all. We were people that were passionate about an idea; down to earth and humble. The only thing we were unwavering about was our commitment to our belief in what we were building."

The "Duke" and "Akebono"

The "Duke"—also known as "Fatty"—the original Xbox controller, started out a bit oversized. Bachus remembers the first time he and Blackley saw it. "It was enormous! We were like, 'What the hell is this?' It was thought that the designers were just trying to fit all the features that Allard had requested, such as six buttons like the Sega Genesis, two thumb sticks, an adapter port, the vibration motor. Which all require space. Apparently, they also said that they had done a lot of testing on it, including biofeedback testing of the electrical impedance of people's muscles. According to Brett Schnepf, who codenamed the Duke after his son, Allard also wanted an LCD screen, but that feature was left out.

Once again, people believed all kinds of things, but Allard disputes these beliefs. "Completely untrue. I threatened to quit over duke. The team didn't work for me and it was the only thing I really lost my shit over on the project."

The "Duke" controller (left) and the smaller Akebono (right)

"So we took it over took it over to Japan," says Bachus, "and the Japanese freaked out. When they saw the console, they said, 'This is the size of one of our houses.' And the controller? 'It's as big as my head.' And they went crazy, to the point that they were starting to say, 'Maybe we won't make games for Xbox because we think this thing's going to fail.'"

Originally, the Xbox Controller S ("Akebono"), a sleeker controller than the "Duke" was introduced only for the Japanese market, but it later became the standard controller. Ironically, the "Akebono" was named after a famous sumo wrestler of the same name. Akebono was the first American born sumo wrestler to win the highest sumo rank of *yokozuna*. What makes it ironic is that apparently the people at Microsoft thought he was undersized for a sumo wrestler, when in fact he was an enormous 6'8" tall and a respectable 517 pounds, although he was somewhat lighter than the first Hawaiian born sumo wrestler, Konishiki, who tipped the scales at a fighting weight of up to 630 pounds on a 6'1" frame.

Again, Allard disputes the idea that Duke was so large to accomodate a lot of features he had wanted. "Obiously, since akebono shipped, with all of the same features just months after duke, the problem was not 'all of allard's features'."

He continues, "had I been more involved in the first generation of the controller, i promise it wouldn't have been duke. don't put that one on me!"

At Launch

At the time of its launch, Xbox was arguably the most powerful console of its time. Featuring the Intel Pentium III 32-bit processor running at 733 MHz, it was more than twice as powerful as that of the PlayStation 2, and was loaded with twice the RAM. The addition of an 8GB hard disk, a first for game consoles, added flexibility and power to the system, and built-in Ethernet

Bill Gates lets loose and plays some Munch.

port set the stage for some of the system's most powerful game experiences as well as digital downloading.

There were plenty of hit games, too, in addition to launch titles like Halo: Combat Evolved, Munch's Oddysee, Project Gotham Racing, Madden 2002, and Amped: Freestyle Snowboarding (Europe), and Dead or Alive 3 (Japan). Later hit games included Splinter Cell, MechAssault, WWF Raw, and The Elder Scrolls: Morrowind. With their purchase of Rare Ltd for $375 million, they acquired the Banjo Kazooie and Goldeneye franchises, not to mention one of the best game developers in the business and a long-time hit maker from the Nintendo stable.

Japan and then Europe

The console launched in Japan on February 22, 2002, but had a harder time catching on there, despite a redesign of the original bulky controller to a sleeker one, the release of popular titles like Dead or Alive 3 and Ninja Gaiden to attract the Japanese gamers—and even 50,000 special edition Xboxes created just for the launch. The Xbox Special Editions featured an additional AV pack and a key chain with Bill Gates' signature on it. On March 14,

2002, the console launched in Europe, but adoption there was also slow, causing Microsoft to lower the price in an attempt to stimulate sales.

Europe

As difficult as it was for Oddworld to adjust to the sudden change of focus from casual game to hardcore focus, they still had a strong game with an established brand and fan base. Unfortunately, the situation got worse in the build-up to the European release of Xbox. Lanning and McKenna were asked to go on a press tour throughout Europe. They were expecting to demo Munch and talk about the game, but according to Lanning what happened was not according to plan. As Lanning recalls, "We were in Europe and we couldn't even talk about our titles on a press tour because the press was so furious at the single price point for the entire newly created Eurozone. So they were really upset with the price and they were really upset that each country was being treated equally in pricing. You had Spanish journalists saying, "Why do I need to drive to Italy to save a hundred dollars on my Xbox? It's bullshit.' They were really, really upset, and Microsoft hadn't built its brand in the console space yet."

Sandy Duncan, Senior Director of Xbox Europe, was John O'Rourke's counterpart in the newly established Eurozone. Everyone knows that the Xbox launch in Europe was a botched affair. But not everybody was at ground zero to explain why. Duncan is outspoken in his analysis. "We launched at £299 (Euro 399). This was totally fucking stupid, as Sony had

In London, Virgin's Richard Branson sells the first Xboxes to lucky buyers.

cut the PS2 price months earlier to £199 in Europe. To understand this stupidity you have to get your head round how Microsoft worked at the time. They were a software company who set budgets once a year. Budgeting concluded in June, and there wasn't a system to review Office and Windows pricing more than once a year. To restate your whole business model during a fiscal year was unheard of."

Duncan says that he flew to Seattle around September/October 2001 to meet with Robbie Bach and argue that they lower the launch price. The problem was the yearly budget cycle. Changing the price would have changed what would be a projected profitable European launch to a one that would project a loss of $200 million or more. As it was, Europe was the only one of the three regions (US, Japan, Europe) that had been projected to be profitable in the first year.

To further complicate the situation, Bach took Duncan's proposal to his immediate superior, COO Rick Beluzzo. The problem was that Steve Ballmer hated the Xbox business model, which was predicated on losing money initially, and so Beluzzo was actually afraid to present the idea to Ballmer. In the end, Duncan proposed a compromise. "I would launch at £299 and 'see what happened,'" he says.

What happened was that the console sold fewer than 100k units in the first week, and the big retailers were trying to send their stock of Xboxes back to Microsoft by the end of week two. "I flew to US to be met by Ed Fries, Robbie and J Allard. Their response was 'How could you let us launch at that stupid price?' It seemed that the shit was only sticking to one person…"

Within five weeks after the launch, they dropped the price down to £199 (EU 299) and gave everyone who had paid the higher price two free games. The price drop helped, but Xbox did not meet its first year projections. It did reach number one in the UK and in the Nordic regions, but did poorly in other countries. Signing an exclusive Christmas 2002 deal (in Europe) for Splinter Cell helped Xbox sales, although they were going up against Sony's advantages, including exclusives of Grand Theft Auto 3 and Metal Gear Solid 2 and double the marketing budget. "Sony's UUEFA Champions League sponsorship alone was about 25% of our total marketing budget."

As Duncan has explained, the initial price of Xbox in Europe virtually destroyed the launch and hurt sales, not only of the console, but obviously of the software, too. And one of the products it hurt badly was Munch's Oddysee. And the price wasn't the only problem. According to Duncan, another issue was distribution. "In 2002 retail was the only way to buy a console (or game). In Europe only EA had good multi-country distribution and would take on other 3rd party titles (e.g. they distributed for Capcom in Europe)." Lanning and McKenna both point out that the lack of console sales, and distribution both hurt them badly. However, both Halo and Splinter cell, according to Duncan, had good attach rates (meaning the rate at which buyers of the console also bought these titles). He also points out, that "platformers were a dying category by then with 3rd person shooters (GTA and MGS) and sports (F1 and FIFA) dominating in Europe."

OFFENSIVE, SHOCKING and in BAD TASTE

Duncan does have what he calls his BIG victory over everyone else at Microsoft (not just Xbox). He was able to produce his own advertising. "We were the only business unit not using McCann Erickson." One of Duncan's TV

Sandy Duncan

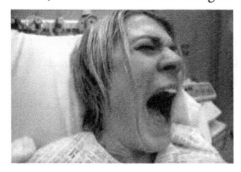

Sandy Duncan's scandalous commercial begins with a woman giving birth and shows the baby flying through the air, aging as he goes, and crashing into a grave at the end. The final message: "Life is short. Play more."

ads was extremely controversial, and even though it was banned in the UK, it won the silver medal at the prestigious *Palme D'Or* in Cannes in the "World's Best Advert" category, second only to Nike, "who always used to win." You can see this remarkable ad at *https://www.youtube.com/watch?v=brsI6z13Su8*.

A June 6, 2002 article in BBC News World Edition reported that Duncan's ad had been banned after getting numerous (136, to be exact) complaints that it was "offensive, shocking and in bad taste". According to the article's (accurate) description, "It starts with a woman giving birth to a baby boy who then shoots out of a window in a surreal sequence. Viewers then saw the boy ageing rapidly as he flies through the air screaming, before violently crashing into his own grave. The advert ends with the payoff: 'Life is short. Play more.'"

The article also states, "Xbox has followed Sony PlayStation's lead in opting for adverts which range from the unusual to the surreal. Its first UK advert featured mosquitoes sucking blood in time to music."

Japanese Launch

People waiting for the Japanese launch of Xbox to begin.

When Xbox launched in Japan early on the morning of February 22, 2002, which was considered to be an auspicious date, Bill Gates took the stage at the Hyatt in Shibuya, the entertainment and fashion district of Tokyo, accompanied by loud music and some pyrotechnics. The event was media only, and he told the assembled crowd that Microsoft was ushering

Mircrosoft gave out special "smoke" Xboxes at the launch in Japan.

めずらしいところでお会いしましたね。

Bill Gates even appeared in ads to win over the Japanese market.

in the next generation of video gaming. Gates said, "For Microsoft it is very important to be successful in Japan." However, the truth is that Microsoft faced an uphill battle.

Still, there was a lot of enthusiasm at the launch event, and Japanese fans had stood in line through the night to purchase the first Xboxes, despite the higher price of ¥34,800 compared with ¥29,800 for PlayStation 2.

In probably the high point of the event it was reported that Gates won an Xbox racing game against Japanese pop star Yoshiki, a member of a group called X-Japan. But that might have been the last win for Gates in Japan because Xbox never really took off there. Whether it was because of consumer loyalty to the Japanese brands like Sony and Nintendo, or loyalty to the games like Final Fantasy and anything from Nintendo, which were not available on Xbox, or for other reasons specific to the Japanese culture, the fact was that Xbox never seriously challenged their competitors in Japan.

Losing the Japanese Market

If Xbox didn't do well in Japan, Chris Phillips thinks he knows some of the reasons why. He offers some personal and uncensored insights into why it failed there. "It was so unfortunate, but more importantly, the fact that they completely disenfranchised the Japanese market before they even had a box built or anything done was stunning. And because of my relationships, I actually knew what was really happening in some of the meetings. Or I would find out after the fact because friends would call me and go, 'Are you guys crazy? You don't understand how this really works.'"

Phillips says that a lot of mistakes were made, such as telling Japanese companies that they were going to have the boxes manufactured, not in Japan, but in Korea. "There was zero cultural sensitivity, where I literally got an earful from multiple people after some of the people you've named went through, big egos, shooting their mouth off and not even realizing that they had completely killed whatever relationship or any deal they could possibly get out of these Japanese game companies because they might as well said their mother was of ill repute or something."

Phillips says that the people he's talking about didn't last very long on the Xbox team, but the damage they did was not repairable. And there was more. He says that the Microsoft people approached negotiations like a movie deal. And, as Bachus has already pointed out, some of the people involved simply alienated the people they were supposed to be working with.

Phillips points out that what the Japanese said to people's face and what they said among themselves was very different. This was true during the negotiations with Square Soft, where there was serious talk on the surface, but, according to Phillips' private translators at the meeting, there was a lot of disdain for the approach Microsoft was taking and doubts that Xbox would succeed at all.

"I'd been meetings with Rick and others in Japan. It wasn't brutal from what was being translated to us, but what being said in Japanese was brutal. And I came in after Seamus and others had gone through Japan, and just… because I had relationships with these companies for years, I got an earful of just how bad we had stepped in it."

Phillips says that one of the major lost opportunities was not using their Japanese engineering talent to meet directly with the companies they were trying to work with. "What was crazy was that we had some phenomenal engineers, many of whom spoke Japanese. I was like, 'Listen. Here's some people you should absolutely hire because they can go and engage directly with Japanese engineers and help land the platform, as well as device manufacturers, peripheral manufacturers." Phillips says that his suggestion was rejected, asserting that the reason was that these people had been part of the Dragon OS team, which the Xbox people looked down on. Phillips is pretty harsh in saying it was ego that stood in the way. "The thing I've learned over the years is that when it comes to your ego on anything, it's stupid if you don't have smart people working for you, and especially people who have deep expertise, and years of experience."

Whether Phillips' claim about for failing to use some of their best assets is valid or would have made all the difference is debatable, but what isn't debatable is that Xbox was a pretty definite failure in Japan.

"I think we let our egos get way too much in the way," he concludes, "and that's always a danger in technology. On the one hand I totally admire the 'willing things into existence' and having that kind of leadership and group of people that can go make things happen. On the other hand, there's a temperance of, hey, leverage all the brains you can. And the humility of that. And I didn't understand that as much in the '90s as I did later on, because I was one of those gunslingers along with a lot of us in the '90s. Because that's what the company really attracted."

Members of the Xbox team recieved a special "ship-it" package after launch.

~24~
Xbox—the First Year

Xbox had a pretty good first year. Of course it didn't even come close to being profitable, but nobody expected that it would be. What it did do is validate that Microsoft could create a console system that could compete in the market against the current leaders—Sony and Nintendo. No American manufacturer had been able to do that since the early days of Atari, Coleco and Mattel. 3DO was the last attempt by an American manufacturer to break the Japanese stranglehold on the console business, and it had failed, arguably due to a lack of good software more than by a failure in design or hardware.

And what Microsoft had that 3DO had lacked was software—notably Halo: Combat Evolved, which was a runaway hit. But there was more. Xbox had the Ethernet port that allowed players to link their boxes together, which was a big part of Halo's success, and even before Xbox Live, was an advantage.

Because it proved itself, Xbox gained more third-party developers and its portfolio of games continued to grow. Before the first year ended, it was clear that Xbox was a marketing success. However, it was not an unqualified success. There were supply problems; they couldn't manufacture enough units to meet demand. It failed in Japan and under-performed in Europe. It had to make quick adjustments to the controller. And despite the fact that there were new third-party developers coming on, Stuart Moulder points out that Xbox didn't have a particularly strong Spring lineup, and their second holiday season was uninspiring, with the exception of Splinter Cell, which helped carry it through.

Fries Takes Third Party

After the multiple staggered launches of Xbox in the US, Europe and Japan, Ed Fries was settling in. His son, Xander (short for Alexander), who was born in March, shortly after the Japanese launch, was named after Xbox. Fries says that Bill Gates signed a Japanese Xbox for Xander on which he wrote, "Ed Junior's First Toy."

Soon afterward, Robbie Bach decided to switch the third-party operations to Fries, who was already in charge of first-party. The switch moved George Peckham's group under Fries. ""So not only was I going around meeting with game developers, would work with our 1st-party team, but also meeting with all the big publishers."

Part of Fries' new challenges involved signing up companies to support Xbox Live, which was in development and expected to launch within the next year. One of their toughest negotiations was, not surprisingly, with Electronic Arts. "EA in particular were very slow to support Xbox Live; they had a lot of demands for their support of that platform. But they were the big guys, so..."

Part of what Fries faced by heading both 1st-party and 3rd-party was that he was simultaneously competing with the very companies with which he was negotiating. "It was a little controversial when Robbie decided to move 3rd-party under me. I think we were the only console that put 1st- and 3rd-party together under one person." One area of potential contention with EA was in the sports franchises. EA was the leader in sports games, and didn't much want competition, but as Fries notes, "We did have a sports division. Fortunately, it wasn't good enough to really be too threatening. I think they were confident enough that they didn't see us too much as a threat. But there were other places, say racing for example, where we were very much head-to-head competitors."

The Strategic Plan

O'Rourke claims that the marketing strategy for Xbox was very well executed. "If you look at it through a marketing lens, the core tenets of any really successful marketing driven company, there's brand at its very center and then a real strategic commitment to the messaging around the brand proposition. That's what we did with Xbox from the very beginning. Where I think some other organizations struggle, everyone on the Xbox team had a shared understanding and shared vision of what the brand stood for."

O'Rourke admits that, in addition to good strategy, there was also luck. "It was a combination of both brilliance and luck, but the brand attributes that we strived to create around Xbox mapped incredibly well to the target audience that we were going after. It differentiated us significantly from Nintendo and Sony." Of course, Nintendo was sufficiently different in their branding and marketing strategy, O'Rourke says, that it was fairly easy to differentiate Xbox against them. "Sony was more challenging," he says. "Sony had that macro brand. Sony stood for entertainment, and the PlayStation had been very successful." For O'Rourke, the big differentiator was connectivity. We talked about what made us the next generation console, in particular being able to tell a story that it is more about connecting gamers, not just to the person next to them on the couch but to a person sitting on a couch across the city or across the state... it gave us a story and a brand position as an innovator that Sony was now having to respond to."

What We'd Never Done Before

As only he can, J Allard looks back at what they had accomplished with Xbox and how much of the effort was brand new to all of them... how he saw the process in some ways as a family affair.

"look, the most complicated msft hw product was the mouse and we outsourced a ton of it. we had never sold product to or through walmart, target or best buy. we had never published a console game. we had never "certified" 3rd party products. we had never had billions in parts inventory. consumer branding? ha. we did product branding for productivity and some bled into the consumer, but never released a major product that was consumer first like this. we never had a million square foot manufacturing facility. the list goes on. we built a whole ton of new competencies. for all intents and purposes, it was a new company that had the full backing of microsoft. how could you say one thing was more important than the other? sure, manufacturing isn't that glamorous to talk about, but what if we missed christmas or had assembly problems? retail seems easy now, but at the time everything we did was through oem's and distributors. no wal-mart? no xbox. we had games from a lot of sources, but no 1st party hit exclusive to the platform (other than halo) then what would our p&l have looked like, 3rd party confidence? no support from EA, no madden? no gamers. i could go on forever. i appreciated every single part of the family we built and we couldn't have succeeded without every single person on the team. there was no wasted energy - no room for it. who's to say any was more important than the other? we love to tell stories with heroes, but this was a story of a family"

An Xbox team photo.
It took, a lot of brilliant, hardworking people to create Xbox,
the project that was once thought to be a pipedream.

PART II:

XBOX GETS CONNECTED

"Playing games through dial-up is like eating pizza through a straw."
-J Allard

~25~
Early Live Visions

We wanted to shift the medium from these rigid narratives with clear beginning, middles and ends to enable people to create worlds that were constantly alive and that participants not just passed through, but left permanent marks while they were there that affected everyone else.

-J Allard

Am I Playing Yet?

-Cam Ferroni

Things were definitely looking good for Xbox, particularly in North America, and in November 2002 they launched something that took them over the top—Xbox Live. Although it launched a year after the debut of the console, Xbox Live was no afterthought. Even the failure of previous attempts at creating online services, such as SegaNet on the Dreamcast, didn't deter Microsoft's visionaries, such as J Allard and Cam Ferroni, from envisioning a truly connected online game experience on the Xbox. Xbox, unlike any console before it—including PS2—shipped with an Ethernet plug-in for broadband, and no low-bandwidth modem. They were banking on features such as voice connections and downloadable content (DLC) to drive people to the system.

Allard described the vision that he and Ferroni shared as "a living entertainment experience powered by human energy." Looking at the history of video games (although this is true of most games throughout history) Allard observed that they had begun by involving people playing together, citing some of the earliest games, such as Pong and Spacewar!, neither of which had a single-player mode. "gaming transformed in 20 years from a social medium to a solitary medium. it shifted from being designed for everyone to games being designed to address the 'most valuable segment.' 16-26 year-old boys was the proxy that most people used." He says that games like Doom, which inspired people to play together in LAN* parties, "rekindled the thinking in

*LAN = Local Area Network

the industry that there was something about re-introducing the ingenuity of the players and 'human ai' into the gaming experience." The problem, as he saw it, was there was no platform to support these kinds of experiences. The effort it took to put on a LAN party was considerable. There was no plug-and-play in those days. It was more like kluge-and-(hopefully) play.

One way they tried to encourage people to play together was to put four controller ports on the box. But there was more to the concept. Allard wanted to build what he called the "virtual couch" so you could "have your friends over" no matter where they were in the world. "we wanted to shatter the limits of physical devices and enable 16-, or 64- or 16,000-player gaming worlds. we wanted to shift the medium from these rigid narratives with clear beginning, middles and ends to enable people to create worlds that were constantly alive... we wanted to rekindle that idea of an arcade and the high-score boards on games that allowed you to see what was possible, or show your stuff even when other people weren't around. we wanted to shift the business to generate revenue beyond the initial sale and to allow publishers and creators to have an ongoing relationship with their audience."

If you haven't already noticed, Allard had very poetic ways of expressing his grand vision, and perhaps this is why he so inspired the people who worked for him. John O'Rourke says that Allard's had an incredible ability to tell a "very good, quotable story. As a leader, he really did a tremendous amount at Microsoft with his ability to paint a picture of the future and get people excited about going to that place in the future that he just talked about. He may not have all the details and all the steps necessary to get there yet, but his passion and his ability to articulate that drew a lot of people to him."

In an email to me, here is a picture Allard drew for me in words about his vision for Xbox and Xbox Live: "until xbox, every game console constrained the designers imagination. we wanted xbox to intimidate their imaginations - like you might imagine the sistine chapel blew away michelangelo - a canvas for his magnum opus that demanded an entirely new way to think without the rigid constraints of canvas or marble and a scale that would allow for a new type of narrative vs. a simple moment in time." Allard's Sistine Chapel for game designers would do away with CD-ROMs, single-player, 3D action button-mashing and introduce instead a world of multiplayer, voice, leader boards, identity, tournaments and serialized, evolving content. He wanted to hasten the game industry's embrace of the Internet. He wanted to inspire masterpieces of player involvement and connection.*

Again, the quotes from Allard's emails are reproduced without alteration. This is how he writes, and as Boyd Multerer told me, "There is a reason we always refer to him as just 'j' with a lower-case 'j'. You should too. He never (or very rarely or just when referring to formal acronyms) uses caps." For convention and easier reading, I do refer to him as "J" or "J Allard" throughout the book, but do not edit his communications with me.

Allard also talked about the promise of the upcoming broadband revolution. He noted that MTV, CNN and ESPN drove cable adoption on TV. "the original value proposition was reception and it evolved to be about selection, we knew broadband wasn't about performance in terms of mainstream adoption, it was about new scenarios - online gaming would be one of the key drivers and someone was going to be the 'ESPN of games' we wanted that to be us. We just wanted to bring gaming back to where it started - as a social medium - using technology that was going to see widespread embrace - the internet. Thus, LIVE…"

Allard would show an old Atari video to inspire people. It alternates images of Atari game screens like Space Invaders, Asteroids, Missile Command, Pac-Man, and more, interspersed with images of manic happy kids and families, starting with two kids, and adding more family members and friends with each new shot. Everyone is leaning forward with their controllers in hand, smiling, laughing, screaming with joy, while suitably energetic announcer's voice, speaking over some equally happy music is saying, "Only Atari makes the world's most popular home video games. The only Space Invaders. The only Asteroids, the only Pac-Man, the only Missile Command, the only Defender. And the only way you can play any of them is on a home video system made by Atari." It ends with the Atari logo and little jingle, "Have you played Atari today?" The link below is bad quality, but amusing.

http://www.youtube.com/watch?v=GU3gHAGbi0Q

"The funny thing was of course that the moment portrayed in that video never really happened," he says, "but that did illustrate both the soul of gaming then and its potential."

Finally, he adds, "as you can see, it was a 10+ year vision that we started and infused in the culture. so many people had so many contributions and so many specific ideas and accomplishments and successes and failures and partnerships to bring it to life there's a million stories to tell. but all of those activities and players orbited a single purpose, a single *raison d'être*. And that purpose still exists today in that culture. it was bigger than any of us, bigger than all of us."

Allard picked his partner and fellow visionary Cam Ferroni to lead the project, and Ferroni's prime directive for Xbox Live was "Am I Playing Yet?" He says, "That ideal drove through everything we did. It both fueled the success, and caused all of the struggle for the next years. We developed an ethos that carried us through the entire lifecycle of what we were building. We obsessed over one core principle—that consoles were simple. They were the original plug and play. It didn't matter what TV you had, you hooked up no more than 3 wires, you plugged it in, and within seconds you were playing a game. You didn't have to download patches, mess around with video drivers, type in activation codes… 2 or 3 clicks and you were playing."

The First Xbox Live Guy

I always like to build things that are going to be relevant when they ship and not relevant when you start. That means you've always got to be predicting where the world's going.

-Boyd Multerer

Boyd Multerer graduated with a degree in mechanical engineering and thermal systems in 1990, but he discovered that his real passion was in software programming. So he decided to "make the fun thing the job and the mechanical thing the hobby." Next, he decided to move to Seattle "because, I don't know… I felt like it." And not being someone who likes being told what to do, he started his own software company marketing desktop publishing tools.

Multerer's company supplied software to large corporations such as Aldus, Adobe, and Microsoft, and one of his contracts was to write code that ended up being used in Microsoft Office 4. While working on that contract he met Rebecca Norlander. He invited Norlander and her husband (J Allard) to dinner one night, and that meeting with Allard led to a job working on II3 (Internet Information Server 3).

While working on II3, Multerer became convinced that "this web thing is just going to destroy desktop publishing." He sold off his major projects, primarily to Adobe, and went to work on web servers at Microsoft under

Boyd Multerer

Allard. He wrote code for iS4 and iS5 as well as some data center management software. Multerer kept in touch with Allard even after he no longer worked for him, and when Allard came back from a long sabbatical in 1999 and became the lead on the Xbox project, he was invited to join the new project. On August 4, 2000 he joined the Xbox team and was once again working for Allard.

Immediately, Allard gave him a mission. "J basically points to the back of the box and says, 'Alright. We decided to put an Ethernet port in the back,' although that was still in debate. He told me, 'Go figure out what it talks to.' And that was my job. I can say I was the first person to work on Xbox Live, although it was called Xbox Online."

From that point and for the next four years, Multerer ran Xbox Live engineering. In the beginning, he was highly selective in his hiring. You had to be more than good to join the team, you had to be exceptional. Like Jon Thomason's Xbox OS team, Multerer built a lean and highly focused team of 15, dedicated to working quietly, efficiently, and with a constant eye to keeping costs down.

Separation

In order to create his vision of the Xbox online service, Allard believed that his team had to be insulated from the Microsoft as a whole. He knew the politics of the company and he knew the propensity for meddling that was common,

213

especially in something as new and revolutionary as what he and his team had set out to accomplish. And so he had fought to move his team off the main campus, to the "Millennium Campus" and specifically into Millennium E.

Even though the Millennium Campus was not far from the main campus, it was light years away from any casual interference from outside the project. Of course it was connected through the networks and phones, but it was a place where the entire focus could be on Xbox and Xbox Live because, in Allard's mind, Xbox was its own company and his team was working for Xbox more than for Microsoft.

JJ Richards, an engineer who came late to the project to work on Xbox Live, credits Allard and Robbie Bach with insulating the Xbox team from the normal predatory culture at Microsoft, pointing out that it wasn't just physical separation that was important, but something far more ideological. "What Robbie and J did was to create a new subset of culture within an established cultural organism. There is a lot of history at Microsoft of projects that had good ideas, and they get crushed by the machine because they weren't Windows or Office or competitive. So the idea that they could create a consumer company, a true consumer entertainment company, out of thin air in a business enterprise company, that cared about beating Sony while no one else at Microsoft even knew why Sony mattered... that was instrumental to the success, because without that, Xbox would have been killed early."

Part of the reason Multerer had favored a small and separate team was that he hoped to avoid an all-out fight with the core team on Xbox, which in time began to grow suspicious of Live's drain on resources. Many at Microsoft, including some on the Xbox team, saw Live as a distraction, at best, and at worst a case of terminal mission creep that could jeopardize the entire Xbox effort. A project doomed to fail.

Projects and Horses

"I heard an analogy at the time, which I've seen applied to many projects," says Multerer. "The analogy is, any project that you're doing, if it's radical and new, it's sort of like having a horse. At first all the other people look at your horse and say, 'Aw, what an old nag, somebody oughta put that horse down.' Then the horse lives on and you move along and you start making some progress. Then they say, 'Oh, why is that horse getting so much attention? We need to kill the horse and not have it as a competitor.' Then it survives and it moves along, and then it's like, 'Hey, this is actually a business driver. I want to hook my cart up to the horse!' I've seen so many projects go through this. It's not just a Microsoft thing. This is just humans."

Meeting the Broadband Challenge

Remember the three bets that Microsoft made on broadband even before Xbox was built?

1. Bandwidth penetration was going to happen.
2. Data center bandwidth costs would fall.
3. Servers would improve so that they could handle the load.

Now that Xbox Live was a real project, it was time to get specific. There wasn't much they could do about broadband penetration in the home, but there was a lot of analysis they could do in planning and analyzing the challenges they faced, such as data center costs and what kind and how many servers they would need.

At the time, they were looking at data center costs at $350 per peak megabit per second. "Let's just say, it would be wildly expensive," says Multerer. The way it worked when you were doing it "in bulk," he explains, they don't precisely measure how much bandwidth you're using. They look at the outgoing bandwidth for a given month. "Because it's all outgoing. What they really care about is, what's the balance? If you're bringing in as much data as you're sending out, then you tend not to pay anything. If it's all lopsided, going one way, then you pay for the difference."

The way it worked was that the data center reserved bandwidth based on expected peak activity for the month. "So you pay for the reservation, not for the actual usage. During any given month, they take the peak amount that you hit, and then some figure slightly below it, and that's what you pay for, as if you were at near peak the whole month. And it was on the order of $350 per peak megabit per second, which is tremendously expensive. We could not have run this business at those kinds of prices, so we had to bet that those prices were going to fall."

The problem with servers at the time was that they were designed to scale up to numbers in the 100,000 client range, but when they discussed the project, they were talking in the millions of users. "We needed internet scale services that look more like a directory service that were traditionally aimed at enterprises, but this didn't exist. And the hardware to run those things was too expensive. So we also placed a bet that hardware was going to get cheaper, and that would allow us to build a web scale system that had enterprise-like technology behind it."

Multerer says, "I think one of the rules we said was over the first couple of years, we would go no more than $50 million in the hole in datacenter commerce. I don't know that we actually hit that. I think we probably went over. But we were trying to be cost conscious. So that was baked in pretty early."

Another area they considered was fiber optics, and they were initially thinking about the oil companies. "Every time they were digging a pipeline, they would put the big pipe in for the oil to go down, and then put a little pipe next to it full of fiber optics that they didn't know what they were going to do with. So it was all dark fibers. It was laid all over the country. And we even toyed with the idea of, 'Maybe we should buy a couple of fiber lines and set up a private Xbox Live channel to reduce latencies and increase the total bandwidth. That was a fourth bet that we made, which was, 'Nonono. The internet's going to get better with us. It will improve. The web is going to push them harder than we are, and the backbone will get good enough that we don't have to go and build a private network.' And that totally worked."

For more on the technical challenges behind Xbox Live, "Moving Information" on page 407.

Developing Xbox Live

Other than the Ethernet port built into Xbox, the development of Xbox Live was primarily about conceiving a clear, coherent and achievable vision, understanding the technical challenges, and writing the code. Lots of code. It was also about preparing for what Allard, Ferroni and their team believed was the inevitable. The Future.

Xbox Live Purpose Statements

"You've got to know why you're doing what you're doing, what are the principles you're going to work by, and then—so many projects don't do this—we wrote down the metrics of what we want to achieve within five years in order to know that we succeeded."

-Boyd Multerer

Multerer remembers a document from November 2000 that spelled out the Xbox Live purpose statement. Here are the main points of the purpose statement with commentary from Multerer:

Games Games Games

"And we had to talk about that. Because this is Microsoft, and are we really just about games? Are we going to put any other things in there? Are we building a service that's about anything other than games? And we said, 'No. We are just games.'"

Lead. Don't Follow

"At the time… go back to 2000… there were no consoles that had a service. The closest was the Sega Dreamcast, which had a browser, and that was it. SegaNet wasn't a really big service. And we clearly decided that we weren't even going to look at anyone else. We were just going to design our own thing and go."

It's an Xbox community.

"We focused in on the word 'community.' In today's parlance, we would say, 'Oh. We were building a social network.' Except we didn't know to call it a social network. And community was the word we homed in on, and we ended up defining a lot of what would become primary characteristics of modern social networks, and that's something I'm really proud of. You've got a list of people you communicate with. We've got good communication channels going through it. At the time, the closest things we were looking at was a little bit of Messenger, but we were trying to do something much deeper than just surface level communications."

Profit generating… gamers are our assets.

"So the most important thing was gamers, but not just gamers… gamers who were going to be buying games. It wasn't going to be a free service, and that was super controversial. Deciding to charge at all for this service… there were more yelling matches over that decision than almost any other decision. Because, you know, 'Oh my gosh. On the PC everything's free, and how can you possibly charge?' 'Well, if you charge for it, you can build a better service.' If you charge for it you can actually invest in servers, especially in 2000. They were wildly expensive. And by setting that precedent, we were able to build a much bigger, more robust, more feature-filled service than we could have otherwise done."

Be fiscally responsible.

"It was also a place where we could have dumped a huge amount of money. We ended up… at launch we had three data centers that we had built pretty much from scratch. And geographically located around the world. A big one in Seattle, one in London and one in Tokyo. And we had to be careful not to spend too much on it."

Crawl, Walk, Run

"J and Cam loved that."

Partner where appropriate

It's a service, stupid, and it just works

"Those were the main principles that we were trying to live by."

From these principal statements, they crafted the purpose statement for Box Live:

Build and manage the safe and profitable online gaming service for the global Xbox community and have fun doing it.

"And we debated every single word. And probably one of the ones that had the most debate was the word 'the'. 'Build and manage 'the'. And 'the' meant exclusive. It meant, 'Look. This is going to be the service for the console.' We're not going to have confusion. We're not going to have different logons for different games. You're going to log onto Xbox Live, and that's going to be your logon, right? And I'd say that led to probably the two most controversial decisions we made in the industry, which now are no-brainers. They're like, 'Well, duh. Of course you do it that way.'"

Gamertags & Presence

The two controversial decisions Multerer is referring to were Gamertags and the concept of Presence. Initially, Multerer says that publishers hated Gamertags. "The reaction was sort of, 'Wait a minute. What do you mean, you own my customer? They're my customer. They're playing my game, and they're logging into my service, not your service.'" But the XBL team wasn't having it. They explained that this was something that would benefit everyone. They explained how players could log into Xbox Live and build a reputation that crossed all the games they played… that XBL was about reputation and community, and if you split people up with different logons on a per game or per publisher basis, you fragment that community, and you're not going to get any scale. "They didn't like that because they wanted to control their customers. They saw it as a very competitive environment, so they didn't want their competitor getting any benefit from work that they did." Microsoft stuck to their guns, though. Gamertags stayed.

The idea of Presence might seem pretty obvious today, but back then the idea that you could log into an online service and see all your friends and what games they were playing (and they could see you and what games you were playing), that you could invite friends into the games you were playing, or they could invite you to theirs, was something new, and to the game publishers, simply a very bad idea. According to Multerer, "Their reaction was, 'No. Wait a minute. First you said I don't own my customer. And now you're telling me that I have to advertise my competitor's game in my game.' I'm not kidding. This was basically the reaction."

These two issues prevented some of the larger game companies from supporting Xbox Live for the first years, but eventually they came to realize that Xbox and Xbox Live weren't going away, and they were missing out. Some larger companies did embrace the new ideas from the start, and Ubisoft fully implemented them when they released Splinter Cell on Xbox at the same time as the launch of Xbox Live in November 2002. "That was the game that kind of proved the point we were trying to make about Xbox Live. Until then, yeah, it was kind of cute and kind of nice, but Splinter Cell really used it and the game was clearly better because of it. And they built around it, and frankly, it helped make that company."

One company that had played hardball all along, and continued to do so with XBL was Electronic Arts, and Multerer remembers an amusing anecdote about Don Mattrick, who, at the time they were pitching XBL to EA was president of worldwide studios, and who became president of the Entertainment Business Group at Microsoft in 2010, before leaving again to join Zynga.

A Don Mattrick Story

When Mattrick joined Microsoft, Todd Holmdahl brought him to meet Boyd Multerer. "Holmdahl introduces me to him. 'Hi Boyd. I'd like you to meet Don Mattrick. And Don Mattrick, meet Boyd.'

He said, 'Oh, it's good to meet you.'

And I said, and this is true, 'We've already met Don.'

'Oh, we have?'

"So it was E3 2002. We haven't shipped Xbox Live yet. Xbox is out. Xbox Live is not. I was in the booth, and we're showing off a bunch of games. We had these little phone booths that were set up, and you could go into booths and you could play against people the other booths, just to prove that it worked. And I was manning the booth at the time, and I was up at the little desk at the front, and this guy walks up who I didn't know, and I read his badge, and it said, 'Don Mattrick Vice President EA' And he's asking a couple of questions about Live, and I'm like, 'Well hey, it's really good to meet you Don. I'm looking forward to EA games being on Xbox Live.' And he says, 'Ptahuogh' and walks away. And I thought to myself, 'Oh yeah? We'll show you.'

"Anyway, so I told this story to Don... the first thing I said to him when he showed up at Microsoft, and he started laughing."

Social Interaction in MMOs

Jon Grande, who worked at the Zone and on MMOs like Asheron's Call, says that the real element of presence in Xbox Live was not fully implemented until the next generation console—Xbox 360. From observation, he knew that a lot of what players did in games was to socialize. It might be to talk smack or compare strategies after a mission, or just to get to know one another.

In MMOs, people cultivated friendships, and even romances. Grande remembers having heated arguments about socialization with people working on Xbox. Based on years of experience with the Zone, Asheron's Call and Cyber Ace, "we knew that people spent more than half of their time—upwards of two-thirds of their time—socializing outside the context of playing the game."

He says that there was some real concern that there would be pressure from other parts of Microsoft to add unwanted elements like a browser or forcing interoperability with other technologies that could dilute the purity of what Xbox was meant to be, and even detract from Xbox being taken seriously as a console. So, when Xbox Live initially launched, the idea of presence was only represented by seeing friends and playing in games with them.

Grande says, "It wasn't really until Live shipped on 360 that it took really a full persona of its own. On one hand I think it was a necessary decision inside the company to avoid having to go back and rehash these arguments about integration with Windows or Internet Explorer or other teams, but I think it was a pretty significant missed opportunity where we could have driven a lot more social interaction in the platform earlier on."

To Pay or Not to Pay

The decision to make Xbox Live a pay service was definitely controversial. At the time they were planning Xbox Live, people who used the internet had to pay ISPs for the service, but after that, they expected to get most other services for free. It's still that way today. Gamers would pay for games, and in the early days of MMOs, they were willing to pay monthly subscriptions for the games they wanted to play. But the idea that a console system could come out and introduce the first-ever massively scaled console-based social service—and charge money for it—was anything but obvious to most people, but not to those who were designing the service, like Cam Ferroni, J Allard and Jon Thomason, who had come over to XBL after completing work on the Xbox OS. "Many felt that because PC gaming was free, we should be free," says Ferroni. "But we believed then—and I think you see it carrying through now—that a high quality, consistent, easy experience, would be something that people would be willing to pay for, and would differentiate the Xbox from anyone else." Ferroni notes that providing a friend list across all games, a single user login/ID, voice chat in all games, an achievement system (Gamertags) that provided a persistent identity as a gamer, as well as ways to play together were services such as they had never seen before on consoles, and worth a small subscription fee.

Thomason says, "The decision to charge for Xbox Live was one of the best decisions we ever made. The thing we knew, even at the time, was that if we didn't charge for it from day one, we'd never be able to. And it was absolutely necessary to charge. The infrastructure cost so much that to have the level of service that people expect, you have to charge for it, unless you have some other way to monetize it, like ads or something else. This was before there was really a robust ad market for online stuff." So they did a lot of math to come up with how much they could charge. Lots of analysis and figuring things out, and in the end, "we just picked a price point because it was the cost of a game. We could explain that."

Despite the initial resistance from some publishers, Ferroni points out that those who did jump on board early were happy to have the extra sales and engagement, and players loved it. "They loved the fact that they could jump from game to game and find their friends easily—and jump right in. They realized our vision—that being in different cities and playing together could have all of the same excitement and quality of experience as playing next to each other in the arcade."

Attacks and Cheating

No online service is immune from cyber attacks, and no online game is immune from attempts at cheating. But speaking about hackers and cheating, Xbox Live's chief engineer Dinarte Morais says, "In terms of the service, I don't think that was too high on the list for people." On the other hand, he says that if players were looking to cheat, they would look for ways to modify their game locally. They might, for example, find a way to modify the game so that they always achieved perfect headshots.

Obviously, this kind of cheating, particularly in a competitive environment was unfair to other players and something to be discouraged. "So Xbox Live was putting in abilities to prevent spying or changing packets on the wire, but we also wanted, as much as possible, to keep the Xbox Live service's reputation high. We never guaranteed that there would be no cheating, but we actively monitored the system and kicked boxes offline so that they can't play with other people who don't want to play with those who are potentially cheating. We also didn't want developers to be the front line of that defense. They have enough work to do to build an excellent game; they shouldn't need to be online security experts, as well."

Morais says that they would look for operating systems that had been "modded" because a modded operating system would make it possible to mod the games, as well. "A lot of the data that was on the DVD was checked for authenticity. If you knew that the operating system was the original then you could, by extension, assume the operating system properly checked that the data it was using was authentic. So if you want to, say, edit a text file that controls how a car behaves in a racing game, and the game checked that the game itself was authentic, and the OS checked that the OS itself was authentic, then what you would have to do to break that change is to modify the OS to allow a slightly modified game to run."

If they detected that the operating system running on your Xbox was not the official OS, they would ban your box. But typically, their integrity checks and attempts to secure the system from cheating started an escalating war between them and those who wanted to hack the system. "We didn't read the DVD itself. We actually just looked at memory. Like I say, the system was dynamic. From the server side, we could change, at a moment's notice, what we would look at. I think the original thing that we looked at was a checksum, adding up all the numbers to see if it matched the types of operating systems that should be on the box. If it didn't, we didn't let them connect. That was the first step in the escalating war. The counter response was to intercept the request and return the hash that the system was expecting so no one's the wiser. Then that began ratcheting up the war.

"I implemented the security gateways, the first servers that you connect to when you log into Xbox Live. Like the key exchange that we did between two Xboxes on system link, we also did a key exchange with the Live service, so I wrote that portion of the front end. I also monitored the logs and came up with techniques for seeing how we were doing, if the detection system was returning valid responses, and then figuring out what the other responses should be, based on the results. The goal was to keep the Xbox Live service cheat free and with as high a reputation as possible. After we launched Xbox Live, I continued to work on that for another year."

Directory Services

Multerer explains some additional challenges they faced, and perhaps some reasons why it was not ready to launch with Xbox. To begin with, they had to build an internet-scale directory service. The existing technology, Active Directory, wasn't, in his words, "going to cut it at the time." So they had to build something from scratch. "When I say directory service," he says, "a lot of people would cringe because it's so enterprise-y and kinda nerdy, right? But at the fundamental core of what Xbox Live is, it's a place that hooks you up with other people to play games, and then furthermore, verify that they're not cheating."

It's actually easy to create something "chintzy" that won't scale to the level required, but it's very difficult to create something that scales into the millions. And it's not just a simple question of design. It gets more difficult when you consider the security issues. "Kerberos is a wonderful protocol that people have been using for a long time. Kerberos is the core standard authentication mechanism that you use every time you log into a Windows machine, and to most UNIX machines. It's a great protocol. And it assumes that there is one user using one machine. I've got four people logged into one machine. You don't mess with security protocols lightly. So ok, I've got four unique users that are using one machine and that needs to be expressed in Kerberos somehow, and have that plumb through the system in a way that you can't DOS (Denial of Service) and take down right away. As soon as you start thinking about attackers, and we know that people wanted to bring the system down, you have to be really careful about what are your weaknesses, what are the bottlenecks in the system, how can you survive a

DOS attack." Multerer further points out that challenges such as these were new back then. Today, it wouldn't take so long to design and implement a system like that. But back then, it did take time to do it and do it right.

Designing the directory services, he says, included matchmaking, leaderboards, a lot of value-added services, messaging systems, invitations systems, user interface design. In fact, he says that the high level vision of the project didn't fully solidify until the end of 2000. "The vision starts to move into strategy."

More and deeper technology information can be found in the Online Appendix under the headings, "Xbox Live Technology" and "A Technical Challenge".

~27~
Completing Xbox Live

At one point, Allard brought Jon Thomason in to lead the Xbox Live team. His operating system group, which he still nominally led, was still cranking out monthly releases, but Thomason's involvement was considerably reduced. "There wasn't much architecture work to do, management was pretty simple. So I went to work on Xbox Live."

During the first week on the project, Thomason went around talking to all the principle people to get a good picture of what was happening in the project. "I was a little in the dark about what they'd been doing." When Thomason realized that not only did they not have a launch date, but they didn't even have a clear schedule, he announced that they would have a complete schedule in two weeks. "So I set a date for a date, which I know is kind of ridiculous, but it had to be done. And we went and decided when we could be done and set a launch date."

Thomason took his schedule and launch plan to Robbie Bach and the other VPs. "I said, 'We can be done this day, but we want to set a launch date right now and get all the clocks ticking towards that. And I got them to buy off that day." Launch day was November 15, 2001. That day, we set that date, and we didn't change it after that. We hit that exact date."

Marketing: Four Points of XBL

Thomason's team then went into high gear, adding some new people and working on the data centers and other important components of the system. The team had grown by this time to 60 or 70 people, but from Thomason's point of view, the weakest link was the marketing team. "The marketing team that was working on this was extremely junior. So not only did I do all the engineering stuff, but I ended up doing all the marketing planning for Xbox Live, as well. I actually wrote the marketing positioning for Xbox Live."

Here are the four marketing points with Thomason's comments:

One: Friends List: "Across all games, see if people are online no matter what they're doing on their Xbox"

Two: Voice Chat: "Talk with any gamer anytime, no matter what they're playing."

Three: Gamertag: "Your online identity and reputation across all games."

Four: Online Multiplayer: Quick match and optimatch. "Play with your friends or play with people your skill level."

"We wanted to make sure that we were clear about what Xbox Live was all about in terms of features, and how better to do that than to emphasize features that we had that Sony did not."

"I remember one meeting where I had all the VPs in there—Ed Fries was in there, and of course Robbie and J and everybody—and I remember, I made these guys memorize the positioning. I had four positioning points that we were going to talk about, and I made them actually recite them back to me because I didn't trust them (heh), and I remember Ed sitting there, 'OK now. Let me say this again.' He said it three or four times, and they all got it, and it worked. Because when we launched that thing, if you looked, you found all those four points in every single article. And I think we nailed it."

Two Styles

Although Thomason credits Ferroni's leadership for getting some things done, he personally thinks that the whole project could have been completed within 18 months, and it had been 18 months by the time he took over. He believes that they could have been doing more work in parallel with the system development and that they didn't hire the necessary people fast enough.

Multerer sees it somewhat differently, however. He agrees that it might technically have been possible to launch XBL with Xbox. He says, "Jon might be right… we could have shipped something by the time Xbox shipped, but it wouldn't have been as compelling as what we did ship." He goes on to say that what they did ship—System Link—"was a precursor. Now if you want to build out a social network, especially when there are no social networks to understand from, I'm sorry that takes more than nine months to do. System Link just barely got done."

Multerer worked alternately under both Ferroni and Thomason. In fact, every several months the situation would change. "I was working for Cam. And then, like nine months later I was working for Jon again, and then a couple of months after that I was working for Cam again. And it just went back and forth and back and forth. I did not have a consistent manager for more than a year during that entire formation." He saw both of them as effective, but in different ways. "Jon is really good at shipping. Cam is really good at figuring out what to ship. They have very different approaches. A ton of work got done while Cam was running it, and yeah, there were lots of distractions. So I'm not saying it was super-efficient."

Thomason spoke about his philosophy of development, which was on display when he ramrodded Xbox OS development. "You've got to be ruthless. You've got to cut stuff. The big decisions were actually setting a time, and then cutting things to make it work. There were millions of little decisions, but the big one was setting an end date and turning it on a schedule-driven project. That's what they didn't do, and that was the missing piece. They hadn't said, 'We're going to ship this thing at launch, come hell or high water,' which with the system software, we had to. We had no choice. So I treated the Live launch like the same thing. Within the first two weeks we had that launch date set and bought off on by all of upper management… everybody."

Thomason says that making an official deadline made everybody work a lot harder, but adds, "I didn't do it by flogging everybody and doing the Office Space thing, you know… saying he's got to come in to work on Saturday. It was more like, we've got to make this date, and to do it we had a work back schedule that got us there, and then people worked weekends because that was the only way to do it. We had to get everybody into a full-on, heads down, mission critical sort of attitude, and they hadn't done that previously." Thomason says that they didn't hire early enough, but by the time he got there the team was pretty big. "Remember, the system software team was only about 20 at that time."

Thomason does give credit to the work the team did, especially Boyd Multerer and Dinarte Morais. "Dinarte Morais wrote all the security software for Xbox Live. He wrote the stuff that copied code down to the console and then ran chief detection code on the console, which at the time was unheard of. Nobody had ever done that before. Everything else had been done on the server before, so you could hack it by hacking the client, but we had a secure environment… secure enough that we could actually push the code down, while it was authenticating the login, and if it didn't look right, he could just fail it. It's pretty cool, and it's worked. There have been a lot of Xboxes over the years, right?"

Some Things Take Time

Looking at the project the way Thomason did, it seemed clear that the project could have been completed more quickly and with better planning. But Multerer points out the many challenging technical aspects of XBL, including making solid peer-to-peer connections; developing the security and exploit measures; designing the directory services, including matchmaking, leaderboards, a lot of value-added services, messaging systems, invitations systems; and user interface design.

"In fact," he says, "the high level vision of the project didn't fully solidify until the end of 2000. The vision starts to move into strategy. There's the pyramid: Vision is at the top, then comes strategy, and then comes tactics, and I'd say Gamertags were at the strategy level."

And that was another thing to keep in mind. It took time to promote the more controversial aspects of the system, notably Gamertags and their concept of presence. They had multiple people and groups doing outreach to developers to familiarize them with these new ideas and try to get them onboard. He specifically mentions several names, including Ferroni, Scott Henson, and George Peckham. "And Robbie was all behind it," he adds. "He stuck by us in that one during an extremely controversial time."

He admits that there was a certain amount of tension between Ferroni and Thomason. They approached product management very differently—in a sense like the difference between a creative style and a more military approach.

To Multerer, both Ferroni and Thomason contributed necessary skills to the project. "Jon is extremely good at shipping things. Very, very good at get-it-done. Spends less time on 'are we building the right thing?' But even today, some of us who've been around a long time will refer back to Jon and, 'Yeah, he was a master at shipping.' But less so on the why are we building what we're building." The "why" came from Ferroni and Allard.

~28~
Promoting Xbox Live

There were several press conferences for Xbox Live ahead of its launch, and both Thomason and Allard were involved. "J and I did a tag team on it," says Thomason. Allard started out by painting the picture as only Allard could do. "He gave a very eloquent talk about the future of gaming and all the kinds of stuff that Xbox Live could enable, and he talked about the cost of the game for the subscription, and then my part was to talk about the four features… the four big features that were in Xbox Live. Analysts loved it." The press events were a whole day that included wining and dining and lodging in fancy hotels.

"It's Good to Play Together"

Beth Featherstone was working on first-party games, not marketing for Xbox Live, but she was aware of the message and the intention behind it. "We knew that it was important to have a presence on Live so people could do multiplayer. That was part of the whole… we had strategies and tactics around getting people to play together, and "It's good to play together" was a tagline at the time."

John O'Rourke knew that part of the challenge was to convince gamers that Xbox was a serious platform, and Xbox Live was a key element in that effort. "What we needed to do was to get into the space of their minds where they viewed us as an innovator and leader. At least someone to pay attention to and listen to versus just being another console there on the shelf. That was where our story helped."

XBL at E3

At E3, they announced several Xbox exclusive titles developed to work with Xbox Live: Unreal Championship, MechAssault, Whacked!, NFL Fever 2003, and Midtown Madness 3, while additional titles include Counter-Strike,

Star Wars Galaxies, Shaun Palmer's Pro Snowboarder 2, Tom Clancy's Ghost Recon, Tom Clancy's Rainbow Six RavenShield, XIII, NFL 2K3, Phantasy Star Online, MechAssault, Meltdown Madness, and NBA 2K3 as well as online enabled follow-ups for Project Gotham Racing, Amped, and Rallisport Challenge with a teaser about the new Halo game. It was also announced that 60 game companies had signed up to make games for Xbox Live.

Ed Fries took the stage and spoke about the power of online gaming. He said, "The games industry is working every day to create a new form of entertainment that is fundamentally more involving, more powerful, and more compelling than anything that has come before." When Allard took the stage, he made this prophecy: "Within five years every important game will be online. There will be new categories of collaborative and competitive console games that are possible only online. The ability to download new worlds, levels, characters, weapons, vehicles, teams, statistics and missions will change the way developers think about creating games, and will change the way gamers play them."

Gaming website IGN seems to have gotten the message. They ended their report on the E3 announcements by saying, "IGN will have more on Xbox Live because it could very well be the all-encompassing future of gaming."

~29~
Xbox Live Beta

The Xbox Live beta kit.

Xbox Live was ready for beta testing by spring of 2002, and kits began going out, first in small numbers, then in larger numbers, all over the world. During early internal tests, members of international teams in Europe, Japan and the U.S. played together. Not only were these tests successful, but they were inspiring, with members of the teams reporting how great an experience they had.

Each beta kit included a headset and a specially modified version of Acclaim's radio-controlled car racing game for Windows, Re-Volt. According to Andrew Walker, who was responsible for the beta title and who got permission from Acclaim to use it, this version of Re-Volt was ported from PC to console by engineers within the ATG and ultimately shipped to 25,000 beta testers. It featured eight-person multiplayer and voice. And, of course, J Allard's *Snow Crash* inspired Hiro Protagonist gamertag was seen often.

Walker remembers showing Re-Volt for Xbox Live to Bill Gates. "I remember demoing it to Bill and he was like 'Oh. This is the game that sold me on the Xbox idea in the first place.'" What happened is that Blackley had used Re-Volt with a console controller long before Xbox had been approved, when they were still using modified laptops. "They basically put a TV on and hacked up a controller and showed Bill, and it was a pretty big deal for Bill to see this."

Beta Hackers

During the beta period for Xbox Live, Microsoft sent out regular updates. At the time, in Xbox everything was linked into a game, so new clients got updated by the beta testers when they ran a new version of an Xbox Live game. Meanwhile, Dinarte Morais was watching the logs and checking out who was connecting. "I was experimenting with the various dynamic challenges that were being sent down to the boxes to see if I could detect any modded boxes, to see if they were connecting to the live service."

Not surprisingly, there were modded boxes, and Morais was able to collect data that would help him deal with various problems that would arise once they opened the service to the general public. "We didn't actually act on the data. I configured the security gateways to ask the questions, but just log the results. No matter what the answer was, people would still be able to connect to the service. When Xbox Live went live, that's when we banned all of the boxes that were known to be modded.

Morais was also keeping up to date with various hacker and modder boards. "People were talking about using their boxes to do different music services and run games that were copied, usually modding them using mod chips that would change the OS and relax some of the security rules. Those were the types of things our system was attempting to discover when you connected to Live, and the modded systems went in a list that would keep them blocked from the service even if they toggled off their chip."

When the service opened officially, Morais activated the list of modded boxes, and there were a lot of complaints from people who couldn't connect. "At the time we shipped," he says, "I didn't have a lot of time to modify the client to say anything like 'The reason you can't connect is because you have a modded box.' It just behaved like Xbox Live was down, it just timed out.

"If you read the hacker boards at the time Live went on there was this interesting effect. Before I turned on the blacklist, everything was fine. People were in beta, they were connecting to Live, they were playing with other people. It was all great. They were letting other people on the modding boards know that everything is fine, there's no problem playing on Live. Then Xbox Live goes live and BLAM—everything stops. Software hadn't updated at the time, and you had this Xbox Live DVD you needed to install to have the service on your box. We just deactivated them to keep them from connecting to Live.

"So if you were to look at the Xbox official forums, people would, by and large, be happy with the service because it appeared to be working and they could connect to other people, but if you looked at these hacker boards there were all these threads of 'I can't believe they let the system ship like this,' 'this doesn't work,' and 'I can't connect.' It was like two different worlds, but they eventually figured it out and realized that they need to switch the chips off on their modded boxes if they want to connect to the Xbox Live system.

"This goes back to the whole thing of us not caring if you want to cheat in Solitaire, but if you want to cheat in a game with other people, then we do care. If you did modify your box, for whatever purpose, and you want to play games solo, I don't really care. As soon as you want to belong to the community, everyone should play by the same set of rules.

"Our Terms of Service says you cannot modify your box, but one thing that is interesting is that the boxes themselves are what were banned, so you could always go out and get another box. There were machine accounts and there were user accounts. So you as the user had an account on Xbox Live and so did every box. When we detected a modified box, we banned the machine, not the user. If someone went and got another box, they could reconnect and play."

~30~
Xbox Live Launch

Xbox Live officially launched November 14, 2002. The private launch party in Hollywood featured celebrities like Samuel L. Jackson and Freddy Prinze Jr. But the real party was online, where players all over the world were discovering the service for the first time. They sold 150,000 Xbox Live Starter Kits in the first week alone.

Hours into the launch, Multerer was told there was a problem. The numbers didn't look right.

"We turned the service on and then went into the cafeteria to watch the numbers. It had a party atmosphere, but only lasted a few hours as the numbers didn't make sense and there was clearly something wrong. It turned out to be a bug in the software that reported the numbers, not the service itself. So no big deal, but it did interrupt the party." No big deal, except that once they fixed the bug it became clear that they had shattered their projections.

In many industry launch stories, the servers are overwhelmed by the initial, and unexpectedly massive, success. Breakdowns on launch were not uncommon. The original Pong coin-op test at Andy Capps famously stopped working, causing all kinds of consternation at Atari, but it turned out that the coin box was so stuffed that it couldn't take any more quarters. Launches of games like Ultima Online and EverQuest featured overloaded servers and last-minute emergency measures. It was a common story, but not with Xbox Live. Even though the launch was far more successful than they had anticipated, they had come prepared. In fact, considerably over prepared.

Thomason reflects on what happened. "We overbuilt the data centers—maybe for the first time in history, and maybe since. We actually ended up shutting down some of the data centers later because we had more capacity than we needed. It ended up ramping up really well, but we were just super paranoid. We didn't think we could live through an experience where we didn't have enough capacity for people playing. We wanted a console experience for Live, meaning it had to always work, it had to be fast, and all that stuff. The Xbox Live launch went extraordinarily smoothly, and people just came up and played, and just played… and it worked."

Rolling the Dice

As impressive as the stability of the initial launch was, perhaps even more impressive was how they planned it. Multerer revealed to me, he says for the first time ever, the very technical process they implemented to determine how many machines they would need to handle the anticipated load. "As we were rolling through the summer before launch, MarkV (VanAntwerp) and I had to provide capacity planning numbers for the services. Very important as if you buy too few machines/services then you can't handle the load when the service turns on, but if you buy too much then you blow the budget.

"The problem was that there was nothing similar to model it against. So we built a big spreadsheet, came up with the best and worst case numbers. Then I got out my old Dragon Dice from Dungeons and Dragons and we literally chose what felt like the right curves and rolled the dice to enter the numbers.

"'This one feels like 20tps + 3d12' (tps = Transactions per Second) (3d12 = A twelve sided die, rolled 3 times and added together) We put that nomenclature in the spreadsheet so we could remember what we did, but never told anyone about it (until now) because the ops and test teams wouldn't have liked the randomness of it. In reality it wasn't very random and was actually a good way to get probability curves for the planning. Worked out just fine."

Xbox LIVE Enters the Arena

January 01, 2002:

Microsoft introduced Xbox LIVE in Nov. 2002, describing it as the first comprehensive, online game arena fully dedicated to fast-action broadband gaming experiences. The company sold 150,000 Xbox Live Starter Kits in the service's first week.

Better Strategy

It was huge. They came up with a better strategy than Sony did, and Sony Corporation was going through a lot of turmoil at the time, and they weren't well led, and they let Microsoft win.

-Brad Silverberg

More Comments about Xbox Live

Xbox Live brought the Internet to consoles in a real and substantial way. Of course it offered game play connectivity, but it also created a community, a medium for communication and a completely different way to distribute games.

I would say that the success of Xbox Live forced everyone else to respond with their own services. Which were successful to varying degrees. Overall, I think Xbox Live was viewed as the best of these offerings and was probably the key differentiating feature for both the original Xbox and the Xbox 360.

-Stuart Moulder

We launched it on the day we planned. Our security stuff has always worked very well. It was all designed very early on, and they're still using a similar scheme today, all these years later. As I understand it now from talking to Marc, Xbox Live is the most profitable part of Xbox.

Xbox Live never paid back much of the loss from Xbox. It was profitable to the tune of maybe $200 million, but we're talking about losses of billions for Xbox. The general number that's thrown around is about $4.5 billion for the original Xbox. It's a staggering amount of money. But to put it in perspective, I think Microsoft lost very close to that same amount of money with the debacle of Windows Longhorn, how it evolved into Windows Vista. I think we flushed at least $3 billion doing that. That's a different story, but Microsoft has definitely lost lots of money over the years.

-Jon Thomason

239

We built a successful, entertainment-based social service before social services were cool. A lot of people they go for a date, they go for reduce your risk, they go for shipping, but it's not interesting to reduce your risk so much that the product you produce doesn't have enough value. You've got to take enough risk, and you've got to do something big enough that success is worth it. Like I said in the beginning—and this is super important to me—I do not want to build any projects that would be successful on the day we start. I want to build products that will be successful on the day they ship, and that means predicting where's the world going to be two years from now, which is how long it takes for anything really big to get done. Really, really big stuff seems to take that long. Like XNA took two years to really come to fruition the first time, and you had to make predictions over what that's going to be. With Live we had to make predictions. You don't know you're right when you start.

-Boyd Multerer

~Epilogue~

The Team

So who gets credit for Xbox? For some, it's a sore point that the stories most often told also most often focus only on certain high-profile players, but in this book I've tried to include the perspectives and stories of as many people as I could reach. There were many who I was unable to interview, but who played significant roles, but I do think it's clear that the initial vision of Otto Berkes, Ted Hase, Seamus Blackley, Kevin Bachus, Nat Brown, Colin McCartney, and Rick Thompson had a lot to do with the ultimate inception and approval of Xbox. Blackley and Bachus also deserve a lot of credit for their evangelism, consistent vision, and passion for the project. Blackley also contributed a key element of the project's success when he formed the Xbox Advanced Technology Group and staffed it with some of the most talented engineers and experts in the company, creating a vision of service to the developers that was of immense help in driving third-party adoption of the platform.

It's equally clear that the team assembled by J Allard did a remarkable job, and Allard, who dislikes personal credit, gives credit to them all. *"hardware, operating system, peripherals, xbox live, 3rd party program and support, vision/ strategy. it was a super collaborative team and high on meritocracy. everyone contributed to everything, no one 'owned' anything. the best ideas and approaches won out and everyone was generally too busy for 'turf wars' - the attitude was much more 'hey, can you help me with this'? i deserve no special credit. we were all 'co-founders'. by the time it was approved there were 20 full timers on it. 19 months and 1 day from that date, it was on shelf. i think all of the ~20 original players were the co-founders of the movement. everyone at that table helped shape our vision and the plan"*

And of course credit goes to Todd Holmdahl and Jon Thomason and their teams for playing critical roles in building the hardware and the software for the first Xbox.

In addition to Allard's team, who were building the hardware and the software, there were people like Ed Fries and Jonathan Sposado doing 1st-party and George Peckham doing 3rd-party, and the marketing team of John O'Rouke, Beth Featherstone, Don Coyner, Jennifer Booth and others who devised and executed an effective marketing plan, Brett Schnepf and Bob Mc-Breen on the business side. Jordan Weisman and Stuart Moulder for leading in-house development and supporting Bungie in their transition.

Ed Fries probably deserves some special mention here because his influence in the decision making was far greater than most people know, and when he supported the small Xbox team over Mundie's WebTV group, or the hard drive, or on dozens of other issues, Gates listened because Fries had a lot of credibility.

And everyone else mentioned in this story as I've told it. From *Game of X v.2:* Alex, Craig and Eric, James Plamondon, DRG and everyone who helped developed DirectX, Cameron Myhrvold, Brad Silverberg, Robbie Bach, Morris Beton, John Ludwig, Rick Segal, and other managers who provided cover.

Jon Tomason for the Xbox OS and for helping set Live on a workable schedule.

To the many engineers, evangelists, designers, and business people, and all the people who contributed without getting any specific credit. It was a large effort, and there's plenty of credit to go around.

And especially Bill and Steve for seeing the vision, and the game developers who made it all worthwhile and provided entertainment for millions of gamers.

And for games for DOS and Windows at Microsoft, whose stories are told, at least in part in *Game of X v.2?* Credit must go to the early pioneers. Special recognition should go the Flight Simulator team, early designers like Wes Cherry, Hans Spiller, David Norris, Tom Saxon, Robert Donner, and Ed Fries. And to some of the earliest games group members like Kathie Flood, Kiki McMillan, and Russ Glaeser, who continued to work on games for Microsoft even after Xbox launched, Tony Garcia, and, again, Ed Fries— for leading the charge to make more and better Windows games, and everyone who made and promoted games at Microsoft.

And most definitely, to all of the game designers and developers who supported PC gaming in DOS and Windows over these many years. They all created fun and entertainment on Microsoft's major platforms, and as someone who has played a lot of games on both DOS and Windows machines, I thank them for the steady work they did to ensure that our PCs would have great games, both from Microsoft and from the many other companies that have used its software.

Xbox Live Credits

Boyd Multerer wanted to give full credit to his main team members, so here are the ones who were not already mentioned along with his comments. "All of them worked incredibly hard to make it happen. (probably in some sort of sub-conscious, but not intentional order)":

Mark VanAntwerp—"Maybe the 3rd person hired? Became the high-level system architect and (as a good senior engineer is supposed to do) wrote all the important parts that the others didn't want to do because they weren't glamorous enough. But the system won't work without these parts! I guess I'll have to do it. We wouldn't have shipped without him and he gets plenty of credit for the overall design. Mark is the engineer I worked most closely with..."

Heidi Gaertner—"She was our representative dev from the game industry and ran development all the software that became the UI for XBL."

Tony Chen—"The first engineer I hired onto XBL. He designed (and wrote) the user login and authentication system (very hard) and worked closely with Dinarte on the other parts of the lower-level systems."

Roxana Arama—"She wrote the code to drive voice and several other important parts of the service."

Sean Wohlgemouth—"The single most important tester of the service. Loud. Opinionated. Not afraid to yell (scream?) at anyone on the team (including me) when we were wrong. Very important contributor to the project."

Daniel Caiafa—"He wrote the statistics server, which kept track of all the leaderboards and more. He and Roxana joined the team at the same time and did great work."

Nataly Pogrebinsky—"She wrote large parts of the dash (UI) and more. Big hand getting the connections to operations to work."

Steve Lamb—"Wrote the first matchmaking / multiplayer for the service. He's up there with Daniel Caiafa in terms of actual coding impact."

Alice Steinglass (then Alice Pritikin)—"Junior (at the time - not any more) PM working across the service. She worked with the devs and helped much of the service make sense. (you should read her linked in page)

Barry Steinglass—"(Married Alice... One of several marriages that come out of XBL)—Another junior (at the time - not any more) who worked across the service and helped pull it together. (you should read his LinkedIn page)"

Tracey Sharp—"Tracy is just as important as Dinarte, but more on the box side than XBL. Whenever there was a critical issue getting things to work at the lowest level of the system, Tracey would debug it. He is still working on Xbox at the lowest level and recent cowrote the bottom layer of Xbox One with David Cutler. Tracy is married to Roxana Arama - the other big marriage to come out of the early days of XBL."

Darren Anderson—"I think the second engineer hired... Wrote and/or managed the tools we used to actually run the service."

Damon Danielli—"PM for audio and voice comms in particular."

Erin Elsasser—"A good recruiter is critical to helping you build a team, but never gets any credit. Erin did great work helping me build the team."

Michio Nikaido—"Worked with Darren to build out the tools to run the service. Also happened to be West Coast champion at playing Unreal Tournament. The team would often play "Everybody against Michio". Michio usually won."

Lit Wong—"Test Manager. My peer, pulled the test team together."

Brian Morin—"Single handedly wrote the first XBL presence servers."

Kelly Altom— "Operations Manager—my peer. He was responsible for the buildout of the data-centers, all the machines, networking etc. This wasn't like it is today where you just rent space in ready-to-go cloud data-centers. Kelly's team had to spec and build out, and run, everything. Kelly, MarkV, and I were in Tokyo for the launch of XBL in Japan. Lets just say the night before was very interesting. WAY more crazy story than the actual launch of XBL in the US. But it also somehow seems normal for Japan."

Eric Neustadter—"Second-in-command (in my opinion) in ops. Huge hand in the design and buildout of the data-center."

Brian Lockhart—"On the ops team, one of the main interfaces and troubleshooters working with the dev team. Worked closely with Nataly, Darren and Michio."

And many more...

"The above people were all reliable and really made it happen. You should look through the LinkedIn links above. I am pleased to see how many of them are now CTOs, CEOs, Engineering VPs, Founders and more. It was a very special team. We held the bar extremely high while hiring (made recruiting's job quite difficult—they rolled with it), and it paid off."

Author's Postscript

So this is the story I decided to tell. I divided it into two volumes: this book and the prequel (*Game of X v.2*) that tells the stories of the DOS and early Windows days, the complex events around the development and adoption of DirectX, and the internal struggles over graphics standards that ultimately had a direct effect on Xbox. Also some good glimpses of Microsoft culture and its relationships both inside and outside the company. It's not by any means the only approach an author could have taken, but after working on this project for several years it became clear that what started out as a chapter in another book now required two volumes, and that I would lead off with the Xbox story because it's the one more people will immediately gravitate toward, and follow with the foundational stories in the prequel..

- I chose to focus on Microsoft as a game company, not only on Xbox.

- I chose to speak to as many people as I could find who would talk to me, to tell the many stories that made up the whole, not a singular story with many actors.

- As much as possible, I used their words, their language, their expressions. I wanted not only to tell stories, but to reveal something about culture and life—the people—at Microsoft over the years. Something about the strategies of massive companies doing business and competing against other massive companies—and against just about everyone, including their own internal groups.

I hope you enjoyed the book, the stories, the people, and will check out *Game of X v.2*. For my part, I thoroughly enjoyed researching and writing these books and extend my gratitude to the many people who made it possible by sharing their time and stories with me.

-Rusel DeMaria

Printed and bound by CPI Group (UK) Ltd, Croydon, CR0 4YY

21/10/2024

01777058-0001